Diagonal Walking

Nick Corble has written over twenty-five books as well as over a hundred articles for the national and local press. Subjects have ranged from walking guides to the history of the English fairground, but he is perhaps best known for his works on the UK's inland waterways system. These include titles such as *The Narrowboat Story*, *Britain's Canals: A Handbook* and, with Allan Ford, a guide to living on the canals called, appropriately, *A Beginner's Guide to Living on the Waterways*.

His very first book, *Walking on Water*, published in 2000, covered a trip down the inland waterways system on a battered ex-hire narrowboat from the northern tip of the canal system down to the south. This not only described the highs and lows of the journey itself, but also attempted to gauge the mood of the nation on the eve of the millennium. *Diagonal Walking* replicates this approach, slicing through the nation, and trying to find out what makes it tick, this time on the eve of perhaps the most momentous event in its modern history.

This is not a book about Brexit, though: rather some reflections on England gathered through the long hot summer of 2018, during which Brexit dominated the headlines, providing the rumble of distant thunder the weather seemed reluctant to deliver. It is a look at England through the eyes of an ordinary man, as confused as everyone else. Neither a political commentator nor a professional pundit, and about to enter a fresh stage of his own life, Nick chose to re-engage with his country, to get out there and talk to people. To reconnect.

This is the story of what he discovered.

Diagonal Walking

Slicing Through the Heart of England

Nick Corble

Matador
9 Priory Business Park,
Wistow Road, Kibworth Beauchamp,
Leicestershire. LE8 0RX
Tel: 0116 279 2299
Email: books@troubador.co.uk
Web: www.troubador.co.uk/matador
Twitter: @matadorbooks

ISBN 978 1789018 356

British Library Cataloguing in Publication Data.
A catalogue record for this book is available from the British Library.

Printed and bound by CPI Group (UK) Ltd, Croydon, CR0 4YY
Typeset in 11pt Adobe Garamond Pro by Troubador Publishing Ltd, Leicester, UK

Matador is an imprint of Troubador Publishing Ltd

For walkers everywhere, but especially
to all my diagonal walkers

Contents

Introduction

This book is a record of my diagonal walk through the centre of England during the summer of 2018. Immediately, that sentence carries with it three caveats.

First, it was my walk not anyone else's, and as such what you are about to read is inevitably biased rather than objective, a record of a trek seen through my eyes alone. Second, it was conducted at a particular point in time, as it happens a particularly interesting point in time, when the country was teetering on the edge of potentially its biggest challenge for a generation.

This was no coincidence. There's no getting away from it, the result of the Brexit referendum in 2016 acted as a powerful motivation to undertake my walk. I had done something similar twenty years before when my children were still young, when my intention had been to try to get a handle on what sort of country they were going to grow up in. With the referendum result I was no longer sure that the picture I'd formed then still held. It was time to take the nation's temperature once more.

The third and final caveat tucked away in that opening sentence is the word 'diagonal'. The route I took was unique. To my knowledge no one has undertaken it before. Again, this was deliberate. I wanted my walk to be a one-off, following my set of rules. I also wanted to create something greater than simply a walk, to give birth to the notion of Diagonal Walking, not just a diagonal walk: to make it both multi-dimensional and multi-media. In particular, I wanted to use as many of the different channels now available on the internet as I could master in order to broaden the project's participation and ownership.

As I approached my sixtieth birthday I also wanted an adventure, to challenge some of my own preconceptions and to place myself outside my comfort zones. Finally, I wanted to write a travelogue about my experiences. Travelogues are funny things. There's a long and distinguished history of them, not just in the UK but all over the world. Explorers like to share what happens to them and the thoughts they collect along the way, while the public also appear to like reading about them, to travel vicariously.

Before setting out on my walk, I immersed myself in some of the most well-known English (and British) travelogues. These included Bill Bryson's *Notes From a Small Island* and its follow-up *The Road to Little Dribbling*, as well as Paul Theroux's *The Kingdom By The Sea*, the last written when the country was in the throes of another crisis, on that occasion the Falklands War. I also delved back in history and consulted J.B. Priestley's 1930s classic *English Journey*, as well as H.V. Morton's post-First World War tome *In Search of England* and, going even further back, William Cobbett's nineteenth-century horseback journey through England *Rural Rides*.

These all had a lot in common. They were snapshots of a moment in time, they were subjective and they were random. This book is all of those, too. I don't claim to be in the same league as others on this noble list, but I can claim to share their intentions. It was time for another look at England.

Diagonal Walking describes what I saw.

Nick Corble, 2018

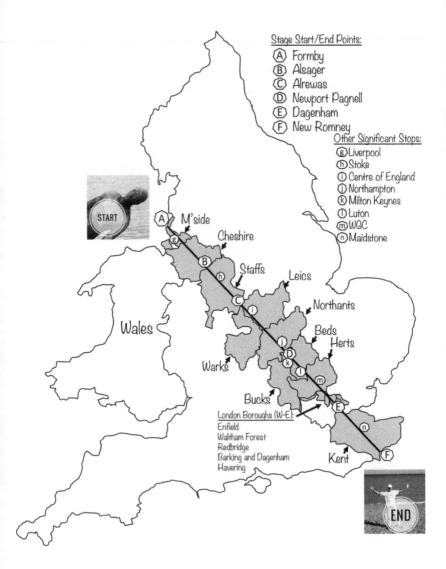

Stage Start/End Points:
Ⓐ Formby
Ⓑ Alsager
Ⓒ Alrewas
Ⓓ Newport Pagnell
Ⓔ Dagenham
Ⓕ New Romney

Other Significant Stops:
ⓖ Liverpool
ⓗ Stoke
ⓘ Centre of England
ⓙ Northampton
ⓚ Milton Keynes
ⓛ Luton
ⓜ WGC
ⓝ Maidstone

START

M'side

Cheshire

Staffs

Leics

Northants

Beds

Herts

Wales

Warks

Bucks

London Boroughs (W-E):
Enfield
Waltham Forest
Redbridge
Barking and Dagenham
Havering

Kent

END

Stage 1

Formby

to

Alsager

98.3 miles
224,124 steps

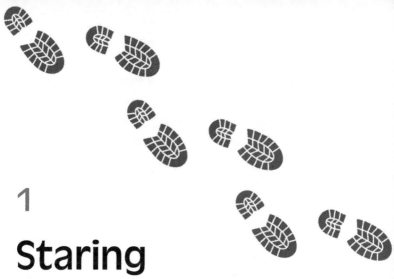

1

Staring
Out to Sea

Sand dunes thick with marram grass clutched the edge of the shore like a giant bear's claw. Below them lay a beach of pristine sand and beyond that, inevitably, the sea, with wind turbines peppering the horizon. It was approaching high tide, and the shallow waves were close to abandoning their twice-daily quest to connect with the shaggy dunes. The vista before me stretched like an extended concertina, the sea breathing in and out, exhaling a restorative briny air which, by then, I was ready to take a few lungfuls of.

That was when I remembered a tradition amongst coast-to-coast walkers. They take a pebble from their starting shore and carry it to their destination on the other side of the country. I wondered if this was something I should copy. After all, wasn't my walk also from coast to coast, even if it did follow a slightly unconventional route? Not for me the simplicity of taking the shortest line between two shores. No, I was going to be walking diagonally, from the north-west edge to the south-east corner, following a line passing through the very centre of England. Even so, I told myself, it was still from one coast to another.

There was a problem though. Not a pebble to be found. The beach at Formby Sands hasn't earned its name by accident, it is just that: sand. Mile upon immaculate mile of it. Besides, I knew from past experience that the beach at the other end of my walk, at New Romney near Dungeness in Kent, is nothing but stones. One option might be to take a bag of sand, but what was the point? It would only slip between the pebbles in an instant. Equally, why carry a pebble all the way across the country to deposit it somewhere where it would be completely unremarkable? I'd already learned one thing in the hour it had taken me to get to this point: I'd overpacked my rucksack. To add more weight seemed madness. Damn it, I resolved. This was my walk, my route, my project, and I'll live by my own rules.

One of those was to engage with as many people as possible. Part of my rationale for the trek was to try to understand what made England tick. It wasn't a particularly original quest, it had been the standby of travel writers for generations, but for me it had taken on a new poignancy for two reasons. First, it was something I'd done before. Nearly twenty years previously, on the eve of the millennium, I'd taken our newly acquired, but long in the tooth and battered, narrowboat down the spine of the inland waterways system. My wife Annette and I had young children at the time, and I was taking a mid-career break, partly to re-assess that career, and partly to get an understanding of what sort of country our children were destined to grow up in.

That resulted in my first book, *Walking on Water*, detailing the voyage in stages, with different combinations of people providing a constantly changing chemistry to the trip. Writing it was cathartic, as well as giving me some insights into parts of the country I would never have visited ordinarily (Chorley anyone?). It also provided insights into both myself and those closest to me, making the experience a seminal one.

The second reason for this fresh challenge was the Brexit referendum, which had pulled me up a bit. Like so many others, I was confused. Rather than stay confused, I wanted to do something proactive, to try to understand, to re-connect, and to indulge myself in some thinking time. My children had grown up and there was the faintest whiff of grandchildren in the air. What sort of country might they grow up in? I wasn't arrogant enough to think that I alone could unpick the Brexit Gordian Knot, but I did want to revisit my understanding of England and the English. Previous experience suggested the best way to do this was to engage rather than become enraged.

The narrowboat was history, sold when the two boys we used to tuck up in its bunk beds alongside their soft toys outgrew their berths. In any case, I wanted to do something different. Along with Annette, I'd completed a number of the country's long-distance walking trails. Maybe the answer lay there? But that presented a problem. By definition, these trails are confined to a particular geography or feature. None offered the prospect of connecting with a cross-section of the population. Besides, they'd all been walked, written about and discussed hundreds of times before. There was nothing for it, I was going to have to create my own route.

At that point, I recalled an old market research technique called the Diagonal Slice. In fact, it was such an old concept that when I googled it nothing came up. It predates the internet. I remembered it as a methodology that allowed researchers to get a cross-section of opinion from a given sample – a company's employees for example – by identifying those at the very top of an organisation and those at the very bottom, and interviewing them along with representatives at every level in between.

In other words, it was pure market research BS. But it sparked a thought. If you took the very centre of England, and drew a diagonal line at forty-five degrees right through it, where would it take you? The first problem, of course, was isolating where the absolute centre actually is. There are a number of claimants to this crown, but only one carries the imprimatur of the highest of authorities – well, within walking circles anyway: the Ordnance Survey. In 2002 they'd come up with their own candidate. The way they did this was complicated, but stick with me for a moment.

What they did was find the centroid or barycentre of the country. A centroid is defined as the intersection of all the hyperplanes that divide an object X into two parts of equal moment about the hyperplane. In layman's terms, the average of all points of X. In layman's children's terms, they did something marvellously cunning. They used maths. At a stroke they added a gloss of science to their conclusions, whilst at the same time making them completely baffling and therefore impossible for the average Joe to contradict.

The point they arrived at was just inside Leicestershire near its border with Warwickshire, a couple of miles east of the canal town of Atherstone. A quick walk to WHSmith delivered into my possession not only a map of England but a protractor, something I hadn't owned since I used the contents of my Helix Geometry Set to flick paper pellets across a crowded classroom. Back home, with the map spread out over the kitchen table, I tentatively drew my line, choosing the north-west to south-west option as it passed through more of the population. At the top left it hit the sea around Formby in Lancashire, north of Liverpool; at the bottom right it did the same around New Romney in Kent. It was as I surveyed this line that coincidences started to reveal themselves.

Shortly after Liverpool it passed through Runcorn, which I'd visited with my brother and nephew on the narrowboat trip twenty years before. An interesting evening there following a curry formed the cornerstone of a chapter of *Walking on Water*. Revisiting the town would give me the chance of a then-and-now comparison. This was a promising beginning. The line then cut through the Potteries, where I'd gone to university; skirted Milton Keynes, where I'd helped build a house thirty-odd years before; edged past a village near St. Albans where I'd once lived, and finally glanced off the edge of Gravesend, where one of our grown-up sons now resided. It was almost as if the line was trying to tell me something. I took it as enough encouragement to take things to the next level.

As I thought about it and spoke with others, it dawned on me that an opportunity existed to fashion my idea into more than just another trip with accompanying travel book. The greatest change that has taken place since I wrote *Walking on Water* is the way the internet has become central to all our lives. Back then the World Wide Web, as we called it, was still a curiosity, something we were struggling to get our analogue-conditioned brains around. In those days, phoning someone when away from home still meant having a pocketful of two- and ten-pence pieces, connecting to the web involved plugging into your phone socket and listening to something Stockhausen might have written, whilst social media meant watching the telly with someone else in the room.

Why not harness this change to create something different, to democratise the whole process? I could ask others to be part of the trip, to follow every step, 'to walk with me' virtually as well as walking alongside me in person, using everything the internet has to offer: blogs, podcasts, videos, Instagram, Twitter and Facebook. And not just sharing the actual walking, but the whole shebang. The planning and preparation, the emotions of the trek, the dubious opportunity to get inside my head as I wrote the book and explored publishing options.

An idea was born that was to take over my life. As the new year began, I started as I meant to go on by engaging with others: notably a local website designer and media students from the nearby university. Together, we created an internet presence, as well as a couple of introductory films for a sparkling new YouTube channel, as well as a handful of explanatory podcasts. The whole project was given a name, gained its own logo and even acquired a theme tune. *Diagonal Walking* was delivered into the world.

Through a combination of talking with others and internet research, I taught myself fresh skills such as how to record and publish a podcast, film editing, search engine optimisation and, most importantly, a different way of thinking. Diagonal thinking, if you like. I needed to consider my walk not just through my own eyes, but through the eyes of others. What would they find interesting? How could I engage with them? Some immediate successes came via social media, which helped form relationships with ramblers and community groups along the route as well as journalists and others. These helped to populate my social media accounts and gave a morale-boosting following wind as I waited for the days to lengthen and for the moment of reckoning to arrive – the day when I would finally get walking.

Interacting with people was a key objective of the *Diagonal Walking* concept, but I hadn't anticipated it starting immediately. Seconds after being dropped off in the centre of Formby I was studying a map of local attractions (bowling club, cricket club, asparagus fields), when a senior citizen approached me, brandishing a stick. Did I know where I was going, he asked. I had yet to perfect my opener of 'Yes, I'm walking diagonally'. I simply replied in the affirmative, omitting to mention that I intended to use the map on my phone to reach my actual start point. My first chance to interact and I'd failed spectacularly, seduced by the screen. Following this early lesson, at my next stop – to pick up some emergency snacks at a local health food store, because my rucksack just wasn't quite heavy enough – I purposely asked for directions.

The reply was so confusing, involving landmarks I had no knowledge of, that I ended up back on the pavement as ignorant as I'd gone in. I discreetly slipped my phone out, pretending to make a call while actually looking up my route. At that exact moment, my elderly friend re-appeared, full of apologies, delivered through tobacco-stained teeth, for his earlier questioning. The only reason he'd enquired if I was all right was because so few people knew how to read a map these days, he explained. I was just preparing to engage with him in conversation when my phone beat me to it.

'Walk north-west on Halsall Lane towards Long Lane,' came the disembodied female voice.

My companion looked baffled and glanced behind his back towards some invisible interlocuter, giving me the opportunity I needed to stride away, embarrassed and defeated once again.

In the end it took me nearly half an hour to reach my starting point. The route involved a road that was clearly proud of its private status, something it proclaimed regularly on signs. Regularly spaced signs. Using bold type. But the green dashed line on the OS map reassured me this was a footpath, so I pressed on, confident that the sands at its end, marked out in flesh-coloured tones on the map, would soon be within my reach. As it happened, a prayer centre ended up standing between me and the sea, and although a swift pray may have been prudent, I opted instead to designate a path to the left through a pine forest as my official starting point.

Caught up in the moment, I once again forgot my wider responsibilities to involve others. Having set off into the woods, I stopped and, retracing my steps, went back to the road. Deep breath. This 'involving others' malarkey would take a bit of getting used to. I reset my step- and distance-counter and framed some words to accompany my first few paces, which I was going to record on my phone. Literally record, on my phone, which doubled up as a camera, voice recorder, compass, pedometer, map and even something I could make calls on, should I be so possessed. Proving to myself that I could walk and talk at the same time, I focussed the camera on my feet and as I slowly raised it to focus on the path ahead, the following came out of my mouth:

'So, there we are, the first footsteps of what might be hundreds of thousands, or let's hope so, or I'll have failed.'

It was hardly 'One small step for man', but at least I was being authentic, whilst also betraying the underlying fear of failure that was now spurring me on. I decided at that point to always say it as I saw it, rather than follow a script. This may have been a mistake as I rambled on, explaining how I was actually not in Formby, but Freshfields, a sort of suburb of Formby, and not, as it name suggested, a branch of a new supermarket chain.

It was probably inevitable that after this significant moment I got lost for the first, but absolutely not the last, time. I've always found woods and forests a problem when walking. Those who erect footpath signs in them seem to work on the assumption that you probably know the way and they don't want to insult your intelligence by making it too obvious. They also appear to be ignorant of phrase 'seeing the woods for the trees'. Buoyed with adrenaline and optimism, I took solace from the serendipity of passing through an unanticipated red squirrel sanctuary. An information board recorded that the species was endangered, and it was easy to see why. Maybe it was time for their mid-morning hazelnut latte, but there were none to be seen. Luckily, no one came past as I lurked in the trees, camera poised like some kind of pervert. I gave up, taking comfort in the thought that I was only technically lost. I had a vague idea where I was, heading for the sea, which could be both heard and smelt, characteristics later landmarks were likely to lack.

A boardwalk eventually delivered me to the coast and the pristine beach that prompted my rumination on sand and pebbles. One of the reasons for coming to this stretch of beach – other than it would have ruined the whole idea of an alternative coast-to-coast if I hadn't – was to visit the old Formby Lifeboat Station. This was the first in Britain, founded by the Liverpool Dock Master some time between 1771 and 1776. Very little of it is left to view, and given the height of the tide even that was currently hidden. Besides, it was a little further down the beach and, although I could see people walking along the sands, I was heavily laden and wearing hiking boots. I didn't want to disappear into the sand. Neither did I want to become 'embayed'. This was a term I'd picked up from Paul Theroux in his book *The Kingdom By The Sea*, and means to be caught by the tide and stuck in a bay. Although the dunes would have offered the chance for an undignified scramble for safety, and the long straight beach was about as far from a bay as you could get, I didn't fancy risking it.

As a result, I executed a tactical withdrawal and headed back down the boardwalk, where I was promptly attacked by a dog, apparently under the impression I'd spent the night before marinating the bottom of my trousers in cat urine. Being English, I assured its owners that everything was all right and that their dog was a delightful playful little chap. In so doing I realised I was displaying one of the timeless features of the English so admired by foreign writers such as Theroux and Bill Bryson, namely our politeness. I wondered if I'd been another nationality, Dutch for example, or possibly German, whether I'd be instructing the owner in no uncertain terms to keep their animal under control. Words to that effect had, after all, been bouncing through my head.

A signpost once again raised the subject of asparagus, suggesting I was on the Asparagus Route, with a circular marker displaying one of these vegetables to ensure I wasn't mistaken. As it was becoming something of a theme, I consulted another of the information boards the area is so well endowed with. It appeared there was a tradition of growing the suggestively shaped vegetable in the area, one that gathered momentum with the coming of the railway in the mid-nineteenth century. If you are someone who enjoys their asparagus, you may wish to skip the next paragraph.

Around the same time as the railway's arrival, there was an escalating problem with the piles of human waste emanating from the growing metropolis of Liverpool. The asparagus growers knew exactly what to do with it. By the 1920s, 200 acres of the stuff was under cultivation in Formby, with crops being sent down to London's Covent Garden market by night train. Formby's asparagus was top notch stuff, winning national prizes (yes, there are such things), even being eaten by the first-class passengers on the *Titanic* during its fateful maiden voyage – much good that it did them. These days there's only a small patch of it left, other solutions having being found to Liverpool's little 'problem'.

Back on the path, I dodged round a MOD firing range, thankfully silent, and followed the Sefton Coastal Path, eventually emerging into dunes beside the green expanse of the West Lancashire Golf Course. Occasional ponds identified themselves as breeding grounds for Natterjack Toads, amphibians distinguished by a yellow stripe down their back. It seemed the Sefton Coast was where up to half the country's Natterjacks bred, usually around April and May, which was exactly when I was there. They appreciated the sand and short grass and liked making whoopee when the sun became warm enough to heat their eggs. Ecstatic croaking was notable by its absence however, so I concluded that like us humans, the toads were still in shock at the arrival of some decent weather after what had been a shocking winter.

The wind was really whipping up as I crossed the dunes and I was grateful when the path gave way to a metalled track leading up to the Coastguard station at Crosby, which reacquainted me with the sea. The tide was still high but on the turn, the shallow beach slowly beginning to reveal itself.

I was gazing over the water when I saw my first one – a stationary naked man, the conventional six feet tall with a deadpan expression, his arms slightly away from his torso, ankles still in the water, somewhat barnacle covered and ramrod erect (although not in that sense). These were the famous 'Iron Men' of Crosby I'd been looking forward to seeing. I'd arrived at the perfect time as suddenly, and somewhat surreally, other bodies emerged from the tide. Some were at angles, others out to sea, with only their heads above water. Some were buried up to their thighs, others up to their waists, and one or two had seagulls perched on top of their heads. All were modelled on the artist, Anthony Gormley, although I hoped for his sake he didn't share their disc-shaped nodules on his nipples and at the top of his thighs. They were all facing out to sea and were spaced far apart, accentuating the bizarre overall effect.

Called *Another Place*, the installation was designed to explore man's relationship with nature. The idea of the artwork is to express how human life is exposed to the elements. It uses the figure of an ordinary man, pitting him against the tides, seawater, sea life and the gritty sand-laden wind, all the while contemplatively staring out at the horizon at the movement of people and materials on ships out at sea. Before coming to Crosby the iron men had been displayed in Germany, Norway and Belgium, and were originally intended to go on to New York after a year on the Sefton Coast. But they'd remained, gazing impassively out towards the city they'd been intended for, the goal for so many people who'd once headed out of Liverpool's docks, leaving their native shores forever.

The receding tide, combined with the falling light, made for a magical end to my first day, and I could have stayed taking photographs and video for my YouTube channel for hours. In the end, I took so much video my phone ran out of battery, necessitating a dash to the café of the nearby leisure centre to top up on juice both for the phone, using an emergency powerpack, and for me, in the form of some coffee. Oh, and a slice of cake.

As the percentage indicator on my phone crept up unhurriedly, I couldn't help but wonder whether the iron men also offered a metaphor. Were they scanning the horizon looking for the trading partners and new friends the country was going to need after turning its back on its nearest neighbours? Were they lost souls, or hopeful? It was difficult to know, and that was probably one of the things that made the installation great art.

It was while waiting in the café that I struck up my first proper conversation with a local. I was wearing one of my *Diagonal Walking* branded T-shirts, revealed after taking off my fleece in the face of the stifling humidity from the adjacent swimming pool. The woman serving the coffee (and cake) came out from behind the counter, business being slow as the end of the day approached. The power of personal marketing was revealed as she asked me what 'Diagonal Walking' meant, and I duly explained. This led to a wider discussion about the need to challenge oneself and, perhaps inevitably, given she was a few years older than me, to the health issues faced by contemporaries and the need to grab life's chances while you could. The year before she'd fulfilled a lifetime's ambition to walk the Kalahari Desert in Botswana, which momentarily cast my own more prosaic efforts into relief. My feet and legs, however, were both reassuring me that I'd achieved something significant that day, but that my hotel now beckoned. Before I went my new best friend spread the word amongst her customers, leading me to do the rounds handing out some of the cards I carried with social media and other contact details.

Diagonally Walking was officially up and running… well, gentle hobbling.

2

Beating
the Beatles

Mention Liverpool to most people and you'll probably get one of two reactions: football or the Beatles. As I passed the unprepossessing building that announced itself as the Aintree Racecourse, I wondered if the Grand National, which had taken place two days before, could be added to that list. Flatbed trucks were queuing to leave, their backs loaded with blue portaloos, and I couldn't help but feel a longing twinge. I'd been walking non-stop for a few hours with steady rain falling for most of that time, with drips tumbling off the hood of my coat and onto my nose.

I'd started early because of the forecast and negotiated a route out of the red- and bronze-bricked terraced houses on the edge of Crosby without too much trouble. A marked footpath sent me down an alleyway opposite the entrance to a primary school where parents, both mums and dads, were dropping off their little ones for the day. Along the way I also noticed a number of empty plots and wondered whether these could still possibly be the result of bombing during the war over seventy years before or the result of more recent demolition.

The alleyway brought me on to the first canal of my walk, the Leeds and Liverpool, which did what it said on the can, linking these two great northern cities either side of the Pennines. The towpath was busy with dog walkers and cyclists; in contrast the water lay still, murky and flat, untroubled by boats, either moored or moving. Efforts had been made by the owners of houses on the far bank to take advantage of their waterside views, with decking and benches placed at the bottoms of their gardens, although quite what there was to sit and stare at was less clear.

The houses themselves tended towards the detached and were reasonably well kept up, even if on this dull day they seemed a little bleak. The areas I'd been through the day before, albeit in better weather, were undoubtedly more prosperous. But prosperity was relative, as my host in Southport, where I'd stayed the night before setting out, had pointed out. Perhaps he was unduly conscious that I came from 'down South'? From my point of view, sand, sea, golf and asparagus – life north of Liverpool didn't seem too bad.

A three-sided milepost appeared on the towpath and suggested that Liverpool was only five miles away, which was encouraging as that city was my target for the day. My route was more circuitous, however, and would inevitably be longer. This was due to the constraint I'd set myself to wander no more than three miles off the diagonal line and to use only footpaths and other public rights of way wherever feasible. It still came as a surprise when the second milepost suggested that Liverpool was now six miles away, until I realised it was telling me how many miles had passed since the canal's terminus north of the city. I remained on track to reach the centre.

Although not littered, the canal wasn't exactly loved either. Locals appeared to enjoy a bring-a-bottle party, the only stipulations being that (a) the bottles were plastic and (b) they were tossed in the canal when empty. Plastic was clearly as much a modern scourge of the inland waterways as it was of the oceans. As I walked along, I remembered the boat owner's mantra of saving one eye for the towpath in order to avoid the perennial problem of dog dirt. Signs everywhere encouraged dog owners to 'Bag it, tie it, bin it' but it appeared even the first of these instructions was too complicated for some. Others got to the end of the second stage and apparently gave up, resulting in regular deposits of small black plastic bags. This came across as a particularly perverse act, doubling the crime rather than solving it.

Near a swing bridge I came across a team of Canal and River Trust (CRT) workers, all in regulation hi-vis jackets, although quite why it wasn't clear (if they fell in the water they'd be difficult to miss). They were busy planting out new flower borders either side of some fresh wooden staging erected to give boats somewhere to moor when operating the bridge. Assuming, of course, that there would be boats along at some point.

Near where they were working, my route joined the Trans-Pennine Trail, a sort of walkers' Leeds to Liverpool. Here, I stopped to envelop my rucksack with its bright orange waterproof cover and to don a lightweight coat for myself against the steady but cumulative drizzle. I suspected this would become a regular habit. The increasingly urban landscape now unfolding felt like it could belong to the outskirts of any major city, with light industrial buildings lining the towpath, interspersed with more modern housing developments. The only thing that placed me was the accents as I greeted people coming my way from under the drooping hood of my coat. 'Maarnin' would come the reply in a distinctive singsong Scouse.

The accent is actually named after a dish rather than an area. Scouse was a sort of stew eaten by the poverty-stricken masses in Liverpool up until the 1900s. It tended to be made up from whatever might have fallen off a greengrocer's stall, maybe with some lamb or beef, but usually an assortment of cabbage, carrots, potato and onion. The accent itself is an agglomeration of those spoken by the various nationalities who came to Liverpool, often with a view to onward emigration. Welsh, Irish and different Eastern European tongues were mangled together and laid over the local English to produce a sound that is both instantly recognisable, but also quite limited in its geographical spread. These greetings would be replaced by others within only a day or two's walking.

Having left the towpath, the well signposted route began to take on a number of other guises as it wended its way past Aintree and then onto an asphalted path, becoming part of

21

both the Cheshire Lines Path and the Liverpool Loop. The former used to be a railway operating between Liverpool and Southport, the very same line that solved Liverpool's poo problem and enabled the good folk of London to enjoy Formby asparagus. The Loop was an old British Rail line, abandoned in 1964 and allowed to become derelict, while plans were nurtured to create an integrated transport system. Efforts to achieve this finally expired towards the end of the 1980s. The route is now maintained by the cycle charity Sustrans, primarily for their principal interest group, but thankfully for walkers too. The only downside of their stewardship was the paucity of places to sit, as the cyclists tended to bring their own seats.

A group of Sustrans litter-pickers were working the route, again all in hi-vis jackets, and I stopped to talk to one of them. They were all volunteers, she said, and were collecting rubbish, of which there was an ample supply. The path runs from Aintree down to Halewood in the south of Liverpool, a spot later on in my route. She told me how they work sections of the path in rotation. An average haul is twenty bin bags, although whether this is per volunteer she didn't make clear. As I surveyed the scene, it looked like a distinct possibility. The ubiquitous small black bags left by dog owners were the worst of it, she confirmed unprompted, agreeing with my earlier thought that they effectively doubled the problem. As we spoke one of her colleagues caught a bag on the end of his litter-picking grab-stick and performed a Liverpool loop of his own, sending it in a perfect parabola into the air, where it lodged in a branch of a tree. There it was presumably destined to stay for some time, a suspended dog dirt question mark.

A few minutes later, I thought I spotted a seat. Notwithstanding the now persistent rain, my feet were lobbying me to stop and take on an energy bar, or maybe some water, anything, so they could have a rest. When I got there, however, it turned out to be a mattress bent double. Initially disappointed, I wondered how the Sustrans people were going to fit it into their black bags.

Around midday the rain decided to step up a gear, and an off ramp to Norris Green beckoned. I hoped to get some lunch and with luck wait out the rain, which was forecast to ease off. Wet and bedraggled, as I made my way into the Pound Café I was concerned I may have looked an unwelcome guest, but I needn't have worried. As it happened, I blended in rather well, the surroundings possibly best described as basic. True to its name, the Pound Café offered the temptation of a coffee for only a solitary pound. Alas, the coffee machine was broken. The thought of turning on a kettle and nipping over the road to get a jar of Nescafé while it boiled had apparently not occurred to them.

I settled for a light lunch and something fizzy, and I don't mean a glass of Prosecco. Towelling some of the worst of the damp off my rucksack cover, I tried to look inconspicuous as a small puddle formed beneath me. Staring out of the window towards the other side of the street, I could make out a bank, a slot machine 'casino', a Poundbuster (which sounded a little threatening, given where we were), a Specsavers, two empty units next to each other and a Bargain Booze. Meanwhile, directly outside the window, a small crowd was gathering around a middle-aged man sitting on an upturned milkcrate (a possible top tip if the Liverpool Loop's policy on sitting down persisted), with various younger 'runners' darting between him and passers-by.

Before I had a chance to work out what was going on, my reverie was broken by a large woman opposite me, her dyed blond hair showing dark roots. She was rapping loudly on the window. I hadn't been taking in the conversation she'd been having with what I assumed was her daughter, largely because I could only understand every third word of it. I paused anyway as she wondered 'What's 'e sellin?' in a loud and squeaky voice. She beckoned one of the runners in, who entered the café, less sheepishly than I thought appropriate, clutching a Morrisons plastic bag to his chest.

His hand darted into the bag from which he extracted a small cardboard strip with a pair of earrings attached to it, mumbling something I couldn't catch. Without so much as examining the goods, the woman demanded "Ow mouch?' They were one pound fifty. She took two in silver and two in gold, enough to buy six coffees if there'd been any going. In under a minute, the lad made a dozen discrete sales from others nearby and exited. Outside, he joined his colleagues, who meanwhile had swollen in number.

The woman opposite me wasn't done yet. She got up and dashed outside, mentioning in passing something about wondering what else they might have. Within a minute she was back. Her daughter asked what she'd bought and was told 'Just some shite like.' I could have told her where she could have got plenty of that for free, but she didn't look the walking type. Her heavy make-up would probably run in the rain, and the sunshine tattoo on her wrist would have been oddly ironic. In the brief moment she'd been gone she'd dropped the equivalent of two or three hours of the minimum wage on some cheap earrings and a pile of imitation super-hero comic books.

'The kids'll 'ave 'em' she declared, although whose kids she was talking about, and what they'd make of them, was less clear.

Back on the path, and with the rain was now less determined, there was a hope of brightness on the horizon. On the ball of my left foot I could feel what was probably a blister rise and fall, wave-like, with every step I took, but I tried to ignore it. The remainder of my otherwise straightforward walk was to Knotty Ash, which to people of my generation means only one thing: the recently deceased comedian Ken Dodd. The way was enlivened by a conversation with a Sustrans warden, who overtook me on his bike before applying his brakes. I wondered if I'd done something wrong.

It turned out he was intrigued by me. The volunteer I'd been speaking to earlier had mentioned me and he wanted to check me out. This was the first time someone had done this – approached me, rather than me approach them – and we had a good chat about the Loop and its origins and about the challenge I'd set myself. Our exchange ended with me giving him a card, and it got me thinking.

That evening I came up with a theory. I'd popped into a Sainsburys and bought a sewing kit in order to perform some self-surgery on my feet. While I was resting them, laid up on the bed in my budget hotel in the centre of Liverpool, I wondered if it might be possible to categorise different types of what I'd decided to call 'encounters'. I'd had quite a few conversations with people by now and I could spot some differences between them.

An Encounter of the First Kind would be when I initiated the contact, either through a greeting or a question. An Encounter of the First Kind might also come about because of a courtesy, a good example being the receptionist in the hotel that morning who'd asked if I was going far, resulting in an exchange of both information and a card. An Encounter of the Second Kind would be like the one that had taken place in the café in Crosby, more of a conversation, natural rather than actively initiated. An Encounter of the Third Kind would be when someone approached me, as happened with the Sustrans warden. I wondered if, later in the trip, there might also be Encounters of the Fourth Kind, with people seeking me out because they were actually looking for me, maybe because they'd read about my walk. I'd already achieved some coverage in the local press and websites, and I'd already experienced the power of my Diagonal Walking T-shirts. We'd see.

Having rested up, I wandered into the centre of the city on heavily plastered feet. I was after something to eat ultimately, but my immediate target was to find the arch marking the entrance to Liverpool's Chinatown, as the weather had cheered up sufficiently to provide a kind light for photographs. This red-pillared, round-tiled-roofed edifice is indeed impressive, at 13.5 metres tall the largest Chinese arch in Europe. It is a testament to the city's Chinese community, who first arrived in Liverpool as seamen plying the route between the north-west of England and Shanghai, supplemented in the 1950s and 60s by migrants fleeing communism.

I wondered whether the community's relative success in getting its culture accepted and integrated into the local scene offered a lesson for us now, but it didn't look exactly thriving. In fact, I was to read later that one of the co-founders of the Liverpool Chinese Business Association described the area as 'not just in decline, but destitute'. It turns out Liverpool's Chinese are no different from any other Liverpudlians. Their young have spread their wings to Manchester and beyond, thereby reducing the community's size and critical mass, producing a declining spiral as fewer Chinese-based businesses serve their own. Maybe this is a success story, I wondered – a sign of absolute integration. On the other hand, maybe it is a shame their identity has become so absorbed.

On my way back into the centre I was surprised, although perhaps I shouldn't have been, by the high number of homeless amongst the polished glass windows and clean pavements that made up the large shopping complex in the heart of the city. No room for Bargain Booze here. This was a phenomenon I didn't remember from my previous deep look at the country twenty years before, and it had been catching a lot of headlines. When the shoppers went home, the homeless emerged, some even erecting lightweight tents. It was possible that they were attracted not only by the warmth from the pavements, but also by the two young volunteers offering free hot drinks (they even had coffee!) along with prepared meals in aluminium containers.

I wanted to stop and chat to these Good Samaritans, but my feet were screaming for me to stop, just stop, anywhere (Chinatown had been a bit further than I'd expected), and the sight of hot food was sending a further reminder to my stomach that it hadn't seen anything hot since breakfast. Maybe I'd be able to catch them the next day, as my schedule included a rest day in Liverpool.

Resting up was the plan, but events took over. By the end of the following day I'd covered my greatest distance yet, over fifteen miles, nearly all of it on hard pavements in walking boots. I set out wanting to see not only the Liverpool the tourists saw, which was inconvenient as I have no interest in the Beatles, but also some of the other side of the city, where people didn't usually roam. I'd been intrigued by a television documentary series earlier that year called *The £1 Houses*. This focussed on an initiative by the local council whereby, rather than knock down some derelict houses, they offered to sell them for a single quid to people prepared to do them up. There was a catch however; actually two. Potential purchasers had to prove they had at least £40,000 cash to do the work with, which had to be done in a year. Then, and only then, would the council transfer ownership.

It was a good idea – something different, an attempt to be innovative and encourage people to take personal responsibility for improving themselves rather than waiting for someone else to do it for them. But it was flawed. Legal problems meant the council was unable to fulfil its promises to a large proportion of those involved. Plus the matter of not handing over title until the work was done required not only trust, but also left those who'd invested their cash vulnerable. One family had had their property robbed of all its valuables just before they moved in, their renovated house a beacon to those on the make. Worse still, because they hadn't yet actually owned the property, they'd been unable to insure their possessions.

The houses were in an area called the Webster Triangle in the Toxteth area. The very name Toxteth carried a stigma. Back in the 1980s it had been the scene of riots, mainly involving young black youths. Paul Theroux visited the area as part of his coastal perambulation. He was greeted with scenes of devastation and an aftershock of dismay from those he spoke to, although he did reflect that what he saw wasn't any worse than rundown areas of New York. This offered some cold comfort I supposed.

I walked from the centre, past the Catholic cathedral – which, with its crown-of-thorns central steeple, goes under a number of pseudonyms, the least offensive of which is probably 'Paddy's Wigwam' – as well as the nearby Everyman Theatre and university. Cutting through a park, diagonally of course, the housing began to take on the form I'd seen the day before, more terraced and less even in quality, but nothing so bad that you'd contemplate giving it away for the price of a cup of coffee. As I approached the Webster Triangle, I was struck by what my Southport host might have labelled 'relative prosperity', although the parameters that constituted that relativity may have shifted. There was a huge high school ringed with a high security fence, a functioning church, a pharmacy, a nursery and a Neighbourhood Centre right on the edge of the Triangle. The last, as far as I was able to make out, was made up mainly of doctors' surgeries.

It was easy to spot the houses involved in the scheme when I reached them. Some, around one in twenty, had clearly been renovated, with sparkling new doors and even cars outside. Others, around the same proportion, were in the process of having work done, encased with scaffolding and surrounded by builders busy doing what builders do – delivering materials, mixing up concrete, swearing imaginatively, sucking their teeth and looking worried. All the rest remained fit for demolition. Doors and windows had all been shuttered with metal; any visible paintwork was flaked; roof tiles were missing and vegetation was growing out of walls, through chimneys, in gutters and along windowsills. A road sign on Bird Street said it was 'Unadopted'. It wasn't kidding.

Looking around the back of the houses, I noticed that one of the renovated properties, identifiable by the fresh tiles on its roof, had erected a high metal wall to prevent people entering from the back – possibly one of those caught in the uninsurable trap? The houses that had been invested in looked good. The owners had painted them, added nice touches like stained glass and, of course, added new front doors. Back when this area was still the subject of riots and it was government policy to sell off council housing, a new front door was always the sign that an ex-council tenant had become a homeowner.

Curious to know how things were going, I called in on the local News and Booze (he was underselling himself, he also sold vegetables, although his shop was an asparagus-free zone) and quizzed the man behind the counter. Young, probably in his twenties, and rake-thin, he was strangely nervous. I supposed that, with my accent and questions he had me down as a journalist – a shout that may have been corroborated by the KitKat I bought to get his attention.

He started by saying it had 'all been a massive mistake', although he caved in rapidly when I challenged this, which made me suspect he was parroting a party line.

'No, okay, it was a good idea,' he conceded 'Just that the council was just too slow like.' In what way I asked? 'In handing over the keys like,' he added, confirming one of the conclusions of the documentary.

The ice having been broken, the young shopkeeper went on: 'I gorra mate who's got one. Made it into six bedrooms like. It's great. But he won't move in like, no' with the kids and that like.' Into his stride now, he went on to say that the council expected people to have too much money up front. That said, his mate had clearly managed it, and the application list was now full, so enough people clearly did have the wherewithal to invest.

I could see where his mate was coming from, though. The scheme needed to generate a critical mass, and while work was ongoing, it looked a way off achieving it. Would the speed of renovation ever gain enough pace to overtake the rate of decay and what appeared to be a growing mood of cynicism? I hoped so and said as much before thanking the jittery young man and moving on.

Before leaving, I called in on the Neighbourhood Centre, which was all shiny new and clean. To my surprise, as my own doctor's surgery would have been heaving at this time, it was almost devoid of people. Those who were there were either asleep or worse, perhaps homeless or under the influence of something. No one challenged me, so I took advantage of the fact that it was probably the cleanest place around and availed myself of the facilities.

I re-set my phone's map and set off for my next destination, back towards the river and the site of the Liverpool Garden Festival. This was the brainchild of the then Minister of the Environment, Michael Heseltine. It was a response to the clamours that 'we must do something' after the riots in various cities of the realm in the 1980s, in Toxteth and elsewhere. It's possible that the then Prime Minister Margaret Thatcher had taken the view that it would keep her troublesome minister off her back for a while, but nevertheless, Liverpool's was to be the first in a series of such annual festivals held in various different cities, and had been open from May to October in 1984.

As it closed its doors for the final time, the festival was seen as a success, attracting more than three million visitors. But its effect was temporary. During the following years a succession of developers put forward plans to build houses on the site, although a portion of it remained for a few years as an amusement park. The focal point of the exhibition, the Festival Hall, was finally demolished in 2006, and after that a thousand new houses were finally built. Four years later, the festival's Chinese and Japanese Gardens were restored. They along with a small pond are about all that remains of the old gardens. It took me half an hour to walk there, narrowly avoiding a brightly coloured coach offering a Magical Mystery Tour along the way. When I reached the site there was only me and a mum with two small boys enjoying it. Pink blossom decorated the trees in the Japanese Garden, and some promised sunshine was tentatively emerging from high clouds.

Nervous of how I might come across, I approached the young mum, who was welcoming and invited me to sit down. Her name was Jacqui, and she immediately informed me that she was home-schooling her boys, which was why they were with her and not at school. I didn't think I looked like a Truancy Officer, but maybe they go around in disguise. One of the boys was taking photographs of the nearby Chinese Pavilion, whilst the other was sketching a coot nesting in the middle of the pond. The obvious question was whether she had any particular reason for removing her children from the school system.

She explained how the elder of the two boys hadn't enjoyed school, indeed he'd become unwell through anxiety. She was told he'd settle, but he didn't. When she raised the subject with the headmistress, Jacqui found her blasé about the boy's problems and unable to offer alternatives. When she brought up the subject of home-schooling, the headmistress offered little insight. After due research, Jacqui decided the best thing was to take both boys out of the system.

She didn't look back. She found a highly supportive network, and of course there was the internet with its opportunities to connect and its access to resources. This sparked a wider discussion between us about rigid thinking in institutions in education and health, how the monolithic nature of the system makes innovative thinking, of the type the council had tried with the £1 houses, so difficult, and therefore the exception rather than the rule. We agreed that we were sympathetic to those running such institutions.

Their job in a time of constrained resources was probably more one of fire-fighter than pioneer. But the issue did raise a bigger question about change and how to bring it about in such important areas, where structures are often stuck using models that are probably at least half a century out of date.

Ours was a meeting of minds. The internet was changing not only possibilities, but how people thought. The educational establishment seemed to see its role as providing knowledge when knowledge was readily available at the touch of a screen. What was needed was a greater emphasis on teaching students how to think, and to think creatively, so they could cope with change, which was coming at a rate faster than most people's ability to deal with it. We agreed this wasn't easy. Teachers these days were forced to concentrate on containing as much as nurturing their charges, acting as social workers and substitute parents as much as educationalists, responsibilities laid on them by external forces beyond their control.

Inevitably, and for the first time during my walk, we got onto Brexit. We concurred that some of the external forces we'd been discussing probably lay at the root of the discontent people felt, not least the pace of change, and they'd expressed this by kicking out at 'the system' at the first opportunity. It was just happenchance that the EU had been the subject made available for a kicking. The subject matter had also allowed a clear level of xenophobia at best, at worst racism and Islamophobia, to surface; even if this was something that had subsequently become the subject that dared not speak its name.

On the way into Toxteth that morning I'd seen a large stencilled graffito on the side of the university posing the question, 'ARE YOU OPTIMISTIC ABOUT THE FUTURE?' It seemed to sum up the question I was ultimately posing, to myself and others along my walk. I asked Jacqui for her response. Luckily, she was an articulate woman and wasn't too fazed by a question I realised later was the conversational equivalent to suddenly tossing someone a medicine ball in a game of French cricket. She was unhesitating in saying 'Yes'. 'You have to stay positive,' she continued, 'to people and to change'. I'd enjoyed our exchange and said so, giving her details on how to follow my walk. It was an excellent example of an Encounter of the Second Kind, the first of many I hoped.

It was time for lunch, so picking up on the mood of optimism I set out in the expectation that something would turn up, and it did. A riverside pub offering the usual fare of something with salad and chips. It was at the end of the long Otterspool Promenade, much of which was constructed as part of the Garden Festival, suggesting its legacy had been more than just a few oriental trees. The day had now turned into a scorcher, and I was glad I wasn't carrying my rucksack. Views out to the Mersey were bracing, while inland there was a marina and fantastic vistas over to the city's two cathedrals, with the larger Anglican version, the Cathedral Church of Christ in Liverpool, dominating.

The playwright J.B. Priestley in his acclaimed 1930s travelogue *English Journey* described the centre of Liverpool as 'dignified and darkish', comparing it to a gloomy Victorian novel. Priestley only ever saw Liverpool in the winter. His description certainly did not apply to the city I saw on this bright spring afternoon. The waterside was populated with shiny new developments, similar to those that line both banks of the Thames in London – all red bricks and blue metal balconies overlooking the water. When Priestley looked for the underside of Liverpool, he headed not for Toxteth but the docks. They wouldn't be his choice today. The docks I saw were abuzz with tourists, many of them with Japanese rather than Scouse accents. I wondered if they knew about the gardens two miles away, but why would someone from Japan come to Liverpool to see something they had at home? No, they were here for the whole Beatles experience and to have their picture taken by the statue of the Fab Four opposite the Liver Building.

The docks themselves, once state-of-the-art freight depots, were now state-of-the-art catering and souvenir establishments, with the occasional museum (very good museums as it turned out) to add a veneer of culture. It was at Pier Head that I finally succumbed and had a coffee at the Fab Four Café. I needed refreshment, and I had somewhere I needed to visit – it had become a case of 'All Things Must Pass'.

Having failed to find the soup kitchen volunteers that evening, I headed for an Italian restaurant. Opposite me were what appeared to be another mother and daughter pairing, although this one clearly enjoyed a more affluent lifestyle than the duo I'd seen in Norris Green. I guessed the daughter was a student and the mother was visiting. Disappointment fizzed between them like static electricity. The daughter sported a fresh tattoo on the inside of her arm and was explaining it to her mother, whose reaction included the word 'disgusting' as she pulled a face to match. Conversation was, at best, sparse. Although intergenerational unease is nothing new, what followed is, perhaps, more recent, as each focussed their attention on their phone, preferring to communicate with others rather than each other.

Only when the food came, and they were forced to put their phones down, was an attempt made to connect. Even then, the daughter picked hers up again to take a picture of her meal. Until that point, whenever one looked like she was finishing whatever it was she was doing on her phone, the other would start up again on hers – an eternal game of cyber-tag. I watched and made some notes, before returning to checking my own Twitter and Instagram followers. Well, at least I had an excuse, I was on my own and carried a duty to keep my accounts up to date.

A young male gay couple arrived and couldn't keep their hands off each other. That such public affection between a same-sex couple seemed so ordinary was perhaps something that had changed in the last twenty years. On the other side of the glass, two young women worked their way through a bottle of rosé sharing a packet of crisps. Although this might have happened twenty years ago, what was different was the reason they were outside. They were both smokers. 'Can't Buy Me Love' came onto the sound system, so I asked for the bill and left, but only after an Encounter of the First Kind with the chatty American waitress while we waited for the card reader to get a signal.

My two nights in Liverpool over, the next day I headed back to Lime Street Station. Standing at the top of the station's steps, I reflected that Liverpool wore its history well. Contemporary and Victorian architecture, such as the cleaned-up St. Georges Hall opposite, sat well together. My wanderings the previous day suggested that Liverpool was really two cities. Whilst this might be true of most places, the extremes had felt particularly stark here. I'd enjoyed it all, though, and I decided that I liked Liverpool, with its efforts to make the best of itself (the regeneration of the docks in the 1980s being a notable example of success, even if the Garden Festival had left less of a lasting legacy), and its 'café society' feel in the sunshine.

I clearly wasn't alone in my fondness. Liverpool has acted like a magnet for travel writers over the years. Perhaps the best-known contemporary one, Bill Bryson, another American, visited in the 1990s, around ten years after his countryman Theroux. While admitting Liverpool was probably his favourite British city (although I liked it, I wouldn't go that far), he also felt it was a city with more of a past than a future, but I wasn't sure I agreed. I thought it had both.

Back on the road, I made a point of greeting everyone like some manic idiot, hoping for another encounter but without success. Were they a particularly grumpy lot in this part of the city? Then I realised why no one was responding. They all wore headphones of one sort or another in their ears. I contented myself with the birdsong and distant traffic noise as I walked past a large solar array in a field to my left. The Liverpool Loop terminated at Halewood Park, a large expanse of grass overlooking a factory with three tall chimneys. I celebrated by taking off my rucksack and stretching. I was wearing one of my T-shirts, so I shouldn't have been surprised when the encounter I'd been fishing for happened unexpectedly, one of the hallowed Third Kind.

'Walk with feckin' me? What the feck's that all about then?'

Two willowy men were standing behind me, one of them brandishing a dog, the other a menacing expression. I turned around and greeted them, before beginning my spiel. When I'd finished, the response was, perhaps, predictable.

'Feckin' 'ell.'

This, I'd found, was a common response, although perhaps not always so succinctly expressed. I'd learned not to start with the details of my quest as it appeared to overwhelm people, leaving them unable to deliver an adequate response. The most common reaction was, 'Are you doing it for charity?' For many people this was evidently the only reasonable excuse for doing something so madcap. Doing it for personal challenge didn't seem to enter their head.

When I mentioned the end point of the walk as near Dungeness in Kent the response was emphatic and immediate: 'Never feckin' heard of it,' as if the speaker's ignorance meant it didn't actually exist.

His name was Andy and interestingly, he'd moved to Halewood from Oxford, where I guessed he hadn't been a professor, unless perhaps of Anglo-Saxon, which he tended to use in the same way other people use commas. I was right. He had been a painter and decorator and had done all right, retiring to be nearer family six years before. I asked him how he'd found it.

'Feckin' terrible,' came the perhaps inevitable reply. Why? 'All they're after is me feckin' money. They found out I had a feckin' pension pot like, and three feckin' times they've feckin' robbed me of it.' Coming from the south, he'd been fair game apparently.

Young people were another target of his vitriol. 'No feckin' respect,' he said, adding that he hadn't found the sense of community he'd expected by moving north.

In an effort to change the subject I asked him if the big industrial plant to the right of the park was the Halewood car plant, notorious in the 1970s and 80s for the strikes by its Ford workers.

He said it was, adding, 'Feckin' thing. Spews out feckin' smoke. See the feckin' flares go up at night, no feckin' idea what they're burning. Even on hot feckin' days like this we 'ave to keep the feckin' windows shut 'cos of the feckin' pollution.

'Still, got to this feckin' age, that's good enough for me,' he concluded, fatalistically, adding as he left, 'Guinness is better here though,' suggesting it was because Liverpool was closer to Ireland, and thereby demonstrating he had at least a rudimentary grasp of geography.

I let him and his mate drift down the side of the park before pulling my rucksack back on and was immediately adopted by a dog walker. If Andy had struggled with Dungeness (and very possibly with the notion of Kent), this elderly gentleman seemed unable to talk about anywhere outside an area of two miles' radius from where we were. We parted ways when his thoughts distilled to the progress of a particular mud patch we were walking through.

Surprise, surprise, 'Mr Feckin'' was wrong when it came to the car plant, which sits, appropriately enough, by the side of a busy road. No longer owned by Ford, it is part of

Jaguar Land Rover, now the country's largest car maker and owned by Tata Motors from India. The plant with the three chimneys was a chemical plant, or possibly pharmaceuticals. The dog walker hadn't been sure, even though it was on his doorstep. Either way, 'Mr Feckin" was probably right to keep his windows shut.

I crossed the road and skirted a large estate, which presumably had once housed many of the plant's workers, although an underpass linking the two was now disused. People were taking advantage of the nice weather to cut their grass; the houses being generally well maintained. There was a church and a doctor's surgery, the latter surrounded by high security fencing. On reaching a corner of the estate I took a detour off the Trans Pennine Trail down the unpromisingly named Dungeon Lane to take advantage of a section of the Mersey Way, a path beside the river, leaving the housing behind me. The road was unloved, running alongside a tall wire fence protecting what looked like an airfield, watched over by an uninterested-looking man in a small van. Things were quiet, with one or two light aircraft and a wooden hut belonging to a local flying club.

I found the river and settled down to a good view of an oil refinery on the opposite shore and speculated on how many more years it would be needed if the current progress of solar installations like the one I'd seen that morning was kept up. Making myself comfortable, I extracted the lunch I'd bought earlier and took on some water. Birdsong regained the air and I absorbed my surroundings. A passing cyclist stopped and trained his binoculars on the water, asking me if there was any sign of the dolphins.

He might just as well have asked me if nightingales still sang over Red Square at midnight. 'I was here the other day and saw them,' he explained, 'but I didn't have my fucking camera.' I sympathised. 'That's the second time that's happened to me like. The other time it was otters.' He finally got around to asking what I was up to, as local wildlife clearly wasn't my speciality. I explained. 'That's a fucking long way,' he informed me, as if this was something I didn't know. 'Anyway,' he went on, 'these dolphins …'

His discourse on the feeding habits of the dolphin was gradually drowned out by the sound of a jet plane, heading straight for us. As it lowered itself over the headland, its easyJet markings were clearly visible. It flew so close I could almost detect the sad expressions on the faces of people in the window seats looking down.

The airport perimeter I'd passed earlier was that of Liverpool Airport, formerly known as Speke, now more commonly referred to as, yes, you've guessed it, John Lennon Airport.

I'd been beaten by the Beatles.

3

Water, Water

The following day was forecast to be even hotter, so I got up early and helped myself to a modest breakfast from the various cereals, bread and fruit juice left out downstairs in the pub I'd stayed in overnight. Having followed the Mersey Way into Widnes, I'd spent the previous evening enjoying the remnants of the sunshine while partaking of the 'Curry Special'– a pint, curry, chips, rice and a naan, all for a fiver. What could go wrong? When I'd asked what type of curry, I'd received a blank stare. 'It's just curry,' I was told.

The final couple of miles into Widnes had been a delight. I met birdwatchers, saw bullfinches and herons and had a few encounters. Maybe it was the weather, but suddenly everyone wanted to talk. One man, holding a dog and waiting for his headphoned-up daughter at Hale

Point lighthouse, engaged me in a conversation about house prices, telling me that his first house, bought in 1970, had cost him £600. 'These days you're looking at two hundred thou' for a starter,' he exclaimed: an impossible sum. He didn't know how his daughter would ever get going on a mortgage. I sympathised, although I wondered if his real concern was never getting her to leave home. She wasn't the most exciting conversationalist.

I didn't dare tell him that two hundred thou' wouldn't get you a garage around my way, but our conversation was a good reminder of the obsession the English have with home ownership and house prices. Throughout my walk, I regularly encountered this fear that a generation was being condemned to a lifetime of renting. I heard news media reporting on it, too, as if it was an epidemic on the scale of AIDS.

The dog walker directed me towards Hale, and on his advice I diverted down the appropriately named Lighthouse Road. He told me that I had to see the statue of the Childe of Hale, who he was amazed I'd never heard of. This is a life-sized statue of a Hale resident born in the sixteenth century, and when I say life-sized, I mean nine foot three inches tall. The 'childe' in question was John Middleton, thought by many to be the tallest man (or Englishman, according to fable) who ever lived. He was said to sleep with his feet sticking outside the window. Presented to King James I he was given the, er, kingly sum of £20 for defeating the King's champion in a wrestling match. Unfortunately, he was robbed of this when returning to Hale, suggesting both that the locals' reputation for scallywaggery goes back a few centuries, and that there must have been a lot of them.

While in Hale I'd shared a park bench with a man with his foot encased in a protective boot following an operation for a metatarsal injury. He was waiting for his mate, who was jogging, which seemed a bit ironic. When he turned up, it turned out his mate was an amateur boxer and knew plenty of professionals who complained that they spent as much time on social media as they did on training, this having become part of the job. It wasn't time-wasting, but vital work, building their brand so they got invited onto fight cards. I sympathised. I'd already found that constantly updating my various accounts was taking two to three hours out of my day.

Twenty years ago, the thought that people could make a living out of writing apps, or indeed that using apps and social media could be considered working, would have been inconceivable, and yet here we were. I remembered a conversation I'd had with a friend on millennium night. Seeing the rate at which traditional jobs were disappearing, he'd wondered how his children would ever make a living. My response was remarkably prescient. I replied that they'd be doing things that hadn't even been invented. What a clever young thing I was back then. Having bemoaned the way the world was going, I parted company with the amateur boxer and his crocked friend, but not before he asked me for details of my social media. He never followed me.

Breakfast over, my biggest concern on this fresh day was getting over the Silver Jubilee Bridge linking Widnes with

Runcorn, which had been a landmark for most of the previous afternoon. The bridge was shut for repairs and had effectively been replaced by the spanking new Merseyside Gateway bridge, a couple of miles down the road. This was the subject of some controversy as it charged tolls. A court case was being pursued by a so-called celebrity lawyer (I didn't know such a thing existed, was this one of the new jobs I'd predicted?), who went under the nickname 'Mr Loophole'. Later in the year the same lawyer got David Beckham off a speeding charge.

He claimed that Halton Council had not specified the tolls correctly and had failed to give sufficient notice of the fees, both charges the council strongly disputed. The case suggested that millions of payments were illegal and would need refunding. I found this whole case fascinating. It highlighted not only the growing use of litigation, of trying to catch someone out and being cleverer than them, but also attitudes towards the funding of public infrastructure. The bridge had cost £600m to build. To me it seemed reasonable to ask those using it to contribute, leaving public money for other more deserving causes.

The underlying logic of the case, other than the smart alec one, appeared to be that these things should be free, that taxes should pay for everything. It was as if ten years of austerity, and the message that the state's resources were limited and choices needed to be made, had yet to permeate. A similar attitude seemed to apply to all public services, notably health and education, and I wondered whether an opportunity had been missed to have a proper conversation on what the role of the state was in the modern world. Meanwhile, politicians and the press connived in maintaining a model of informing and engaging people that was stuck in the pre-internet age, something thrown into stark relief by their conduct during the Brexit Referendum so-called debate.

Luckily, and perhaps ironically, I was able to cross the new bridge for free, using a shuttle bus laid on by an anonymous benefactor. This deposited me at a spot in Runcorn that held a dear place in my heart – and that's not a phrase I thought I'd ever type. It was here, under the Silver Jubilee Bridge and at the terminus of the Runcorn Arm of the Bridgewater Canal, that I'd moored up twenty years previously with my brother and nephew, where our experiences formed a chapter of *Walking on Water*. These centred on impressions of a Saturday night in the town and a visit to a curry house and its inevitable intestinal aftermath in the confined spaces of a narrowboat. It's fair to say that my impression at the time wasn't favourable. I'd described it as 'a bit of a hole', and if anything, twenty years later, that hole looked like it had deepened. The town felt flat, existing rather than excited, long rows of terraced housing speaking of a different century. Okay, it was early morning, and maybe the closure of the bridge had depressed trade, but the regular arrival of the shuttle bus appeared to offer the only signs of life.

I resolved to walk on, but immediately got lost following signs for the Trans Pennine Trail (for it was back). It was difficult to escape the conclusion these signs had been designed to indicate a vague direction and then leave the walker to it. After forty-five minutes of wandering around identical-looking houses I spotted two things on the map: first was a series of contours suggesting a climb; and second a shortcut to the canal. I opted for the second, confident that it was pretty difficult to get lost on a towpath.

On reaching the water, I stopped to rehydrate. It was already getting warm and the back of my T-shirt was feeling decidedly moist. The canal was my second of the walk, but by no means the last. Because the canal system had originally been designed as a 'Grand Cross', linking the four great rivers of the Mersey, Trent, Severn and Thames, it too had a long diagonal going north-west to south-east, and for long stretches its towpaths were often more or less contiguous with my route.

After a couple of miles, I took a footpath over some fields to hook up with the main arm of the Bridgewater Canal, the country's first since Roman times, and the brainchild of the civil engineer James Brindley. This clings to the edge of a hill and passes under the M56 motorway linking Manchester and Chester. I felt like I was making real progress as I headed southwards, past the entrance to the Runcorn Arm and the portal of a tunnel.

A black and foreboding hole, whose exit wasn't visible, suggested that, contrary to rumours, there wasn't light at the end of the tunnel. This was Preston Brook, marking the point where the Bridgewater meets the Trent and Mersey. A sign aimed at boaters joining the former highlighted the Bridgewater's unique quality of being privately owned and the licence restrictions this imposed. Like so many canals, the Bridgewater was initially bought by a railway company, but it was sold in 1885 to the Manchester Ship Canal, which now belongs to The Peel Group, a privately owned investment group. Unlike other canals therefore, it had not fallen into public ownership with the nationalisation of the railways, making it an oddity in the system.

Still, I was leaving it, heading uphill over the top of the tunnel, where I spotted the first mile marker of the new canal. Similar to those seen earlier on the Leeds and Liverpool, these marked the distance to Shardlow, near Derby, where the canal linked up with the River Trent. As I climbed up, brick air shafts dotted the top of the tunnel and the scent of wild garlic growing amongst the trees filled my nostrils.

After about a mile of this new canal, I diverted right through some fields on a track called the Delamere Way in order to course-correct onto my diagonal. This brought me down onto another waterway, this time a natural one, the River Weaver, although much of the course was channelled to make what is known as a 'Navigation', fit for boats, sometimes quite big ones. This made for a pleasant change of scene. The waterway was much wider, with grand black and white painted locks to match.

This was turning out to be a day of water, and I stopped to take some more on for myself. Having passed through the 'damp' stage my T-shirt was now firmly en route to 'sopping'. Ploughing on past Dutton Locks I came across the wreck of an old boat called the *Chika* or *Chica*, according to a nearby man I asked who was carrying out some maintenance on his narrowboat. He hinted at a colourful history, and subsequent research backed this up. The boat was constructed in Norway towards the end of the nineteenth century when she'd been called *Flora* and was rigged as a yacht. After having a number of owners and operating as a salt fish carrier, the boat was commandeered by the German Navy in 1940, by which time she'd been fitted with a diesel engine.

After the war, some reports say she operated in the Mediterranean, smuggling tobacco and guns, whilst others say she shipped logs for the rebuilding of Norway. This phase of her history is a bit shady, but what is known is that by the 1980s she ended up in Liverpool and was bought to operate a passenger service up and down the River Weaver as well as operating as a gourmet restaurant. In 1993, just shy of her centenary, she started taking on water and as no one was on board to operate the bilges, she listed and there she remains to this day, rotting and rotten, and something of a blight on this lovely stretch of water.

Other than the *Chika*, the water was populated mainly by mallards and swans. At the magnificent Acton Swing Bridge, which was capable of swinging the A49 out over the water, although thankfully not without stopping traffic first, signs told me I couldn't continue, but were less forthcoming in providing alternatives. Luckily, my OS came to the rescue, offering a steady trudge up a hill on a minor road, where I reacquainted myself with the canal. The spongy turf of the towpath was welcome after the road, while several tens of feet below, the Weaver tracked a parallel route. The mile markers returned, although they registered only a disappointing four miles since Preston Brook.

Further tunnels emerged as I approached Barnton: the Saltersford and, appropriately, the Barnton. On the far side of the former a small and self-important looking man was busy gathering the ropes of his narrowboat, as it was within five minutes of the allotted time for boats to pass through east to west. I told him I'd seen a boat going in bang on the deadline the other end. He immediately turned to announce to others waiting behind him, as if he alone was the source of this intelligence, 'Looks like we've got a rusher'. In that single moment he summed up one of the characteristics of certain boaters, and perhaps certain people (I didn't think it was a particularly English characteristic, although a Scot or Welshman might disagree): that of the self-proclaimed expert.

Around half past four I reached my target for the day, the Anderton Boat Lift, and celebrated with a long swig of water. Reports were suggesting these were the hottest April days for seventy years and it felt like it. We'd seen the Boat Lift in the process of being restored twenty years before, when I'd been cynical about its chances of success. I said as much to my brother and he'd told me not to be so pessimistic. I said then that time would tell, and it had. He'd been right. The structure was now one of the waterways' star attractions.

The lift, consisting of two cassions, or chambers, used to lift boats to and from the Weaver and the canal. It had been built in 1875 to facilitate the transport of pottery and salt. It hadn't been an amazing success. Problems started with an accident seven years later when one of its cylinders burst, sending a chamber, complete with boat, to a premature rendezvous with the river below. Subsequently, the lift's hydraulics faced a constant battle with the corrosive effects of salt, causing them to be replaced with an electrical system. The lift finally closed in 1986, but had reopened in

2002, only three years after I'd been so disparaging about its chances. It was, I thought, a prime example of the English talent for taking one of our prime assets – heritage – and converting it to another use: leisure, a bit like the canal system in general. I'd hoped to visit it, but it turned out to be shut.

I wandered into Northwich where my bed awaited, passing a chemical plant with a round blue plaque stating that Polythene was invented on this site in 1933. It was now a sodium bicarbonate plant owned by Tata Chemicals, owners of British Salt and part of the same Indian conglomerate which owned the old Halewood plant I'd seen the day before. A derelict site next door exemplified the wider decline of the salt industry in the region.

Northwich had been voted one of the best places to live in the UK in a *Sunday Times* survey in 2014 and, superficially at least, it was easy to see why. There are lots of half-timbered buildings, a large and impressive marina and quay, and even a Waitrose, normally a dead giveaway for an affluent area. It is also home to the country's first electronically operated swing bridge, although I doubted this often featured on local estate agents' descriptions. Later, however, I was to hear a report on Radio Four of a different side to the story. The town had recently opened an £80 million new shopping centre called Barons Quay, built on the site of an old salt mine (naturally). This has failed in its primary purpose of attracting any shops. A cinema and a restaurant had become established, but these were symptomatic only of a wider trend in high streets across the country away from the selling of things to the consumption of experiences.

As a result of this initiative, Northwich's traditional high street, where the half-timbered buildings are, was stuck in a sort of limbo, along with the rest of the town. When the development's original developer, a private company, pulled out after the 2008 economic bust, the council had taken over, allocating a further £1.3 million to kick-start its spanking new showpiece, doubling down on its bet that retail had a future. The jury was out. Northwich's experience said so much about both the decline of traditional industries and, in turn, the fundamental shift in the nature of the type of employment it had been hoped would replace them.

The next day I meandered on along the Weaver, a cool breeze now taking the edge off the sun's heat. I made a detour at the spectacular Hartford Bridge, known locally as the 'Blue Bridge' because it is, well, bright blue, in order to call in on Jerry, an old school pal I hadn't seen for decades. Jerry and I used to cycle together to school (remember when children used to do that?), but alas Jerry's cycling days were ended by a terrible accident which broke his neck, confining him to a wheelchair.

Prior to his accident, Jerry was a fighter pilot in the RAF, seeing service in the Iraq War, and later as part of the Battle of Britain Memorial flight. To mark the fiftieth anniversary of VJ Day, he piloted a Dakota down the Mall, dropping a million poppies over the crowds below. He was flying commercial jets in 2007 when he'd been caught by a freak wave on a Mexican beach during a layover. Lucky to have survived, Jerry had not let his misfortunes get to him, becoming an after-dinner speaker and charity campaigner. A keen runner before the accident, for the past ten years he has organised a 'Big Push'[1] around the Manchester 10k run, raising money for a number of charities. As such, it seemed fitting that after our chat Jerry should accompany me to the top of his road in his motorised wheelchair, becoming the first person to 'Walk with Me', metaphorically, if not literally.

It had been great to catch up, but time was ticking on so, topped up with liquid, including some much-appreciated ice, I hit the road again, returning to my route beside the Weaver. This took me through a long 'cut', made to ease navigation, and through the outskirts of Winsford, past active salt works, with veins of salt visible in the soil on the opposite bank. A slight detour then brought me back to my diagonal and a new canal, the Middlewich Branch of the Shropshire Union. These towpaths were proving to be excellent for keeping me on track, and it was along here that I ended up having an encounter with a 'liveaboard' as those who live on their narrowboats are known, although this individual didn't live on his in the winter, and I couldn't blame him. The local landscape was open and I suspected it could get very cold when the wind got up.

His mooring was on a farm, with the farmer treating his liveaboards as a ready supply of informal labour, an arrangement that suited everyone involved. Tall and wearing a flat cap my new friend was happy to talk, probably encouraged when I told him I used to have my own boat, bringing us into a conspiracy of waterfolk. His biggest concern was the number of boats on the canal. On the face

---

1   See http://jerryward.co.uk/Home.php

of it this came across as incredible, but he was insistent that during the summer holidays you could practically walk across the canal over the tops of boats. His other concern was costs, with it costing him £1,500 a year for the mooring and £800 a year for licences, and that was before he got to maintenance and other odds and sods.

Like many other liveaboards, he lived a life that might be described as semi-off-grid, with wider changes taking place in society barely touching him. For him and plenty like him, life was much the same from one year to the next, with its rhythm of winter on-shore and then the agricultural cycle to get stuck into when he got back to his boat. When I asked if he used the internet, he replied that he had little need for it, so giving him a card would have been a waste of time. He must have been a member of one of the very few groups in society for whom the internet was largely irrelevant.

He was also useful in giving me instructions on how to get into Middlewich, the towpath up ahead being closed. I'd heard about this, a major breach in the canal, which had resulted in a huge section of it now bearing more resemblance to the Somme than Flatford Mill. I followed his instructions and made my way into the town, where I'd planned another day off.

If Northwich was having problems with its shopping, at least it had some shops. Middlewich was distinguished by a complete absence of anything useful other than a Tesco Express and a Tesco Superstore, which turned out to be less than super, tucked around the back of the main street. Combined, these had sucked any life out of local retail scene, leaving in its wake only a string of takeaway fast food outlets and a pub or two.

Middlewich's population had doubled since 1970 to roughly 14,000, and indeed, my new billet was in a recently built housing estate. Like Northwich, it too had been voted as one of the most attractive postcodes to live in. Its Wikipedia entry though is nicely ambiguous, and hints at a deeper truth, suggesting that with the decline in local employment, many people live there because it is cheap rather than for what the town actually offers. Even an Ideal Standard factory had recently closed. Even toilet manufacturing had gone down the toilet. My Airbnb hostess worked in Salford and spent most of her weekends in Wales. She referred to Middlewich as 'the village', rather than 'the town', and admitted she had no idea where I could eat, an appreciation of the place that appeared to confirm the Wikipedia entry.

The one thing the town can boast however, is waterways. Not only does it have three rivers, the Dane, Croco and Wheelock, but it is also home to three canals, the Trent and Mersey, the Middlewich Arm of the Shropshire Union (although this was, for the moment, a moot point), and the Wandle. I'd never heard of the Wandle, and when I eventually found it I didn't feel the need to reproach myself. At around fifty yards long, it is the smallest canal in the country, capable of fitting into one photograph. It was cut by the owners of the Trent and Mersey to retain control over the junction with the Middlewich Branch. Clever.

The next day I was back on the towpath, coming up to a series of double locks and the flight of twenty-two deep locks boaters know as Heartbreak Hill. I'd been there and done this twenty years before and remembered being pleased when it was over. At least we'd been a crew of three. As I was wandering, I caught up with another liveaboard I'd spoken with in Middlewich the previous day, and he was taking on the locks alone. Unlike the first liveaboard I'd spoken to, this one was what was known as a continuous cruiser, which meant he had a licence which required him to move on every two weeks. He was on his way to Cambridge – eventually, as he put it. We'd spoken previously when he was negotiating the notorious three locks on an elbow of the canal in Middlewich, when his conversation had consisted mainly of griping against the Canal and River Trust, which he called the Cyclists and Ramblers Trust. This echoed a complaint I'd heard before from liveaboards, that the CRT didn't have the boaters' interests at heart.

'God, we thought British Waterways was bad, but this lot …' He left the sentence unfinished.

The CRT was created in 2012 with the remit to become self-financing. This meant taking a more commercial approach to its property and other assets and, inevitably, the raising of prices for things such as moorings and licences. It also meant interpreting its role more widely than its predecessor British Waterways, embracing and encouraging all users of the canals, including, you've got it, cyclists and ramblers, as well as dog walkers, anglers and so on. This doesn't seem unreasonable, unless of course you are a boater and are used to being seen as the primary users of the waterways, plus the fact that you pay a licence to be on the water whereas no one else did.

In this regard, the CRT is like many other government bodies, or quasi-government bodies, and actually quite late to the 'having to justify your existence' party. The friction between them and boaters perhaps underlines how, in the twenty-first century, there are few places left to run away from the modern world, and how the real world has finally caught up with them. When we'd spoken before, we'd been approaching one of Middlewich's traditional boatyards, and a series of information boards were testament to the town's, or village's according to taste, attempts to carve out some kind of niche for itself. It also held an annual folk and boat festival.

The problem was, although Middlewich was undoubtedly trying hard to make something of its waterside heritage, it was, if you'll pardon the phrase, swimming against the tide of change. Even one of its boatyards had recently gone bust. Perhaps the breach in the canal offered another metaphor? Something had finally given. With its large housing estates and people working away from the town, it must have been hard work to foster a sense of community.

Continuing along the canal, I bumped into a couple from the Isle of Wight out on the water for a week. Before I knew where she was from I mentioned I was from 'down south', a description I'd fallen into using as my home town of High Wycombe rarely featured on anyone's mental map. She remarked how where she came from they regarded the rest of us as coming from the 'north island', which certainly put me in my place.

It was time to get away from the water outside Alsager in Cheshire, where the promise of a pottery on the OS map lured me to make a detour. Immediately off the towpath, I came across a lorry driver with his wagon, staring blankly at the canal bridge and the sign that said there was a seven-ton weight limit.

'Satnav bring you here?' I asked. He nodded and said something I couldn't quite make out above the sound of his still revving engine. We were both looking at the bridge. 'What's your weight?'. Lip-reading, I made out the words 'Nearer nine'. I looked down to the farm where the pottery was supposed to be and suggested he could turn around there. He nodded in resignation, and I left him in order to check out the pottery, as a little something for the wife might be in order. It was shut.

Meanwhile, the silence-shattering sound of the 'beep, beep' of the lorry's reverse filled the air and I checked to make sure I wasn't in his path. I needn't have bothered, as at that moment, the beeps stopped, the engine gunned, and he took the bridge at a speed too great for me to get his licence plate, even if I'd thought of doing so. In three seconds, he'd gone. I checked the bridge for cracks, but he'd got away with it.

I entered Alsager via the Salt Way, which unsurprisingly was another old railway line, used to carry salt, as well as products from the local chemical industries to the potteries in Staffordshire in the 1850s, bringing back coal for those industries on their return journeys. Later, towards the end of the century, it had been used to take passengers to Trentham Gardens in Stoke, a service that continued until 1930, with the goods line closing in 1970.

Alsager is a pleasant small town with a side line in ethical trading (it's a Fairtrade Town), and I reflected that this sort of direction, looking forward rather than to the past, might be more effective than Middlewich's strategy. An information board for Milton House in the middle of the town, whose grounds are now a public park, told how in the 1860s the house belonged to John Maddock Jnr, whose family owned an earthenware factory in Burslem in Stoke. The house's next owner, one William Young Craig, made the house self-sufficient in not only fruit, vegetables and flowers, but also eggs and coal, even producing its own electricity. Perhaps this was where the town got its green credentials from? Alsager still has a high street and even a Costa, something Middlewich couldn't offer, which must make it the only place with a population above three men and a dog that hasn't. It also has a huge modern health centre, although its defining feature, its lake, or Mere, was hidden behind housing.

Alsager also still has a rail line, and a station it is proud of, with a number of plaques screwed to a wall commemorating various wins as 'Station of the Year', something it has achieved without having either a ticket office or even a ticket machine. What it does have is a level crossing and an efficient service to Crewe in one direction and Stoke to the other, and points beyond. It was time to let the train take the strain. The first leg of my walk had come to an end.

Stage 2

Alsager
to
Alrewas

54.7 miles
127,831 steps

4

Pot
Luck

The next section was going to be tricky, with my diagonal line cutting a neat north-west to south-east transverse through a largely rural Staffordshire. Much of the route was through open moorlands, some hills and considerably less convenient places to stay. To ease matters, my wife Annette had agreed to ferry me around and we'd taken a cottage for the bank holiday May Day weekend, a decision swayed by a good weather forecast after the first day. The route also offered an opportunity for some catching up, not only with the course we'd followed twenty years previously, but also with both Annette's and my alma mater, Keele University.

Annette thus became the first person to physically 'walk with me' as we negotiated an open stretch to Newcastle-under-Lyme, where both previously-left car and a bed awaited us. On reaching exposed fields, I immediately spotted an owl flying low over the newly sown crops, and I wondered whether this might be an omen. Maybe it was, as the next few days turned out to be challenging, not so much because of the walking, more for the obstacles put in our way.

Without the reassuring presence of towpaths, it became more important to track our route, both on the map and by following footpath signs. When planning the walk, I'd decided against investing in a handheld GPS, partly because I thought my phone could do the job, but also because I wanted to spend my time looking up, rather than down at a screen. This strategy depended on there being a full complement of signs of course, but as it didn't take long to discover, the local landowners delighted in making life difficult for walkers, either by failing to replace missing signs or by pretending footpaths didn't exist at all. The nominal width of a public right of way is a metre, but it looked like whoever was responsible for maintaining them in Staffordshire had got their metric and imperials mixed up and settled for a foot. Crops were also sown right up to the edge of fields, creating a quagmire along the edge, which in turn made for heavy walking.

Surviving any initial obstacles put in our way only meant being confronted with others. Electric fences turned out to be a popular choice. These fences looked benign, a thin strip of fabric stretched over flimsy plastic poles, but they packed a punch. At one point, Annette slipped in a pool of mud so fresh we suspected it had been deposited there especially that morning, and in trying to regain her balance grabbed a fence that turned out to be live. Luckily for him, the local farmer didn't make an appearance at that point, but as we negotiated a way across his land it felt as if he was tracking us through binoculars and having a damned good chortle.

To top things off, in line with the forecast it began to rain. This was just as we were approaching the highlight of this stretch, the Wedgwood Monument, propped proudly on top of Bignall Hill. Classified as a sub-HuMP (yes, the initialisation is correct), a prominence over 100 metres high, the monument turned out to be a stone edifice with three steps leading to a tall stone plinth with a pointy bit on top. From here it was supposedly possible to catch views out over Cannock Chase, the Peak District and Snowdonia, although we could barely make out Newcastle through the gathering mist.

Quite naturally, given the area we were about to enter, we'd assumed the monument was to Josiah Wedgwood, but we were wrong. It was in fact to a John Wedgwood, a local coal mine owner who, rather modestly, left a sum of money in his will for the construction of a grand obelisk overlooking his old mine. The executors of his will duly fulfilled his wish and, in 1850, eleven years after his death, the monument was completed. According to some sources it also included his tomb, although where they'd kept the body for over a decade remained unanswered.

Imposing though the monument was, until fairly recently it was much more so. It toppled in a storm in 1976, and what's left now is but a stump of what it once was, a sympathetic representation perhaps of the local coal industry, once a huge part of the Staffordshire economy.

Decaying concrete posts were scattered around the monument, suggesting that in the recent past it had served a greater purpose, as a lookout post during the war perhaps, although I could find nothing to support this theory. Maybe it was just to deter visitors, a theory more in line with our experience of Staffordshire so far.

We continued along our path, and were just congratulating ourselves for having left the domain of our malevolent farmer when we were confronted by a large pool of water that had reclaimed the footpath for ducks and anglers. We walked our way round this and, slaloming through some boulders left at the entrance to a path, found our way into Apedale Country Park. This, it turned out, occupies the site of the late John Wedgwood's colliery, now home to a Heritage Centre. Discarded railway tracks and rolling stock were scattered amongst disused buildings, where coal was still mined up until the 1980s. It's still possible to go underground, but only as a paying tourist.

We were approaching the outskirts of Newcastle, and as I'd already discovered, whenever you approach a stretch of open land near a town, so dog walkers start to appear. Before long, these were complemented by two youths, each clutching a can of cider, who left behind a strong smell of something aromatic and illegal. Passing a Speedway Stadium ('70 mph, no gears, no brakes'), a sport I hadn't realised still existed, we entered some housing. A recently built care home on one side of the road faced an uninspiring-looking industrial estate on the other, where signs offered 'Professional Battery Solutions' and 'Dynamic Pump Services', which did leave me wondering about our modern attitudes towards the elderly if this was the best we could offer them as their final view. Still, it could have been worse. A little further on, and totally randomly, a cemetery had been carved into the hill.

A young man pushing a baby buggy walked past us as we entered a housing estate, the buggy containing an infant with two cans of Stella at its feet, presumably for later.

It was then that it happened. An older man, walking at his own pace, and possibly returning to the care home hoping to smuggle in a can or two of his own, uttered the universal Staffordshire greeting: 'Hello me duck'.

We were homing in on the Staffordshire of our memory.

That night, we chose a chain pub to eat in, both for convenience and because there was little other choice. After Annette had given our order to the waitress, who then proceeded to type what looked like the opening chapter of her autobiography into an iPad, a woman on the table next to us cleared her food debris onto her partner's plate and then swiftly lifted up her own to examine the base. Not only were we in Staffordshire, we were also close to Stoke, for this was a characteristic of 'Stokies': checking out the provenance of their crockery.

'Churchill,' she announced, adding 'I'm impressed.'

Churchill is one of the few local potteries still going. It operates out of Tunstall, one of the five towns made famous in the novels by Arnold Bennett. The others are Hanley, which operates as the main centre; Burslem, which is regarded as the mother town and birthplace of the pottery industry; Longton and Fenton (not the dog in the famous YouTube clip). Absent in that list are Newcastle-under-Lyme and, you may have noticed, Stoke itself. Use of the name Stoke-on-Trent to cover the whole area began in 1910, primarily because Stoke was where the train station happened to be.

Stokies tend to have a self-deprecating attitude towards their city, and if my walk into the centre from Newcastle was anything to go by, this might not be an unreasonable approach. Devoid of both a footpath and of my wife, who'd nipped off to do a bit of shopping, I had little choice but to walk alongside some busy main roads, lined with small convenience stores, tattoo parlours, tanning salons and other salubrious establishments. I'd hoped to pass somewhere where I could buy some oatcakes, that rare example of a local food speciality, but I was disappointed. There was one shop dedicated to them, but perhaps inevitably, it was shut. Seemingly for good. A savoury pancake around eight inches in diameter, oatcakes are made using oatmeal, flour and yeast and are generally cooked on a hot plate. They provide a good base for both sweet and savoury fillings and I'd been looking forward to sampling them again after discovering them during my time at university. I'd last tasted them the last time I'd passed through this way in 1999.

Stoke's polycentric nature doesn't do it many favours, with little to distinguish between Bennett's different towns to the outsider, although apparently there's a lot of snobbery between the different locales. Inhabitants of Burslem for example, would not want to be confused with someone from Longton. This was almost ironic, in a sort of 'It may be a dump, but at least it's my dump' kind of a way. Large, dirty civic buildings in rust-coloured brick dominated what I assumed was the centre. The grandeur and optimism they must once have expressed was now diminished by their surroundings. Brown tourist signs offered a Cultural Quarter in what appeared to be a cruel joke.

Not surprisingly, these supposed attractions focussed on the city's Potteries heritage, providing another example, after the Anderton Boat Lift, of the country's talent for tapping into its past in an attempt to underpin the present. When J.B. Priestley passed through the Potteries at the start of the Great Depression, he'd regarded them as unworthy of the potters, who he saw as craftsmen, masters of a skilled and difficult profession. That may well have been true in his day, but my own experience of working in a pottery as a student in the early 1980s was rather different. It was a dehumanising job, ruled by conveyor belts and systems that, even to my innocent eyes, looked inefficient and doomed to be carried out by people earning even less than I was, probably on another continent.

Even in Priestley's time, the writing had been on the wall. In his tour of the area he visited what was regarded at the time as a cutting-edge factory making ceramic electrical insulators. Back then, this had represented the future. In fact, what he witnessed was only a passing phase at the very dawn of an electrical and electronic revolution we are still living through today. Perhaps the future is always out of reach, with change coming faster than our ability to adapt to it?

Given my quest to understand brink-of-Brexit England, I'd taken the fact that Stoke sits plumb on my diagonal line as one of the deciding factors to undertake the walk. After all, Stoke has earned itself the sobriquet of being the 'Brexit Capital of Britain'. Journalists being journalists, this label had stuck, even though it is factually incorrect. Sure, Stoke voted 69.4 per cent in favour of leaving the EU, a high proportion. But less than the nine other areas whose vote had exceeded 70 per cent. The tag had in fact been created by the ex-leader of UKIP (a not terribly exclusive club) Paul Nuttall, when standing in the 2017 parliamentary by-election in Stoke Central. So when anyone, including a journalist, uses this term to describe Stoke they are actually propagating UKIP 'fake news'.

Although Brexit continued to dominate the newspaper headlines during my walk, and to dominate politics, there was little evidence anywhere I went that it was the burning issue on people's minds. It was difficult to escape the impression that people had been asked a question and, in the absence of a proper debate, had responded instinctively; after which they'd just got on with their lives.

Conversations I'd had so far with those favouring Leave had emphasised a wish to protect what they had against perceived outsiders. Walking around Stoke, it was hard to see what was so precious it needed to be preserved. Stoke was a poor city in Priestley's time, and is a poor city now. A survey[2] commissioned by the BBC just prior to my visit revealed that in a listing of average weekly wages in the 64 areas with a population of more than 135,000, Stoke came 54th, with an average wage of just £455, against the national average of £539. A few days later I had a conversation with a woman called Julie, who recounted that she'd grown up in Stoke in the 1950s and like many people there she'd been raised in dire poverty. Where she lived there was no inside toilet and she didn't have a bath until she was fifteen.

---

2   Source: BBC. See: https://www.bbc.co.uk/news/business-43729508

I found myself comparing Stoke with Liverpool, which in the same survey came out pretty much in the middle of average weekly earnings. Both had experienced fundamental changes in the basis of their local economy; both had struggled to come up with a replacement. But Liverpool had come across as having more heart, more soul. That heart was its centre, including its civic buildings and its industrial heritage, where the local authorities had made an effort to spruce the place up, as if it was expecting important visitors. Stoke suffered from having no discernible historic centre and looked resigned to its fate. It had lost its coal mining, most of its potteries, a steel industry and even the vast bulk of employment at one time offered by the tyre manufacturer Michelin. It felt like Stoke had run out of luck. It was punch drunk, a washed-up fighter incapable of stopping further blows. To make matters worse, in the same way that one of the ways Liverpudlians defined themselves was through their football teams, so Stokies coalesced around the magnificent new stadium of their local team, Stoke City. As a final blow upon a bruise, during our time there the team was relegated from the Premier League.

Also like Liverpool, Stoke had attempted to become a European City of Culture, bidding for the status in 2021. They made the shortlist and, in an attempt to publicise their bid, had launched a plastic duck into space as a homage to their local greeting. There is a video of this on YouTube, and when I watched it I'd anticipated seeing a small rocket blast off from a field somewhere. Instead, it was little more than a powerful drone, which following a less than dramatic 'three-two-one' slowly meandered its way into the upper atmosphere, smiling benignly at the camera in front of it, before coming down, probably over somewhere like Latvia, the reaction of whose locals could only be imagined. Stoke eventually lost its bid to Coventry, and, in an ultimate twist of fate, in the end wouldn't have been granted the status even if they'd won – because of Brexit.

More hopeful was something else the two cities had in common: an attempt to regenerate a rundown area by offering houses for sale for £1. Like the Webster Triangle in Liverpool, Stoke is offering houses in its Portland Street Estate for that sum on the condition that new residents stay for a minimum of ten years. Instead of expecting incomers to raise their own £40,000, Stoke offers loans of £33,000 per house. Although, as with Liverpool, it is too early to tell whether this scheme will work, the early signs are encouraging. Although those incomers taking up the scheme were initially viewed with suspicion, they have since started to take the initiative to turn the community around, including turning an abandoned pub into a community centre, and creating a Social Enterprise based on ceramics, once again using raw clay to fashion something Stoke could be proud of.

I didn't actively dislike Stoke, it's more a case of there wasn't much to like. At one point it was fashionable amongst politicians to talk about JAMs – people who were 'Just About Managing'. I wondered if Stoke was an example of a GUM – 'Given Up Managing'? I hoped not. A recent documentary made by *The Guardian* newspaper[3] for their

---

3   Source: The Guardian Online. See: https://www.theguardian.com/cities/ng-interactive/2018/jan/08/made-in-stoke-on-trent-episode-1-we-have-lift-off

website had been castigated locally for taking too negative a view of the place, forcing the filmmakers to re-visit the city to present a more positive message. It was hard to say they'd succeeded.

Another way of looking at Stoke's predicament was to see it as suffering from post-PMT – a reference to its local bus company, the quaintly named Potteries Motor Traction, which provided most of our transport during our time at university. It is now known by the more prosaic name of First Potteries.

It was time to move on. The volume of traffic on A-roads in the heart of Stoke mean that this wasn't a walker's city, and I was keen to get going. But before then I had a couple of excursions lined up, and I met up again with Annette. The first shared yet another Liverpool connection, but this was one where Stoke fared rather better.

Liverpool hosted the first of the National Garden Festivals in 1984. Two years later Stoke was the venue for the second. As in Liverpool, I was keen to see what had happened to the site. This is located just north of the city – between Hanley and Burslem if that helps – where the Shelton Bar British Steel works used to stand until 1978, when steel joined the list of industries deserting Stoke. Known as Festival Park, it is now mostly devoted to retail. When I asked Julie from Stoke a couple of days later what people did now in the city she remarked how it was all distribution and retail, and this temple to consumerism supported her thesis. It wasn't just shops and warehouses. There was also a cinema, a ski slope, a toboggan run and a waterpark, as well as a marina attached to the nearby Trent and Mersey Canal. There were also some offices, including those of the betting firm bet365, in premises that once belonged to the local newspaper.

As for evidence of the Festival itself, we found this round the back of the Morrisons car park. You can still wander around a substantial portion of the site, which includes a slight climb up to a trig point, which no doubt helped save it from the developers' machines. In a nice piece of symmetry, a statue by Anthony Gormley, our friend from Crosby, had once stood at the top of this hill, but wisely perhaps, it had been removed. Called *A View, A Place* it consisted of one of Gormley's trademark single figures looking out over the Fowlea Valley.

What had once been a suspension bridge over one of the main walkways of the site was now closed due to rotting timbers. Scattered elsewhere were the remains of sculptures and flower beds and, with a bit of imagination, it was possible to make out some of the park's layout. In one corner, we found a ring of old palm trees, somewhat the worse for wear. Still, the Festival had been more than thirty years ago, and that there was anything at all left to see was something of a miracle. The site originally had its own railway, but this was sold off lock, stock and sleepers to a Bygones Museum in Norfolk, while two of the four locos used on the track were sold to a safari park in Spain. The site was well maintained, but not developed. You could say it was just about managed.

As we needed to stock up on provisions before moving on to our cottage for the weekend, we took advantage of the Morrisons. Disappointingly, this too was devoid of oatcakes, although what it did have was a lot of (how shall

I put this?) generously proportioned people. It can be a fun exercise to look in other people's shopping trolleys, but I do not recommend doing so in the Morrisons on Festival Park in Stoke. At a time when obesity is a very live topic, we were shocked by how little heed many of the good people of Stoke were paying to what they put in their mouths. It's easy to be judgemental I know, and I too could do with losing a few pounds, but there's a difference between carrying a bit extra and being positively suicidal. It was their ages that troubled me the most – people still in their thirties who were clearly obese, if not morbidly so. It was probably unlikely that many would ever shift that sort of weight. Like their city perhaps, they had given up and accepted that they were what they were.

Having loaded our car with our relatively meagre purchases, we had one more stop before we could put our feet up. This was to visit the campus of our shared old university of Keele, just outside Newcastle-under-Lyme. We'd both failed to recognise any of Newcastle when we'd passed through and were hoping for better luck there.

Our immediate reaction was of shock. Not only had the main entrance been moved, but we felt as if we were back in the commercial area next to the Festival Park. Large sparkling new concrete and glass buildings, including a whole new Medical School, occupied the side of a hill where, during our time there forty years before, there'd been a lone observatory used by a few equally lonely Astronomy students. Yes, there were Astronomy students. There was a rumour during our time that the hill remained undeveloped because it housed a secret nuclear bunker, one of many supposedly dotted alongside the motorway system (the M6 used to be visible from my room), designated for Very Important People. Or possibly not that important if they were destined to eke out the last days of their lives underground in Newcastle-under-Lyme. It was a fun theory, but if it was a secret bunker, how come everyone knew of it?

We started by revisiting our old Halls of Residence. The one I used to gaze out of onto the M6 had been condemned as it started to slide closer to the service station that shared the university's name. The one I'd lived in during the second year had already gone. Vamoosed, demolished, a victim of mining subsidence. Annette, meanwhile, was having better luck. All of her old homes were still intact, although there were signs of impending redevelopment. It was sobering to think that the buildings – well most of them – had been around for longer after we'd left them than they had been before we'd lived in them. Maybe, like parts of us, they were due for renewal. In fact, there was building going on everywhere, almost as if the university offered a Construction degree, with an emphasis on the practical.

Also noticeable was the sheer diversity of the student body. In our day, there were foreign students (as they were called) but broadly the university was the preserve of the children of the white middle classes. The student body now constituted a regular United Nations, with a spectrum of different tongues spoken, skin colours and ethnicities. As a campus university, Keele offers a comforting community feel for those coming to the country for the first time, but this offered only a partial explanation. This mix isn't unique, in fact, around one in five of university places in the UK are now taken by non-nationals.[4] It was sobering to wonder what might happen if this flow of students, and money, dried up in a post-Brexit Britain. Combined with demographic trends impacting upon the sheer number of home-grown eighteen-year-olds, institutions like Keele could be in for a hard time.

One of the most significant changes that has taken place in recent years has been the expansion of higher education. When we went up to Keele around one in seven eighteen-year olds went to university.[5] By 2000, when I'd last passed through the area on our canal boat, it had risen to 35 per cent and now it was closer to 50 per cent. Whilst this has undoubtedly had its benefits, it has also brought problems, not least the issue of how to pay for it all.

Tuition fees were first introduced under a Labour government in 1998 in the teeth of much opposition. Fees then were *up to* (a point often forgotten) £1,000 a year. At the time of writing they are *up to* £9,250, having been capped. In our day, there used to be a queue to collect your student cheque (remember those?) from a desk in an old Nissen hut. We then trotted down to the on-site bank branch (remember them?) to pay the cheque in. Each Friday we'd return to take out a 'Five and five ones', or ten pounds, which was supposed to see us through the week. If we were

---

4   Source: UK Council for International Student Affairs. See: https://www.ukcisa.org.uk/Research--Policy/Statistics/International-student-statistics-UK-higher-education

5   Source: The Revolution in England's Universities 1980-2000 by Peter Maitlis. See: http://warlight.tripod.com/MAITLIS.html

feeling particularly adventurous, we might even use the new-fangled Cashpoint to get the money, but there was no guarantee of getting the 'five ones' that way.

The rapid rise in tuition fees has undoubtedly contributed to a growing sense of inter-generational friction, expressed both financially, and in terms of fairness. And who can blame today's students? Whereas their parents (if they went to university, which, remember, most didn't) had everything paid for them, the young adults we were seeing on the campus would leave with a degree that might or might not get them a job and be encumbered with a massive debt, in some cases rising to as much as £50,000.

In a country where so much value and status is invested in home ownership this is a major problem. Just when they should be accumulating cash to get on the housing ladder, first-time buyers find themselves fighting to raise a deposit. I recalled the conversation I had outside Hale with the man who said he couldn't see how his children could ever afford their own home. In theory, getting a good education and increasing your life chances should be making you happier. So why is it that research by the charity, The Princes Trust,[6] has showed that the happiness of young people (defined as sixteen- to twenty-five-year-olds) is currently at its lowest point across every area since the annual survey was first conducted in 2009?

Whether or not getting an expensive degree will enhance their job prospects is another issue which receives insufficient attention. In the rush to 'get big or become irrelevant',

---

6   Source: The Prince's Trust annual UK Youth Index

universities have been selling to a naïve and loaded market. Not only have schools been incentivised to increase the numbers of their students going to higher education (it is another measure against which they are assessed), but the buyers, the students themselves make decisions on the basis of poor information. In a double whammy, they are influenced by parents who are simply proud that their child is going to university when they didn't, even if this means they have very little real knowledge with which to guide them.

As a result, for many choosing both the best course and the best institution is often a case of pot luck, and even if you get both right, the job market is precarious and changing in the face of technology. Concern about future prospects was one of the areas highlighted in the Prince's Trust report, with over half those surveyed saying they were worried about jobs and their finances. This didn't come across as progress.

Equally, there is evidence to suggest that reaching the fabled target of 50 per cent of eighteen year olds going to university has created its own divisions, which in turn may be contributing towards the fault lines emerging in English society. In some parts of the country, such as Barnsley, east of Liverpool in Lancashire, only 10 per cent of disadvantaged young people make it to university.[7] This isn't to do with their being disadvantaged, it's to do with where they live – 50 per cent of similarly disadvantaged young people in Kensington and Chelsea do make it to university. It felt like a case of pot luck again.

---

7   Source: The Social Mobility Commission. See: https://www.gov.uk/government/organisations/social-mobility-commission

Going back to the Brexit referendum, this imbalance came through in the results. I'm not saying that only stupid people voted to leave. That would be to deride those with deep-seated and well-argued objections to the EU, and ignore the fact that intelligent people are just as capable as anyone else of making poor decisions (the financial crisis anyone?). But I will point out what the Social Mobility Commission[8] has reported: of the 65 areas of the country identified as 'social mobility cold spots' – that is those with the worst education and employment prospects – 62 voted for Leave.

This lack of social mobility, of being able to spread wealth and opportunity, which back in 2016 led many to kick in the teeth the elite that governed them, has to be worrying. Perhaps those lacking prospects and social mobility settle for what they've got and grab another cider and slice of pizza? Or perhaps they are attracted to the comforts of popularism or take to the streets, much like they had in the 1980s. Never mind, perhaps another kindly government minister will come up with a scheme like the Garden Festivals to take the sting out of the situation?[9]

Keele was, and still is, unusual in being a campus university, indeed it boasts of being the largest campus university in the UK. It was, and remains, unusual also in offering a wide breadth of education, including its fabled Foundation Year and an insistence on dual-subject degrees.

---

8   As above

9   In her speech to the 2018 Conservative Party Conference, the Prime Minister Theresa May announced plans for a post-Brexit National Festival inspired by the 1851 Great Exhibition. It didn't go down well.

When Annette and I attended, half the students studied the history of Western civilisation, sampling everything under the sun before making their final choice for three years of study. That's right: these were four-year courses. These days the university offers half a dozen more streamlined Foundation Years and most degrees are single subject. The essence of the old philosophy is still there, but it has been diluted. It is also unusual in having an old Victorian hall and a park complete with its own lake and an arboretum.

Given these differentiators, perhaps Keele is not a good example for extrapolating wider trends. For one thing, its campus status means that the local town of Newcastle has largely escaped the blight of low-grade student accommodation, which mops up cheap housing that might otherwise offer a route to young people looking to buy their first home. It also means that the students there have time to regard the campus as their neighbourhood, rather than an area they occasionally visit.

The closer we looked, the more we were convinced that the essence of the old Keele, the one we remembered, was still there. The Students' Union was relatively intact, and still acted as a focal point for the student community. This isn't automatically the case nowadays as we'd learned during Open Days at other universities when looking with our sons. Where once we'd played Space Invaders was now a Starbucks, and where we'd once clustered round pigeonholes organised by surname (and where I often used to bump into my future wife) was now a reception area. I doubted these students got much in the way of 'snail mail' anymore, although presumably there was some way of collecting Amazon parcels.

Being a long-distance walker, I naturally took advantage of the facilities while I was there (grab 'em when you can), and was delighted to find that my feet no longer stuck to the floor due to spilled beer. Mission accomplished, it was time to remove ourselves from nostalgia and back into the real world. But first there was time for one more reflection.

Shortly after we left Keele, in the mid and late 1980s, the university was used as the set for a slightly surreal television comedy series set in a medical practice within a modern university. Called *A Very Peculiar Practice*, the plotline of the series was about some Americans coming in and attempting to run the university like a business.

It ended in anarchy.

5

Ambulatories
Non Gratae

'Tear that bit of cardboard off. It's rotten anyway.'

A couple of minutes before, I'd recklessly walked right through a pool of cow cack wide enough to require four stretching strides and deep enough to go over the tops of my boots. I'd made it to the gate, but that was only a staging post to our ultimate destination of the field beyond. An equally wide expanse of bubbling manure still lay before us, and I was reconnoitring the scene before me to see if there was a drier route out.

Meanwhile, my companions for the day, my cousin Simon and his wife Judy, were yet to even reach the gate, and Simon was stranded halfway. He'd found a wide strip of cardboard by the side of the pool and placed it, like a giant snow shoe, one pace out in an effort to provide a temporary stepping stone. He was stranded, and needed more material. All I had in front of me was a railway sleeper, and as well as not really relishing picking it up, the thought of the collateral damage it could do if I tossed it in his direction wasn't worth contemplating.

Meanwhile, Judy was casting around for anything her side of the poo she might be able to use, watched by a gathering herd of young brown and white heifers, the source of the problem, if you discounted the farmer who hadn't kept the footpath clear. No gate or fence separated Judy from the cows, and any sudden decision by them to nudge forward a bit would prove disastrous. Stoic and defiant, Judy tore more cardboard off the old hoarding by the side of the hedge and handed it gently towards the outstretched hand of her husband. He, in turn, plopped it in front of him and took another dainty step, the green and brown sludge oozing out around the edges. Like someone in a corporate team-building exercise, he had shown his initiative. I stayed stuck on the gate, oblivious to Simon's suggestion that I could swing out and collect him. I didn't trust the gate's hinges, and besides, I didn't want to freak out the cows. Eventually, Simon made it, and Judy was able to follow on using his stepping stones.

With the three of us now committed to further progress, islands in a sea of crap, Judy explored the option of going up the side of the hedge to our right, while Simon and I contemplated a more complicated, but manly, route via some farm machinery. The railway sleeper was not mentioned again. Just then, the steady chug-chug of a tractor in the nearby farmyard stopped, and an angry farmer started yelling at us that the footpath was via the hedge. Simon's diplomatic responses, thanking him for the advice, were admirable in the circumstances, and I wondered how I might have responded if I'd been on my own.

The day had started pleasantly enough, with two more people to add to my now growing list of those who'd 'walked with me' along the diagonal. They had been early volunteers, but by this stage they may possibly have been regretting their offer. We'd met just south of Stoke and proceeded along the Trent and Mersey canal for three miles, generally catching up and talking about this and that. We'd already passed a reed-lined pond with a family of swans and come across a newt haven, so, initially at least, my new companions, both nature-lovers, were happy.

We'd also passed by the Wedgwood complex in Barlaston outside Stoke. With a refurbished museum and factory tour, this is now as much a visitor attraction as a true manufacturing plant. Most of the company's wares is now produced in China. An iconic British brand, Wedgwood's story is more international. After initially merging with the Irish firm Waterford, the joint company was bought up by a New York-based equity firm when it went into administration in 2009. Six years later, the new owners sold it on to a Finnish consumer goods company.

Back at our gate, we eventually made it back to terra firma and continued our walk, looking out over ploughed fields of the distinctive red soil that presumably reflects the quantity of clay within it. Our path took us gently uphill, and briefly along a road, where a strange sign indicated we were outside a farm with a name that came across more as Stalinist

Five-Year Plan than the more traditional 'Green Acres' or 'Manor Farm'. The ever-informative Simon remembered that this reflected Staffordshire County Council's policy of owning farms to let to start-up farmers, an admirable idea they spoiled a little by giving them names such as 'Holding Number X on Estate Y (Z).'

We were approaching Barlaston Common outside Meir Heath, where my eagle eyes spotted a shortcut across the common that would lead us to a pub. The day had turned out to be hot again, and a pint was suddenly a very good idea. As we approached the gate to the common, however, we spotted a problem. The path on the other side was distinctly churned up, and as we were now wary of anything brown and liquid, and our boots had by then dried out sufficiently to form a thick crust, we hesitated.

At that point a half-naked man – well, stripped to his waist anyway – appeared, a cacophony of barking dogs in his wake. He was yelling at us, and first thoughts returned to the belligerent farmer earlier, which just goes to show you shouldn't rely on first impressions. He was, in fact, sympathetic to our plight, bemoaning the recent practice of allowing cows to graze the common. Cattle had been reintroduced a decade before on the basis that grazing would stop the common, mainly marshy grassland, being invaded by scrub. No one had spotted the equation that heavy cows plus wet ground equals mud.

Our new friend duly invited us to walk through his field and onto a more convivial section of the common, from which we could make our way to the pub. He did issue a warning however: 'It's gone right downhill recently.' When we got there, the pub, The Swynnerton Arms, was just what we needed, friendly and with good facilities and an outside seating area. More of a gastropub than a locals' pub, we agreed that our recent friend's definition of going downhill was different from ours.

Suitably refreshed, and with a podcast recorded, we made our way through Meir Heath, past its windmill and on through fields to Fulford. Along the way, Simon reflected how when he'd taken some New Zealand friends walking they were amazed that we were able to just walk across a farmer's field. I was reminded of how lucky we were to have our network of footpaths, something that made the entire Diagonal Walking enterprise possible. Coming in a number of different guises, from footpaths through permissive paths, byways and public rights of way to bridleways, 140,000 miles of such paths criss-cross England and Wales, according to an estimate by The Ramblers.[10] And that excludes the 10 per cent of such paths not shown on OS and other definitive maps. Many of the paths are thousands of years old and may represent old drovers routes, or simply how people used to get from A to B in an age before cars, or indeed an age when owning a horse or a donkey was a luxury. These rights of way are one of the country's largely unsung assets, especially valuable when there is an imperative for people to exercise more.

It was a shame, therefore, that, if my experience of two days of rural walking in Staffordshire was anything to go

---

10   Source: The Ramblers. See: https://www.ramblers.org.uk/policy/wales/rights-of-way/public-rights-of-way.aspx

by, they were under-appreciated, under-loved and under-maintained. In this county anyway. Actually, it was more than a shame: it was downright dumb. If a footpath is ill-defined, then the walker has no option but to trample wherever they can to find their route, which is in neither their interest nor that of the local landowner. At times it felt as if a policy of benign neglect was, in fact, deliberate. No paths, no walkers, means no need for paths. If this was how things were going to be for the rest of the walk, I was in trouble.

The next day I gained two fresh diagonal walkers: one of my sons, Ed, and his partner Lydia, as well as Annette, who'd already earned her spurs. With two cars now at our disposal, we were able to take one to our intended end point and drive to the start point, where I'd left off with Simon and Judy the day before. Once again, the day started well as we absorbed the local countryside at its best, with freshly budding shrubs and trees, and the deep lime-green of grass now growing steadily after a wet winter and being enjoyed by gambolling lambs. After walking during the hottest April day for seventy years, we were now about to set out during what proved to be the hottest May Day since the holiday was created forty years before.

After shuffling the cars, we found our starting point, but the gate protecting it was padlocked and impassable. This went beyond the usual local practice of providing a sign at the start of the footpath and then leaving you to figure out your own way. The locals appeared to have adopted a strategy of trying to stop walkers even starting, a theory supported by the fact that once we found our way onto the path, taking a diversion through some dead hedging that ripped my T-shirt, the stiles and waypoints were, at best, antiques.

We persevered, but it was hard going. Obstacles placed in our way included electric fences, electric fences over stiles (something that required a special sense of hostility towards walkers), crops sown right up to the edges of fields, making it difficult to walk, pointers that had been discarded or removed, fingerposts left to fall and rotten stiles. Occasions when we found a stile that wasn't either rotten or unstable became the exception, and even when they were whole they frequently contained rusty nails sticking out of them. Every nasty trick in the book, in other words.

Then there were the sheep. Never get between a protective ewe and her young, that's my advice. I'd always thought sheep were timid creatures, easily frightened. Not when they have young to protect, they're not. Negotiating a way over a dodgy stile only to be confronted by a cantankerous sheep is no joke, especially when the next stop is another death-trap stile a hundred yards away. A horned and extremely woolly sheep can be quite threatening when it looks like it's prepared to take you on. Incidentally, simply yelling 'Mint Sauce' in their angry faces only serves to antagonise them.

We survived, and shortly after a picnic lunch pretty much bang on the diagonal line, overlooking a solitary, and eerily quiet, wind turbine, we met a woman sitting on a camping chair in the middle of nowhere, studying a map. She looked like she was enjoying the sunshine, but wore a concerned look on her face, so we checked to see if she was okay. It turned out she was a Duke of Edinburgh Scheme invigilator, there to track the progress of a group of innocent sixteen-year-olds. Both Ed and Lydia had taken part in such expeditions and a knowledgeable exchange took place before I picked her up on something she'd said.

'You said tracked ...'

'That's right, we have trackers on them.'

Visions of criminal tags came to mind, but on further questioning, the invigilator seemed to think this was perfectly normal. Her greater concern was that they'd barely moved for nearly an hour and a half and they'd phoned through to say one of their number was suffering from a 'gammy-toe'. Wait a minute. Phoned through? With this news, my young companions enjoyed an early opportunity to revel in one of the pleasures of adulthood by muttering something along the lines of 'Back in my day ...', before we wished her well and got on our way.

Within minutes we came across the dishevelled party, finally on their way, it appeared. Whilst there was little sign of any gammy-toe-afflicted member, there was one lagging at the back, constantly complaining, who may or may not have been the injured party. Ed assured me this was normal practice for a 'DofE exped', as he called it. There was always one, it transpired. They'd just negotiated a stile with heavy rucksacks, so we empathised, telling them their tracker up on yonder hill was furious with them, just for devilment. They didn't look too bothered, although at least one of them may have been less nonchalant when they later realised they'd left behind a bottle of Tizer. They'd also dropped a solitary crisp, speculation on the nature and flavour of which provided us with conversation for a full three minutes.

We continued along our route, the various challenges being thrown our way now representing a new normal. This trend was pleasantly bucked when we came across a large prairie-like field freshly sown with wheat towards the end of the day. Uniquely, it had been treated with weed-killer, leaving the footpath clearly visible. Cutting a diagonal through the field it also provided a wonderful photo opportunity, and I handed my camera to the proficient Lydia. This was more like it. A farmer who 'got it'. A nice wide strip through, and not along the edge of, a field. If only he'd fixed the stile at the end of it, which was a double one through a particularly painful hedge, he could have been up for a Staffordshire Farmer of the Year award.

Just before reaching our final destination, things reverted to normal – a fingerpost pointing straight into a field of waist-high rape, as yellow as sunshine, but not as welcome. We'd all had enough. Locating the car on the phone, we walked down a track and along a seemingly endless B-road, arriving hot and not a little bothered at our transport. A good, but hard, day's walking, made bearable by the fact that it had been completed with family. Later that night, we recorded a podcast after a barbeque and a couple of beers, during which Lydia suggested that one reason why the paths might be in such disrepair could be because most serious walkers probably headed for the Peak District, a National Park, only twenty minutes drive away, allowing Staffordshire to hide in its shadow. Later, I was to post a blog on the state of the county's footpaths, which received a lot of reaction, including a piece on the website of one the main walking magazines. It was reassuring, but also a little disconcerting, to find our experiences weren't unique. It was going to be interesting to see if this was an issue everywhere.

This opportunity for reflection also revealed that, other than the DofE expedition, we'd seen no other walkers all day, a gloriously hot and sunny Sunday on a bank holiday weekend. Whether this was a coincidence, or an indicator of a wider trend we didn't know. Whether the state of the paths played a part or landowners' attitudes reflected the wider local population's indifference was a riddle.

One thing I'd discovered after three days of walking with others was just how different it made the experience. When I was on my own I tended to give reign to my internal dialogues, requiring frequent stops to take notes. I was also more diligent in stopping to take photos for my social media accounts, and in shooting video for the YouTube channel. The advantage of walking with real (rather than virtual) others was, of course, that it is more companionable. It also proved useful to have people to share the frustration with when the local landowners set up a game of 'Find The Footpath' for us.

The following day I was back on my own, and I immediately missed this interaction. I started by getting thoroughly stung by stinging nettles along an overgrown path. Shortly after, I was challenged to avoid some particularly aggressive Canadian Geese guarding of all things, a moat. The moat enclosed a small copse of trees and it was impossible to see if there was anything inside it. An MP perhaps, calculating his expenses? Having ducked under one electric fence and climbed carefully over another, I made it to the pretty settlement of The Blythe, which sits on the River Blithe (yes, with an 'i' not a 'y', and no, I don't know why), around 11:30, in time for a quick refresher at the local pub. It was shut. A local informed me they were still cleaning it. I wondered what sort of party had taken place the night before that stopped it opening before 12 on a sunny bank holiday Monday, but just managed to stop this thought spilling out of my mouth.

Given their tardiness in opening, I felt justified in using one of their picnic benches to dump my rucksack while wringing out the back of my T-shirt and taking on some fresh water. A scattering of caravans decorated the back of the car park, into which a car now turned, pulling up just in front of me. A couple who looked like they were in their sixties got out and started unloading plants and potting compost. The woman of the pair spotted me and asked:

'Are you having a nice walk then?'

This was my cue. 'Well actually …'

I told them about my route and how far I'd come and when I mentioned Stoke, her face lit up. 'I'm from Stoke,' she said, 'lived there all my life. Fancy a cup of tea or coffee?'. The kindness of strangers had struck, and we settled down. This was Linda, the woman who'd grown up in poverty in Stoke in the 1950s. While her partner Dave potted up plants, we exchanged life stories.

In his book *The Kingdom By The Sea*, Paul Theroux suggests that saying you're a writer to anyone tends to be the kiss of death on a conversation. I disagree. In my experience it tends to open up a chat. This was particularly so in Linda's case, not least because she too was a writer, although on spiritual matters rather than walking. With her agreement, we recorded an interview for my podcasts and, thanking her and wishing her well, I went on my way.

The following stretch was relatively straightforward, and included a picture-book half-timbered farmhouse of the sort that would suit a jigsaw or the cover of a tin of biscuits, the sort of thing you might see in an airport, in a shop called Souvenirs of Ye Olde Englande.

Another travel writer came to mind, H.V. Morton. He began his book *In Search of England*, originally published in 1927, by summoning up the memory of an idyllic England he'd had when he'd thought he was dying in Palestine during the First World War. It was an image of thatched cottages, wood smoke coming out of chimneys and church bells being rung. It was not dissimilar to the picture of England used by the then Prime Minister John Major in a speech to the Conservative Council for Europe in 1993. In this he'd pronounced that 'fifty years from now Britain will still be the country of long shadows on county grounds, warm beer, invincible green suburbs, dog lovers and pools fillers'. The last of these was a reference to the favoured form of gambling at that time, the football pools, so on that one at least he was wrong. This is an image many writers have tried to express – for example, George Orwell when he talks of 'old maids cycling to communion through the morning mist',[11] a reference thought to have inspired John Major's speech.

Next up was Abbots Bromley, which epitomised the sort of place summoned up by such ruminations. On the surface at least, the village looked well kept and affluent. During

---

11   *England, Your England* by George Orwell (Essay)

my brief time there (I stopped for a pint and to top up my water at the pub, where I also made some), I saw at least three expensive open-top sports cars glide gently by, but I suppose if you have an expensive sports car, a sunny bank holiday is the sort of day to go out in it. Abbots Bromley was rated the best place to live in the Midlands by the *Sunday Times* in both 2013 and 2016 (the *Sunday Times* seems to do an awful lot of these polls). Although some may cruelly regard this as a backhanded compliment, its wide main street, succession of half-timbered buildings, fine school and decent pubs certainly looked alluring.

The locals were on the warpath, though. Notices everywhere implored people to spruce up their surroundings, as the judges for the Best Kept Village competition were due in town. Abbots Bromley is a regular winner of the East Staffordshire section of this competition, but it has yet to win the county-wide award, something that rankles, just a bit. The village is also the location for an annual Horn Dance. With claims to be the oldest folk dance in Britain, this tradition dates to way back when and takes place on the first Monday in September. It involves six dancers carrying a set of reindeer horns: three white and three black, with some of these having been radio-carbon dated to over a thousand years ago. Other dancers include someone playing Maid Marion, a fool and a hobby-horse. This felt in total keeping with the Abbots Bromley brand, if I can call it that. One of those nutty traditions that people will fight to the death to defend but serve no contemporary purpose. A bit like the royal family, it's harmless fun, makes people feel happy and brings in the tourists.

I checked in to see how Annette was getting on. It turned out she was still some way off being able to collect me (having decided that one day's diagonal walking was enough, my companions of the previous day had chosen to immerse themselves in the delights of the Wedgwood Experience), so I decided to push on to my next destination, Yoxall. Only later did we realise that the texts I'd received had arrived in the wrong order, and she was, in fact, ready to get me. It was an error I was to rue.

The footpath away from Abbots Bromley included the by now traditional impediments, with the added bonus of some curious alpacas to spice things up a bit. I made an error when presented with a 50:50 choice at one footpath, but was soon able to course correct, and passing through the grounds of a large farm, I was cheered to see something I'd thought I would never see in Staffordshire: brand new stiles and gates placed at the correct point on the footpath.

Maybe I got lulled into a false sense of security, maybe I just became complacent, but at the next farm things went badly wrong. I thought I'd followed the right signs and where these were absent that I'd made intelligent choices, but suddenly I was completely and absolutely lost. Wherever I went I was unable to pick up the footpath. At one point there was an option to either walk straight through a field of wheat, in a reckless, Theresa May kind of a way, or be responsible and walk round the edge to find the footpath to the next field. I'd taken the latter option, and this was my big mistake. Everywhere I went was either ploughed up or tall grass. Barbed wire, hedges and electric fences protected every boundary. I was trapped in Staffordshire Hell. Having walked up and down one field three times looking for an exit, I stopped and hailed someone in a tractor mowing one of the pastures.

He returned my friendly wave and then, his smile turning into a look of concern, suddenly realised I wasn't waving but drowning. He stopped and climbed out of his cab.

'I need some help here mate,' I pleaded, showing him my remnant of map. 'Do you have any idea where I am?' His answer wasn't reassuring.

'Haven't a clue,' he said, 'I live twenty miles away.' He looked at my map. 'Is that a footpath?' he asked, nodding towards a gate.

'I've no idea, there's no sign, but that doesn't mean much round here.'

Equally lost, I asked him how he'd got here, on the face of it a reasonable question. He couldn't remember. This was becoming one of those conversations that could go on all day. I got him to think back, and eventually he recalled a road by a farmhouse in the distance which he thought linked to the main road. It wasn't much, but I took it.

On reaching the farm there was someone brushing the yard. I thought it politic to ask if I could climb over the gate separating us. The nonchalant brusher wasn't sure. The farmer was at the other end of the field. My feeling at that point was that if the farmer wasn't prepared to maintain decent signs, as was his legal duty, then I was going to take the initiative and climb over his ruddy gate. The time for cousin Simon-level diplomacy had passed.

Now talking face to face with the brush-armed farmhand, I asked, nay demanded, where the road was. This also appeared to be a tricky question. Getting to the road meant walking through the yard, and while I was prepared to do this, my informant was less keen. Not wanting to get him into trouble, I followed his instructions to walk across a field, duck under an electric fence and climb over another gate. On finding the road I came across another house and was presented with another 50:50 choice.

I stopped to consult my map and the compass on my phone. Someone came from the garden of the house, which I now saw had a swimming pool. He heard my story and assumed a look of concern. I clearly looked distraught, and he was keen to offer me some water. What I really wanted was a lift into town, ideally preceded by a dip in his pool, but when it became clear neither of those was on offer I got my phone back out and called Annette, giving her instructions on where I could be found. For the first time, I needed to be bailed out. I'd come to the conclusion that in Staffordshire it wasn't so much a case of personae non gratae, but ambulatories non gratae – walkers not appreciated.

Reunited with Annette, I learned that she'd been waiting for quite a while, taking sanctuary in the cool stone interior of the local church. Her time hadn't been wasted. She'd picked up the local parish magazine, in which an article by a correspondent who called himself, somewhat self-deprecatingly, The Country Bumpkin explained that Staffordshire has over 3,000 miles of footpaths and that the County Council was responsible for working with landowners and others to keep these public rights of way open.

With the county under increasing financial pressures, they'd undertaken a consultation and were proposing to categorise the footpaths as A, B or C in order to prioritise maintenance. It came as cold comfort that at least there was an acknowledged problem. Further research revealed that the council receives 2,000 footpath complaints a year – that's forty a week, or more than five a day. I wasn't surprised. But wait a minute, wasn't there something a bit at odds there? The council worked with landowners? But as cousin Simon had pointed out two days before, in many cases the landowner was … the council. Some dots in my head joined up. Now it all made sense.

Fed and rested, the next day I completed a relatively short seven-mile stretch into Alrewas. This was to be the end of this leg of the walk and I was keen to get as close as possible to the edge of Staffordshire, if for nothing else to find out if the footpath problem was contagious. The day started in Yoxhall, a clear competitor with Abbots Bromley for the Best Kept Village competition, with my route following a new long-distance path called The Way for the Millennium, and as such it was refreshingly easy to follow.

Just as I was coming into the village at the end of a long meadow I stopped by a gate, where it looked for a moment as if I was back into the cow manure scenario: an ocean of the brown stuff. As I was soon going to be getting into our car I didn't really want to get my boots caked up again, so I worked my way through some trees. Just as I made the track on the other side a Land Rover pulled up, towing a trailer. The back of the trailer was lifted up and the driver released half a dozen fresh young cows. Just to apply the finishing touches.

Stage 3

Alrewas
to
Newport
Pagnell

94.3 miles
210,934 steps

6

Out of
the Woods?

Mention Alrewas to most people and I can pretty much guarantee you'll get a blank look as they wonder why you've taken to swearing in Romanian. That is unless they've visited the National Memorial Arboretum, which sits just outside the town, situated a few miles north-east of the cathedral city of Lichfield in Staffordshire.

Planting began at the Arboretum in 1997 and it was officially opened in 2001. Recent major investment has seen the building of an impressive Visitor's Centre. The Arboretum has since become a favourite with coach parties and individual visitors. They don't come just because it's free, or at least I hope they don't, but to pay their respects to those who've fallen in combat, not just in the armed forces, but civilians too.

Annette and I had visited at the end of the previous leg of the walk, on a swelteringly hot day which demanded use of a glacial 'noddy train', with its running commentary, both from the loudspeaker and from others in the carriage. Although the set pieces to each of the three main branches of the armed services were grand and impressive, a feature of the vast site that hit us both was the variety of memorials to other groups. These are as diverse as the Bevan Boys, War Widows and, appropriately enough, the National Association of Memorial Masons, who possibly have a vested interest in the whole enterprise. Established as a living tribute designed to last for generations, there remained a slight sense of having been here before. Perhaps it was the newness of it, the impressive display and large car park, all built on reclaimed land. We both hoped we were looking at something more lasting than a modern-day National Garden Festival.

It was interesting, this relatively recent refound respect for the armed forces, which has undergone a revival since the millennium, with further evidence coming in the shape of the foundation of the charity Help for Heroes in 2007. As a nation, there's a sense that we've become more comfortable with public grief and remembrance. When I was a schoolboy, there was Poppy Day and a minute's silence by the school war memorial, but these days recent wars have become exam subjects, with trips to the First World War battlefields almost obligatory at some point in a child's education.

The Second Gulf War in 2003 and a wider recognition in general of the devastating impact of Post-Traumatic Stress have undoubtedly played a part in this revival, but

I wondered if it was something more fundamental. The national mourning for the untimely death of Princess Diana, for example, suddenly made it okay to grieve in public, as did the collapse of the Twin Towers. Was this a permanent shift away from the traditional reserve of the English or, on the contrary, should a symbol like the National Memorial Arboretum instead be seen as an archetypal English expression of considered respect, expressed through that most English of things, a love of gardens?

Another possibility was that it was linked to a broader harkening back to a glorious past, to a time when things were better and we enjoyed a prominent place in the world, sentiments that no doubt fuelled some of the voting in the Brexit referendum. This could also be seen in a growing vogue for all things 'retro' (or, to you and me, old tat), and an ostensibly endless stream of films and plays about Britain standing alone during the Second World War. These sentiments had escalated to the extent that people actually believed that a nationalised railway was better than the alternative. To be nostalgic for British Rail you either had to be too young to remember it, which is forgivable, or wearing spectacles with the deepest shade of rose tint available.

This suspicion was supported by a survey published by the BBC[12] while I was walking, which suggested that half the country thought that England was better in the past (rising to two-thirds amongst Leave voters), with only one in six thinking its best days were ahead. An immediate reflection

12 Source: The BBC. See: https://www.bbc.co.uk/news/uk-england-44142843

on this finding was how it highlighted the general state of confusion in the country – that we were better off on our own, but having secured that status feeling pessimistic about it (with Leave voters more pessimistic about the future than everyone else). Perhaps all this was saying was what a load of old moaners the English were. After all, the same research indicated that a majority of people in each of Scotland, Wales and Northern Ireland thought their country's best years lay ahead of them.

My acquaintance with the Arboretum on this leg of the journey was supposed to involve following a footpath around its edge. This being Staffordshire, things didn't quite turn out that way. Having taken a train and bus to where I'd left off, the start of the walk was straightforward, a track down the back of some houses which led me out onto a busy dual carriageway. My map indicated a path on the other side so, taking my life in my hands, I crossed, not leaping the crash barrier so much as clambering awkwardly over it like a spineless hedgehog, before waiting for the next break in the traffic. A fingerpost told me my eyes weren't seeing things on the map, and I proceeded down a narrow road which led me to a sewage farm, pausing momentarily to wonder why they were called farms.

The location was apposite, as the path was supposed to take me round the edge of the fence surrounding this facility, but was obstructed by six-foot-high nettles and other vegetation as effective as any Trumpian wall. There was no choice but to turn back, treading a treacherous path down the side of what I now knew was the A38, before picking up a side road, passing the disused Alrewas signal box by a level crossing, resplendent in cream and emerald green paint, and finally emerging at the entrance to the Arboretum.

It hadn't been the greatest of starts to this third portion of the walk, but at least I was making progress. Preparations for this leg back home had been time-consuming, leaving me with little choice other than to plan for long daily treks of around fourteen miles. I'd done similar distances earlier in the walk so I wasn't particularly fazed by the prospect, but these totals had usually resulted from diversions and getting lost.

As such, planning for these distances left no room for error. The thought of potentially undertaking treks of sixteen or seventeen miles a day – and on consecutive days – was going to stretch the limits of my comfort zones, especially as I was now reacquainted with my old friend the rucksack. On the positive side, this planning did remove the need for a car. All my overnight stops were more or less on the route, and overruns on time and distance in the past had usually resulted from underestimating links and transit times.

As my fresh leaving date got closer the more a chemistry set of emotions brewed – excitement and trepidation combining to leave a fog of anticipation. Yes, comfort zones were being tested, but wasn't this part of the point of the whole exercise? Things weren't helped by the weather forecast a week before I set out, which wasn't good, including thunderstorms and a lot of rain. The thought of having to complete those miles, togged up in wet weather gear while lightning forked into open adjacent fields, wasn't an enticing one. Up until then, I'd been very lucky with the weather, experiencing record temperatures. Too hot if anything, I'd reasoned, displaying my own streak of particularly English moaning.

I was comforted by two thoughts. The first was my established belief that weather forecasts are about as reliable as an appointment with British Telecom. Bitter experience over the years suggested that any weather forecasted a whole week out was almost certainly the one type of weather you were guaranteed not to get. Maybe modern weather forecasters are simply overwhelmed with data, to the extent that they can't see the clouds for the rain. Even the BBC had sacked the Met Office as its weather supplier, allegedly on the grounds of price, but I think we knew better. As each day passed, the forecast swung back and forth like the pendulum in an old grandfather clock. Adopting the principle that there was no such thing as the wrong weather, just the wrong clothes, I made sure I was suitably equipped and hoped for the best. It was only worth worrying about things I could influence.

The second comforting thought was the fact that I would be leaving Staffordshire within a day's walking. Were the county's footpaths the exception or the norm? Was I out of the woods, or was there more to come? For the remainder of that first day back, I decided not to take the risk. Building work at the Arboretum had already provided another diversion, so I took to the sides of country lanes. These were relatively traffic-free, but also, understandably, bench-free. As a result, I was forced to unshackle my rucksack and slump to the ground on frequent water-stops, before finally entering the refuge of the small village of Harlaston, where my bed for the night awaited above the local post office. Yes, it still had a post office.

A 2008 article in the *Birmingham Post*[13] described Harlaston as 'the quintessential English village', and it has won the Staffordshire Best Kept Small Village award five times (how many of these awards were there?). Walking around it, it certainly had all the ingredients. Manor house? Check. Half-timbered houses? Check. Neat gardens? Check. An old phone box converted into a library? Hold on, a what? Yes, an old red phone box on the main bend in the village, its gold crown freshly repainted, had been converted into an informal lending library by the Parish Council. A sign instructed users to return books when they'd finished with them and gave details on where to leave donations. I learned later that the box itself was actually listed. It was a neat idea which warmed me to the locals.

I soon met one of them, Tony, who was also my host for the night, as well as being proprietor of the local shop and postmaster. What he wasn't, was a cook; but I supposed that might have been asking for the moon. When he asked if I might be wanting a cooked breakfast in the morning and I replied in the affirmative, reckoning it came as part of the whole 'bed and breakfast' deal, his face took on the aspect of a man who'd been given another job at the end of a long hard day in the stamp-dispensing business. He said he'd make a few calls, and I went up to my room for a much-needed shower.

First impressions suggested Harlaston as one of the parts of England probably the least touched by progress over

---

13 Source: The *Birmingham Post*. See: https://www.birminghampost. co.uk/lifestyle/house-homes/idyllic-harlaston-unspoilt-by- time-3957312

the previous twenty years. Certainly, I experienced trouble getting the WiFi to work, despite trying every possible permutation of the proffered password. I took my life in my hands and sought out Tony.

'Hi, I'm having trouble logging onto the WiFi.'

'Well yes, you will,' he offered, a little unhelpfully, I thought, sighing a little as he did so. My slightly raised eyebrows encouraged him to continue. 'BT promised me they'd be here last week, and when I called after they failed to show up they said it would be a few days. However, one of my customers works for them and he says they're actually coming tomorrow.'

This twisted logic sounded about par for BT. If even a post office gets this sort of service, what hope was there for the rest of us? For a company whose entire raison d'être is communications, it really is surprising how bad at it they are. They are the modern equivalent of Flanders and Swann's gasman, or, if you're of a different generation, Monty Python's cheesemonger. Their terrible attitude to customer service is one of the few things that has remained unswervingly the same over the previous two decades.

Harlaston's pub, The White Lion, was my next stop – having had the foresight to phone ahead to make sure they served food on a Monday, which, to my relief, they did. A ramshackle brick building painted white, set off with a pair of fetching red parasols outside, my first impression was that this was a real locals' pub, and my instincts turned out to be right.

Four burly tattooed men, still in their working clothes, were sitting inside on two pairs of chairs, facing each other, like the back of a London bus. The language was ripe, but the beer good. I placed a food order and allowed the first pint to slip down easily, as it always did. When offered the chance to go through to the deserted restaurant, I said I was fine where I was, watching the entertainment. By entertainment, I didn't mean the large flat screen TV showing *Emmerdale* with the sound turned down, something that's crept into pubs in recent years. That said, I guessed the screen in this pub would soon be useful in showing the forthcoming World Cup.

In between glances at my phone (unlike the post office, the pub had WiFi – it seemed BT did have priorities after all), I watched as a rotating cast of characters came in and out, with two of the original four acting as mainstays. Some left forever, some returned, bringing a whiff of nicotine with them, the habit of smoking outside a definite plus to twenty-first-century pub-going. Topics of conversation swung from activities at a village event the previous day, to arcane details of different types of car engine, and although these were both outside my orbit of understanding, they were nevertheless strangely absorbing. Perhaps I was just delirious, or demob happy at the thought of leaving Staffordshire? Impressive amounts of alcohol were being drunk, matched by equally impressive beer bellies. There was no mystery as to how this pub serving a village of a mere 400 souls managed to stay open.

A cook had been recruited for my breakfast the next morning, and I was well into my rant about the state of the county's footpaths when she informed me, just too late, that she was a local farmer's wife. Somewhat indignantly, she assured me that her husband always sprayed the footpaths on his fields, and I can only assume it was his handiwork I was walking along shortly after. They were beautifully laid out, just the right width and exactly where the map said they should be. He was a paragon, an example to the rest of the county, his work a fitting testament on which to leave it. Just to top things off, I was privileged to see a hare scamper past in full 'there's a bunch of mad greyhounds chasing me' mode, its powerful hind legs building up a remarkable speed.

When I'd set out some principles for my walk, I'd decided against acquiring a portable GPS, naïvely reckoning a map would suffice, and failing that, the map apps on my phone. My experiences on the previous stage had disabused me of this idea, and following my blog on the troubles I'd had, I'd taken up a suggestion to download the excellent Pathwatch app from The Ramblers. Not only does this allow the user to see where they are against a footpath map, but it also includes the facility to report blocked paths and dodgy signposting. Revenge was going to taste sweet.

Unfortunately, I'd also acquired a new phone, and the two hadn't wanted to play together the previous day, which was one of the factors behind the decision to stay with the roads. I'd fixed this in the pub by employing the classic fix for anything computer-related, deleting it and reloading, and it was now working again. Its value wasn't just in indicating wrong decisions, but also in providing succour, reassurance that a decision made was the right one. My hope was the app would minimise any mistakes and allow me to keep as close to my daily itinerary as possible.

It immediately guided me out of Staffordshire without mishap, bringing me out onto the road that marked the border. As if to confirm matters, a large sign welcomed me to Warwickshire, although to be honest I think it was aimed mainly at motorists. And, it seemed, some motorists had taken aim at it, for it was peppered with buckshot, with a bullet-sized hole at the bottom of where the 'C' and the 'K' met.

On the other side of the road, on the Warwickshire side, a clean and prominent fingerpost pointed me down a bridleway. Everything was going to be all right. I celebrated by drinking a bottle of water, most of which immediately seeped through onto the back of my T-shirt.

7

Searching for Middle England

The sheer undiluted joy of walking down a path and being absolutely certain you are going the right way is one of walking's under-recognised pleasures. Just by doing the simplest of things like erecting wayfinder signs on the edges of fields away from a road makes such a difference. Warwickshire, take a bow! This also meant I was now making good progress, even if by the time I entered the small village of Warton my trousers looked like I'd been competing in a bog-snorkelling contest. This was no mean feat in what had so far been one of the driest early summers on record, and was the result of having to walk quite literally *through* a rape field that the last farmer on the other side of the border had 'forgotten' to spray.

My target that day was Atherstone, a historic town between Tamworth and Nuneaton, four miles inside

Warwickshire. In one of many coincidences, my route for the next few days straddled the border between this county and Leicestershire. It also followed the route of the A5, the old Roman Watling Street, as well as the M1 motorway. This wasn't too surprising given a straight line is the shortest distance between two points. Those Romans were no slouches when it came to roads and shortening distances. Equally, canals and railways would feature strongly in the coming days.

Before Atherstone however, there was a massive solar array to negotiate. Generating a total of 15MW, this most modern type of farm had recently been acquired by a joint venture which offered local residents and communities the opportunity to buy bonds with a 6 per cent annual return, which on the surface at least, came across as quite a good deal. More immediately, I was faced with a problem, or rather two. The first was, my path cut right through the array and there was no obvious way in. The second was sheep. Again. Four of the sheep grazing amongst the panels had escaped from the wire fence surrounding the array, and were chewing contentedly by the edge of the field where I needed to go.

A Land Rover appeared on the other side of the fence and a man in a blue boiler suit got out and beckoned me over. I could see security was tight and sensed a difficult encounter coming up. He didn't look the type you could enter into an academic discussion about public rights of way with. I wandered over.

'You the shepherd?' he asked.

Yeah, as if shepherds regularly walk round with large rucksacks on their back.

'Only there's some need rounding up.' His tone suggested that even if I wasn't the shepherd, maybe I'd like to have a go.

I disabused him of this notion and got on my way, ironically towards the sheep, which promptly ran off, getting even more lost. I got to the end of the long field and turned left, heading for the next corner on the assumption I could pick the path up there. I could, but on reaching the corner spotted a fenced-off path right through the array. The footpath had been respected, cutting a diagonal (of course) path through. How had I managed to miss it?

Wandering through Atherstone later that evening, I got a positive sense. It felt compact and with some interest. Primarily a market town, Atherstone also used to be known first, as a centre for making first leatherwork and cloth and, later, for its hats, in particular felt hats. At its peak, the town's hat-makers employed 3,000 people, which was not an inconsiderable number. Atherstone hats were particularly popular amongst West Indies slaveowners for supplying protection from the sun for their slaves working in sugar plantations. With the abolition of slavery, plus cheaper imports and less people wearing hats in general, the industry declined. The last factory, Wilson and Stafford Ltd, finally closed as recently as 1999.

Since then, Atherstone has benefitted from its position on the A5, which has also helped to define its main street. This is both long (with a disappointing lack of imagination it's called Long Street,) and, it was good to see, is occupied mainly by local shopkeepers, rather than the anonymous chains, although there is, of course, a Costa Coffee. Tiles on a wall showed three hands, pointing towards London, Holyhead (the top left tip of the A5) and nearby Daventry. Just off Long Street there's a small market square, and here Atherstone has its own re-purposed red telephone box, although in this case housing a defibrillator. What this says about the relative excitements offered by Harlaston and Atherstone it's hard to say.

Back in the nineteenth century the town benefitted from the arrival of the railways (it still has a station) and, before that, the canal, in this case the Coventry Canal. After checking in to my hotel, this is where I headed next. Traffic on the water was leisurely, as tended to be the case, made all the more so by a short flight of locks. By the bridge stood the old Wilson and Stafford factory, now an empty shell, although some enterprising locals had found entertainment in breaking in and spraying graffiti tags. Although our acquaintance was brief, I liked Atherstone, both for its history and for the sense it enjoyed some kind of community. It had been various things over the years, and although it couldn't be defined by a single industry any more it appeared to have settled into just being itself.

Wandering back to my hotel, I couldn't help but notice a profusion of lemon-yellow ribbons tried in bows around all the bollards that lined Long Street. I asked what it was all about at reception, wondering if a lost soul had been found. The truth was sadder than that, yet at the same time quite uplifting.

'Oh, they're there to mark the anniversary of someone who was murdered in the town a year ago,' the receptionist told me, continuing before I had time to take this piece of news in. 'It's typical of the town really, it's a very close-knit community.' I asked him what made him say that. 'I'm from Tamworth,' he began, 'but every time I come here I get the sense that everyone knows everyone else. Many of them went to the same schools. They come to this hotel for family events.'

It was interesting that he'd picked up on the same vibe, even if it was less comforting to know that someone had been murdered in the high street I'd just wandered down.

Something else Atherstone is known for is its Shrovetide Ball Game, and although this is a community event, friendly it ain't. As its name suggests, this takes place every Shrove Tuesday. It involves a heavy ball (too heavy to kick) made of thick leather, to which ribbons are attached. If anyone is able to grab one of these ribbons, they can be exchanged for cash, but the real object of the game is to be the last person hanging onto it. The ball is thrown out of the window of what is currently Barclays Bank at 3pm and the game goes on until 5pm, although the ball can be deflated and hidden anytime from 4:30. In the previous century, the game was played between two teams from Leicestershire and Warwickshire, but these days it's just a free-for-all. There is only one rule: no one can be killed. Which was something, I supposed. It sounded more anarchic than the Horn Dance, more of a participant rather than spectator sport.

The following day offered the potential, in every sense, to be pivotal for my walk, for it was just outside Atherstone, in the neighbouring county of Leicestershire, that the middle of England awaited. I was aware that there were various contenders for this title, with the most widely recognised being Meriden outside Coventry. A tall sandstone pillar has been erected there claiming the centre, in much the same way that colonial explorers used to claim countries with flags. Some say this pillar is over five hundred years old, throwing legal precedent into the mix, but in truth it's probably nearer two hundred.

Another claimant is Weedon Bec in Northamptonshire, which was chosen during the Napoleonic Wars as the place furthest from the sea, and therefore likely to be the last place Old Boney would reach should he undertake a successful invasion. Such was the level of perceived risk that a royal getaway was built there, along with a canal to speed the King on his way (if anyone can speed on a canal), along with a huge barracks and arsenal, presumably on the basis that if we were going to go down, we'd go down with a bang.

As I've already described, the matter was settled once and for all by the Ordnance Survey in 2002, when they settled on a point in a field located on private land belonging to the Lindley Hall Farm, just outside Fenny Drayton.[14]

On paper, it looked a short walk from Atherstone to Fenny Drayton and then onto the farm, but in the event it was anything but simple. A herd of cows stood in the first field I came to, drinking lazily from a water trough. Twenty bovine heads looked up as I crossed a stile into their

---

14   See: https://www.bbc.co.uk/news/uk-england-
     leicestershire-22890463 if you don't believe me.

territory, and they didn't go back down again. I began to walk, my mind on other things: would I be able to get to see the plaque that signified the middle of England? Had the farmer received the letter I'd sent beforehand? Had I been right not to try to phone them first? Why were these cows following me in a line?

Two or three of the cows in particular were keen to make my acquaintance. Was it milking time, I wondered. Did they think I was leading them to the milking parlour? Did farms still have milking parlours? It seemed a weak theory. These were very young cows, at least I thought they were cows. I thought it was impolite, and perhaps impolitic, to turn around and check.

I upped my pace slightly, causing the cows to up theirs, before they paused. Maybe they'd lost interest? No, they were taking a run-up. Until then, I'd never realised it was possible for a cow to jump up in the air, cross their legs mid-jump and quite literally, hit the ground running. I was in trouble. I tried soothing noises and putting my palm out towards them. This had some effect and they kept their distance, even if this distance was only around ten yards or so, ground I'd recently discovered they could cover quicker than I could.

I was never so glad to see a stile, even if it was three fields away and the cows followed me all the way. If my initial theory was right and they were ready for milking, the farmer must have been mystified by their absence when he turned up to collect them. That was his problem; mine was getting my heart rate back to normal. I hoped these cows didn't belong to Lindley Hall. Antagonising the farmer might impact my chance of seeing his plaque. Later, I was to come across a Twitter account called Killercows. I recommend it.

After the feisty Friesians I'd have taken anything, even another field of nasty rape. This was just as well, as this is what I got. The farmer here had sprayed a meagre path but it had become overgrown. Getting through it was like wading through a shoulder-high ocean current, with the added bonus of ankle-high shoots to trip over and tug at my laces. I limped into Fenny Drayton and rested on a convenient park bench. One last chance to make that call. No, I'd trust to fate.

The entrance to the farm was obvious to find, largely because there was a sign saying its name, painted in the shape of a tractor. Beyond it stretched a long drive, which I began to walk down. Just as I was approaching its end, an elderly woman appeared from a small bungalow, accompanied by a loud barking dog.

'Can I help you?' she enquired, and I explained my quest.

She didn't look convinced, but when I said I'd written in advance she deferred to her daughter-in-law, who'd taken over the farmhouse. She let me continue and I felt like I'd passed the first test. Having turned a corner I walked up to the farmhouse, and then around another corner into the farmyard. I was now deep into potentially hostile territory. I could see that the front door was open with people chatting around a kitchen table inside, one of whom I presumed to be the daughter-in-law.

I approached a gate to the sound of another angry dog. I waved and introduced myself, repeating the letter story. She knew nothing of it. We were now in no man's land. I explained my mission and how critical reaching the centre was to my project. I was even wearing a Diagonal Walking T-shirt and baseball cap as evidence of my earnestness.

'I don't know,' she hesitated. 'We got fed up with people coming to see it. People used to turn up at all hours unannounced. Some turned up at 9:30 at night.'

I sympathised and reminded her again of the letter, allowing us to bond over the failings of the Royal Mail. She was cracking, I was sure.

'We have kids here,' she added.

'Yes, I saw the bike,' I retorted, although quite how this was going to help matters I didn't know, other than building empathy. I looked longingly over to where I thought the relevant field was. Maybe it was the cow eyes (something I'd recently become only too familiar with) that did it, but she caved.

'Oh go on then.'

'Thanks,' I said, 'I just want to say I've been there and take some photos,' again not sure if that was helping.

By then however, she was walking towards the corner of the yard, and for a moment I wondered if she was personally going to take me to the spot. Instead, she pointed out a field boundary and a tree where she thought the plaque was. It clearly didn't feature largely in her life, other than when strange, unkempt, muddy-trousered, rucksack-carrying strangers turned up and asked to see it.

I made my way to where she'd pointed, and after around five minutes spotted the plaques I'd seen in postings on the internet. Plaques in the plural, because there was more than one, in bronze, with black indented lettering. The first simply stated that 'In 2002 the Ordnance Survey defined this spot as the Geographical Centre of England', and gave the co-ordinates and grid reference. The second was erected as recently as 2013 and gave the names of a Councillor, the Chair of the Hinckley and Bosworth Tourism Partnership and someone who gave his title as Cultural Services Manager, a wonderful designation that meant very little. The logos of the Tourism Partnership and the council were included in the corners, along with thanks to the Farmer family. That's right, the farmers were called Farmer.

The first plaque also had the logo of the local council, but more importantly sported a postcard-sized St George's flag and an arrow. The arrow was pointing to a spot 150 metres (not yards) to the left. I glanced over. Another field of unremitting rape, chest high. No way was I going to wade into that just to say I'd stood on the exact spot. Not only would it finally do for my trousers, if not my sanity; it would have been a betrayal of the goodwill I'd been shown by the farmer's wife: Mrs Farmer.

I paused for some selfies, took one final look around and left. On the way back, I tried to spot both the current and former farmer Farmers, but there was no one to be seen. Not even a barking dog. It was a rather low-key way to conclude this seminal moment, but I took it. I'd done the best I could and was glad I hadn't phoned on ahead and that the letter hadn't arrived (or been opened), as it would have been so much easier to turn me down remotely. By turning up in person I'd taken a risk, but it had paid off.

Later research suggested it was doubtful that my cow eyes had been the decider, or that the killer cows from earlier belonged to the farm. The farm had been a victim of the foot and mouth epidemic early in the century and was now entirely turned over to arable. This research also revealed that the farm got its name from a hall that had owned the land roundabouts since the sixteenth century, the final iteration of which was demolished in 1925. An aerodrome occupied the land in 1943, but was disbanded shortly after the war. Where once planes had taken off and landed then became the proving ground of the Motor Industries Research Association. All of which went to show that it's a mistake to assume that things are always what they seem.

That the Ordnance Survey should have designated this spot as their middle, or centre, was in some ways highly appropriate. Not far from here the Battle of Bosworth Field took place, during which Henry VII had defeated Richard III in the culmination of the Wars of the Roses. This event marked the end of one era, and the beginning of another. Defeat for Richard meant the end of the Plantagenet line, and more importantly for him personally, marked him down as the last English king to be killed in battle. The crown was reputedly found in a hedge and placed upon the head of Henry, marking the start of the Tudor dynasty, on a spot now called, you've guessed it, Crown Hill. Still, at least it wasn't Coronation Street. Richard's body of course, was famously lost for centuries, until it was dug up under a car park in Leicester, thereby making him the only king to be buried in a car park. So far anyway.

My next port of call was Stoke Golding, with its sign proclaiming it as 'Birthplace of the Tudor Dynasty', which was probably pushing things a bit. The sign was also proud to announce the village as a 'Neighbourhood Watch and Smartwater Village', which sounded slightly less impressive. More importantly for me, Stoke Golding was where I could allow things to calm down a bit, as it sat on an arm of the Coventry Canal last seen in Atherstone the day before, grandly called the Ashby-de-la-Zouche Canal, or more commonly the Ashby Canal. This thirty-one-mile stretch used to connect a coalfield to the main canal network, but these days is busy with leisure craft plying the twenty-two miles that remain navigable.

I was walking along, collecting my thoughts and banking my achievements, when I was interrupted by the sight and sound of three excited young women, practically running down the slight incline by a bridge onto the canal.

'Water!' they exclaimed, like deprived explorers in a desert. 'It says here there's water.'

'Not just any water,' I told them, 'but the Ashby-de-la-Zouche Canal!'

All three looked relieved. They were each around the same height, with one wearing an army T-shirt. I couldn't guess their ages, which is one reason why I'd never make a good barman. In fact, two turned out to be seventeen and the third nineteen. We quickly fell into conversation. The three, Orla, Ailsha and Keira, were all Public Service Students. When I asked what this meant two of my new friends were suddenly stuck for words, but the third, the oldest, tried to explain it to me.

'We focus on going into the army, police, firefighters, all the uniformed public services. We do various tasks to help us get into them careers,' she said.

One of them was keen on going into the fire service, one to go into the CID and one to become an army or police dog handler. They learn various skills on the course, and their challenge that day was to master map reading, following a pre-assigned route simply by following a map, eschewing use of their phones. Their route was five miles long, and seeing as a good mile and a half of that was along the canal, it didn't appear to be too onerous a task. I told them my schedule, and the awe this inspired instantly broke any remaining ice.

This was a golden opportunity to hear from a group of people dedicated to helping run the social fabric of the country, who, at best, had barely been conceived at the time I'd undertaken my previous country-wide trek. So I took it. Their views were interesting. When I asked them to come up with what they thought were the biggest changes they'd faced in their short lives, they started, unsurprisingly, with technology. What was more surprising was the ambiguous relationship they enjoyed with it. They took some of the wonders technology offered for granted. For an old duffer like me, who'd grown up in an age when pocket calculators and digital watches where the height of modern technology, this sense of wonder was renewed on practically a daily basis, but for these young people it was just something routine.

More significantly, they saw the threats technology brought with it, particularly in the shape of social media and photographs, and specifically the pernicious impact on them as young women. One told how she used to be on twenty social media apps (I didn't realise there were twenty), but had cut back severely when she'd realised keeping up-to-date was ruining her sense of connection with her family. They were also slightly scared of it, pleased to be out of school before iPads came in. This comment surprised me. Surely iPads had been around for years – were they only just filtering down to schools?

They were also concerned about a lack of respect, both from their own age group to others, and from older age groups towards them. To some extent, this maybe wasn't surprising, given they were probably undergoing some advanced indoctrination in social values on their course. On the other hand, maybe they'd chosen their course because they held these views? I didn't know.

We then moved onto climate change, a subject on which they were remarkably well informed, from the state of the oceans to problems with palm oil production in Indonesia. I was impressed.

It was only after an interlude involving much stroking of dogs belonging to a fellow towpath walker, and after I'd summarised what they'd told me and asked if there was anything else on their mind, that they uttered the B-word. Brexit. Only one of them had been old enough to vote in the referendum, and she'd voted Leave. She expressed a fervent belief in the capability of the country to stand on its own two feet, but also to an ignorance of what the EU actually did. The other two readily admitted they knew very little about the issue, beyond knowing theirs was the generation most likely to be affected by it. When I pointed out that sixteen-year-olds had been given the vote in the Scottish independence referendum this blew their collective minds.

Both this inability to grasp the complexity of the whole EU debate and its low position in their list of priorities was, I suspected, a common experience. Nowhere on my travels so far had I seen, or heard, evidence of an ongoing debate. Although Brexit dominated the headlines, people appeared to regard it as yesterday's news, the referendum result as an end, rather than the beginning of a long, long road.

I thanked the women and wished them well, as they posed for a photo outside a KFC – not for social media they assured me, but as evidence that they'd actually walked the route. As we finally went our separate ways, we agreed that our exchange had been interesting and helped pass the time, as well as miles, along. As it happened, we left the canal at the same bridge, with the women going right and me left, to explore Hinckley. Not strictly on my route, this was an opportunity to take the temperature of another town. As a parting shot I asked my companions if there was much there. In retrospect I wished I'd listened to them. Maybe I was tired (it turned out to be a lot further than I'd expected), but when I got there Hinckley had little to offer.

Like Atherstone, it too was once dependent on a single industry, in Hinckley's case hosiery. That's stockings to you and me. These days it is supposed to be a hub for more creative types, but if this is so, they were keeping a low profile that day. It is also home to Triumph Motorcycles, which occupies a large factory on the opposite bank to the canal. If ever an industry typified the ups and downs of British manufacturing, motorcycles is probably it. These days, the town's position near a number of motorway networks makes it a favoured spot for warehousing, a story that was becoming familiar. Maybe I didn't give Hinckley a fair shot, after all it had been an eventful and emotional day, but it wasn't exactly throwing itself at me, so I gave up and found a taxi to take me to my bed and dinner. Oh, and possibly a pint.

I completed three more miles of the towpath the next morning, an overcast day with little traffic on either the canal or the towpath. My main problem was actually the wind, and not because of the cooked breakfast I'd enjoyed. There'd been veiled hints on the TV that morning of a storm to the north and I could feel specks of rain on the air. My concerns about the weather at the start of this leg of the walk resurfaced, but as I'd always known, there was no option but to press on.

Having passed through the pretty village of Barton Hastings, a more immediate challenge presented itself: crossing the M69. My map suggested an underpass, but when I got there it was flooded, and I couldn't be certain all the liquid I could see was water. Time to improvise. I could see there was a footpath along and just above the motorway, and that this led to a bridge, so I followed that. Curiously, this wasn't a particularly popular path, and as a result it consisted mainly of tall grasses and the occasional hidden badger set as trip hazards. Stinging nettles were also another popular option, meaning the couple of hundred yards to the bridge took at least half a painful hour to complete. On exiting the path I was greeted with whatever the collective noun might be for a mass of burst bin liners full of rubbish, along with enough dumped mattresses to furnish a hostel.

I was free of the nettles, though, walking along the sides of fields ploughed to create eighteen-inch-high trenches of red-tinged soil nurturing seed potatoes. My day had settled into a routine, of pretty small villages followed by stretches of fields, some passable, others less so. A good early example was Wolvey, where thatched cottages were scattered randomly around the village and a decorated sign proudly displayed the village's name on a small triangle of carefully tended land opposite a doctor's surgery. This was located in a decent-sized house, where it had moved in 2002, having previously been located in the Village Hall. On the one hand, it was quite impressive that this small village, with a population of around 2,000, has its own practice; on the other, it could be considered incredible that delivering twenty-first-century healthcare from a converted house is still seen as acceptable.

A small statue, or maybe it was a trophy, sat below the village sign. Made of bronze and about two feet high, it was a bear and ragged staff, the motif of Warwickshire county. This was for the 'Dr. Flack Memorial Award for a Village With Over 500 Souls'. There were no further details, and I couldn't find out anything more about it afterwards, so I decided to settle for being suitably impressed it wasn't a Best Kept Village Award or another *Sunday Times* recommendation and pressed on.

Equally bucolic was Monks Kirby, where there was a delightful pub opposite the impressive church. I paused here to gather my wits and my breath, as well as to slake my thirst. The wind had died down, the day once again a hot and sunny one. A group of what might once have been called pensioners, but who were probably more accurately called local residents, were enjoying a convivial meal inside. They paused only to glance up at the strange unshaven man, with elderflowers stuck to his sweaty arms, the remnants of stinging nettles on his boots and a large blue rucksack on his back. They weren't glances of encouragement. I decided to prolong my stay a while by ordering a sandwich and using the facilities, in that order. That I was expected to produce a jacket and tie and remove my two-day stubble in order to eat inside wasn't expressly stated, but felt implicit. I therefore ventured outdoors where the sun shone and the WiFi failed.

My afternoon took me along the edge of Newnham Paddox, where Capability Brown had designed a large mansion for the fifth and sixth Earls of Denbigh in the eighteenth century. The house was eventually demolished in 1952 after flood damage caused by the thawing of frozen water pipes. The current Earl, for there still is one, lives in a modern house in the grounds, while the surrounding lands have steadily been sold off in blocks. Oh, how the mighty eventually fall, undone by a combination of plumbing and death duties.

My final stop that day was at Churchover, yet another delightful small village, where the pub marked on the map had been replaced by a bar in the Village Hall. I waited here for a taxi into Rugby, the nearest place I'd been able to find a bed for the night. As I waited a tall man, probably not that many years older than myself, dragged himself over and initiated an encounter. He opened by apologising that he suffered from Parkinson's Disease, although I assured him there was no reason to say sorry for that. He clearly wanted to talk to me about his treatment, our conversation developing quickly as I happened to know a bit about the subject. Our discussion about recent advances in medical science was eventually curtailed by the arrival of my taxi, so I wished him well and headed for my latest digs.

Although not strictly on my route, and my stay there was by necessity limited, I took to Rugby. It has a range of restaurants, which was important to me at the end of an exhausting day, as well as some interesting streets. The area I was staying in was dominated by Rugby School, where football wasn't invented. Every second property appeared to be part of the school, which even had its own Sanatorium. Not the headmaster's secretary and a first aid box mind you, but a whole Sanatorium. It must be all those playing-field injuries. I reflected how these fee-paying schools (private, but public, just to confuse foreigners) had, if anything, become more entrenched over the first two decades of the century, in part through an influx of overseas students. Private education, it seemed, was just as much an export industry as our universities, while at the same time making it okay for nationals able to afford it (7 per cent of the country's schoolchildren are privately educated) to pay for the 'decent start in life' that would more or less secure their middle-class status for another generation.

My hotel was run by a couple of Chinese origin, who were delightful, if a little eccentric. On checking in, I was told that breakfast was £6 extra, cash preferred, but my 'eat when you can' philosophy meant I was in. So it was that the next morning I found myself alone in a decidedly retro-looking dining room, alone that was except for a young man also of Chinese origin. After he'd left I asked the proprietor if this was his son and he laughed. No, he was a customer, here for an interview at the school. He was still laughing as he went to fetch my toast, leaving me sensitive to any further ethnic faux pas.

Returning with a full toast rack, my easily amused host decided to engage me in conversation.

'So, you walk it, yes?' he asked.

'Yes, off to Long Buckby today,' I replied, slightly bemused, as we'd gone through all this the evening before.

'No, walk it?' he insisted.

'Yes, walking,' I confirmed, correcting his English.

It was only then that I realised that the T-shirt I'd pulled out of my rucksack that morning proudly stated, 'I have walked the Great Wall of China' (which I have, although not all of it, obviously). I confirmed my status as a Great Wall Walker and he picked up my dirty cereal bowl before retreating once more into the kitchen, looking decidedly less jolly.

Another taxi trip later, I picked up the route and came upon Colton House. This was once the management training centre for the Royal Mail. Yes, they actually had one; it even had its own sub-post office. The centre burned down in 2010, and the grounds were being converted into a high-end housing development, which of course provided an opportunity to 'lose' footpaths while no one was looking. This led to an early battle around a field edge. Insects upset at being disturbed seemed to take solace in the fresh source of nutrients offered by the open scratches all along my arms. This was followed by another motorway crossing.

Luckily, this one was dry, and after passing through the village of Newton via some fishing ponds, I set a course for the A5, Watling Street, a few hundred yards ahead. The passage ahead was enclosed by tall trees and wooden fences on either side and was occupied entirely by tall leggy stinging nettles striving for the light. I could hear the road ahead, but first I had to get through these. My map and Pathwatch app were all well and good, but whilst they could confirm I was on the right path this couldn't guarantee the quality of said path. Sure, I now had the capability to report it, but this came as little immediate consolation.

I managed around 95 per cent of it and, just as I was congratulating myself and reflecting on how awful it would have been to fall into the nettles, I did just that. Too busy looking down, I'd missed the overhanging branch which caught the top of the head pouch of my rucksack, pulled it back and then flung me with extra motive force to the left and the embrace of mother nettle. It was quick, and yet it was also in slow motion, if that makes sense. Strangely inevitable, really. Once free, I sat by the side of the road and smothered myself in sting relief cream, before negotiating the A5 and pressing on, trying hard not to scratch too much.

The following paths were relatively straightforward, and it hit me how footpaths are a bit like technology: great when they work, but amazingly frustrating when they don't. They both present a perfectly reasonable scenario, the difficulty being in the execution. I also mused (I was spending a lot of time on my own) on how it was possible to tell when you passed from one landowner's jurisdiction to another by how well the footpaths were maintained. They may own the land, but the footpaths were there before they were and would be so afterwards. Managing them is just good practice, as well as making economic sense. If a path cuts an angle across a field, why sow crops over it – people with a right to walk that route will either trample the crops down, or go around the edge of the field and probably do even more damage that way. And that is just the economic argument, putting aside simple goodwill and manners, before even touching on legal obligations.

Still, as I'd already reflected, we English are remarkably lucky to have our footpaths at all. It's just a shame they vary so much. The Ramblers Association recently cited a figure of over 100,000 reported problems,[15] based on a survey of sixty-eight councils. So given that's not all councils and only covers reported problems, the real figure must easily be in the hundreds of thousands, or around a problem per mile, all in all a fairly damning statistic. At a time when we are all being encouraged to exercise more, and the CRT (the body responsible for the canal network, remember) has rebranded itself as providing 'Wellbeing for Everyone' in recognition of the value of the increasing need for peace and quiet (it was Hippocrates himself who declared that walking was 'man's best medicine'), this comes across as counter-intuitive. It was a good example of decision makers in cash-strapped councils and beyond being too tied up in simply surviving and dealing with the day-to-day to be able to think outside the box.

---

15 Source: The Ramblers. See: https://www.ramblers.org.uk/get-involved/campaign-with-us/past-campaigns/footpath-funding-cuts.aspx

All this was going through my mind as I passed through the village of Lilbourne and followed a diverted bridleway through a vast bank of wind turbines outside Rugby visible from the M1. I crossed this iconic modern artery via an ancient agricultural bridge, after which my route largely bypassed Crick, home to an annual narrowboat gathering, before heading south to Watford. No, not that one, but the one that gives its name to the Watford Gap, which in turn people probably recognise because of the motorway service station there. It is this Watford, not the one further south, that is the source of the phrase 'north of Watford', the traditional demarcation point between the north and the south of England. There is even a signpost at the service station pointing to the north one way and the south another. The gap in question is one between two hills and is significant, channelling transport links through the ages, from ancient roads, through canals (there's a flight of locks a mile from the village) to modern highways (hence the service station).

I'd headed to Watford both out of a sense of homage (it may not be Watford, Herts where my football team was from, but I felt a completely irrational obligation to visit), and to see if this distinction between north and south might make it a better candidate for the middle of England. After all, if a place is the pivot between the north and the south it is surely the middle, right?

The village was picture-perfect. I was now in Northamptonshire, and many of the buildings were in Northamptonshire ironstone, a gold-coloured stone, or more traditional brick. A village of only around 320 souls (it would qualify for the Dr Frick Memorial Prize, if it had been in the right county and if anyone knew what it was for), this Watford has a fourteenth-century church and a long history going back as far as the Romans as well as evidence of Anglo-Saxon settlements, a mention in the Domesday Book, and links with the earliest American settlers. A Watford man, Thomas Rogers, was one of the passengers who left for the New World on the *Mayflower*. There's even a Thomas Rogers Society in the USA which meets every three years, all descendants of this Watford resident.

Naturally, Watford has its local Lord of the Manor, most latterly coming from the Henley family. The second Lord Henley was married to the sister of the Victorian Prime Minister, Robert Peel. The local 'big house', Watford Court Manor, was demolished in 1975, which acted as a significant economic blow to the village, but probably a bigger blow to the Henleys. I passed through some of the grounds of the old house, along an avenue of young oak trees, making a wary detour round a herd of cows on the way, and before that under the ornate Lord Henley's Bridge. This iron construction, painted a vivid green and bearing the Henley coat of arms, sits on the estate's northern ride, and was built to carry the Hanslope-Northampton-Rugby Loop railway line. The story goes that it was designed as a feature to placate the locals, although the fact that it also acted as a halt to take the Lord to Westminster in order to vote is probably a coincidence.

So, was this the real middle of England? In part, yes, I concluded; but only in part. In being so busy looking for what has changed in England, I'd missed spotting what hadn't. This village, along with many of the others I'd passed through, represented a crystallisation of the heart of England. The sort of image people held onto when they were away from the country for a while. The sort of place H.V. Morton summoned up when he thought he was pegging it in Palestine, of wood smoke, thatched cottages, church bells and happy farmers.

Many of those features have endured (except the happy farmers bit, obviously), and offered a sort of foundation myth for the rest of the country. Change could happen elsewhere, on the coast, in the grand cities; but things would remain pretty much as they had always been in these villages of Middle England. Their farms may consolidate, their manor houses be knocked down or suffer from water damage, their pubs disappear (never mind, we can always set one up in the village hall), and their post offices survive without internet access. They were resilient. They were at England's core.

8

Shoetown, on a Cloudy Day

The following day, I was due to meet up with some more diagonal walkers: Moira, another cousin, and her friend Lesley. As such, I set off from my overnight stop in Long Buckby relatively early, my Airbnb host Gilly joining me with her dog for the first couple of miles. It was going to be a companionable day.

The previous evening had already been very sociable. I'd planned to look around Long Buckby, a reasonably sized town, which I'd hoped might give me further insight into my Middle England ruminations. In the end the only sight I got of it was wandering through the village green and high street and the inside of the local pharmacy to get some more sting cream. On first appearance the town looked like it was well provisioned with amenities such as shops, eateries, a Co-op supermarket and a selection of pubs. Once I got inside the door of the Airbnb however, I never left it again, other than a quick trip to the supermarket, of which more in a second.

I'd had an email exchange with Gilly beforehand as I wanted to see if she'd let me use her washing machine. This had been a ploy to reduce the amount of clothes I needed to carry with me and had worked, although I was now down to my final pair of smalls. She was intrigued by my walk and we spent some time talking about it before I could get away to my room, have a shower and fill her laundry basket.

I asked about the best place to eat, and she suggested a deal. She and her husband Richard would provide the meal if I provided the booze – hence the short trot to the Co-op. I'd liked what I'd seen of Long Buckby, and Gilly described it as 'Cotswolds-lite'. There were good transport connections and a good community vibe. Gilly was originally from Canada, but has lived in the UK for thirty-five years and she and Richard run a cattery in the village. This explained the clutter of felines around the house, all of which were theirs, not guests at the cattery (or, indeed, the Airbnb).

She claimed that 75 per cent of Long Buckby had voted Leave in the referendum,[16] something I put down to locals wanting to maintain what they had. I was slightly taken aback when she shared that she was one of them, on the grounds that she was a libertarian. This didn't mean she was

16 The result was actually 58.6 per cent in favour of Leave in the District of Daventry in which Long Buckby is located, although it may have of course been higher in the village itself.

a fan of a certain London garage punk band fronted by Pete Doherty, although she may have been, but that in her eyes the removal of any tier of government was a good thing. Her language was also thought-provoking, including references to 'those in the south-east' who didn't understand how everyone else felt. This jarred a bit with me, not least because pleasant picture-postcard Long Buckby would probably qualify, for most of those earlier in my walk at least, as in 'the south-east', or 'the south' anyway. In my experience most English people's appreciation of their country's geography was on a par with that of the shipping forecast areas.

I snuck a look at local house prices on my iPad. A brand-new five-bedroom house on the edge of the village was available for £650,000. A comparable house in my neck of the woods (ahem, the south-east) would probably cost half as much again. What about a starter pad? A two-bedroom Victorian terraced house, a perfect first-time buyer's place, could be had for £160,000, which with two earners in reasonable jobs would probably be affordable. Life wasn't so bad in Long Buckby.

Gilly's motivations for voting Leave spoke of something else, too, I thought. This was a distrust of elites, of being ruled by faceless, unelected, bureaucrats, a perception that had haunted the EU for decades. Trust of politicians in general has also loosened, weakened by things such as the MPs expenses scandals, and of elites in general, finding its ultimate expression in Michael Gove's infamous comment about 'not trusting experts' during the referendum campaign. Add to this mix the way the EU, or those in the Euro-zone at least, handled the banking crisis and their imposition of austerity on the so-called PIGS (Portugal, Ireland, Greece and Spain), perceived by some to have been heartless, and a growing sense of not wanting to be associated with 'that lot' is perhaps unsurprising. Besides, it was easier to hate those you could not put a face to.

Gilly and Richard were perfect hosts and I enjoyed our discussions. Having said my goodbyes to Gilly and her dog, I carried on alone for three miles to Little Brington, passing copses of pines trees last seen in such density outside Formby on the first day of the walk. The path was covered in cones, and as I stopped to take a picture a pair of squirrels leapt out of the adjacent wheat field, raced across my path and up into the trees.

Moira and Lesley joined me outside the pub, where a wedding reception was in full swing – a good effort seeing as it was only 11am. I'd been slightly concerned about dragging these two women through nettles and fields of ripening crops, but as it happened our route coincided with a stretch of long-distance path known as the Midshires Way, a name offering further evidence I was in the middle of the country. As any experienced walker knows, a marked long-distance path represents something of the Holy of Holies of walking, usually clearly marked and well maintained, the sort of path that even Staffordshire would keep up. This proved to be largely the case, the route leading us through obvious stiles and gates rather than obliging us to seek them out.

Taking advantage of the fact that for once Moira and I weren't meeting at a funeral, we caught up on each other's family news and all too quickly we were meeting up with another friend of hers and Lesley's at a garden centre. After that, I was back on my own and walking through another large pine plantation. The pines seen earlier had simply been an amuse bouche. This was Harlestone Firs, part of the Althorp Estate owned by the Earl Spencer, better known as the man who won 'man of the match' at his sister, Princess Diana's, funeral where he stuck one to the royal family, and thereby captured the mood of the country.

Twenty-foot-wide paths made it impossible to get lost, and when I did reach open fields there was a sense that wheat crops were finally triumphing over rape. I hoped so. In fact, the vista that lay before me just outside Northampton was of a vast prairie over a mile wide with a single tree on the horizon, as if it had been planted to give the tractor drivers something to look forward to when it came to ploughing. The scene was a brooding one, with dark grey clouds gathering over that horizon and I could feel a few spots of rain on my cheeks. While my next bed was the only one I'd booked for two nights on this leg, I didn't want to arrive there sopping. I had to press on, and quickly.

Two miles of urban walking, dipping into bus shelters when it looked like the clouds were finally going to empty, felt heavy on the feet; but then again, most days when the finishing line came into view, the miles magically doubled in length. As it happened the rain was just playing games with me, and I arrived at my hotel in an unexpectedly dry state.

The hotel was perfectly decent, and ridiculously good value. Clean, with my own bathroom and breakfast thrown in for £40. Okay, it was ten minutes out of town in an area with a prominent Co-op Funeralcare centre (shop? outlet?) cheek by jowl with cheap fast-food emporia, exotic shops selling fatty sausages which might hasten demand for the Co-op's services and a Polish off-licence with a recent delivery of whole watermelons outside (four cans of Tyskie please, and go on, I'll take a watermelon while I'm here). The hotel was family run, with a silent matriarch holding brooding court in the reception area, making sure that everything was done just so, and a pair of identical twins apparently doing everything else. At least, I think they were twins.

Suitably refreshed, I wandered into town to find the best bit of Northampton, and I think I succeeded, although it was difficult to be sure. Everywhere was surprisingly quiet for a Saturday night, although to be fair it was still early. Some decent architecture offered variety, but most of this was at least a 150 years old. The most recent attempt at something interesting was the Northgate Bus Station, the effect of which was diminished by some pretty hideous multi-storey car parks. These looked as if the architects had delegated their design to their children, with the help of some Lego bricks, lolly sticks and shirt cardboard.

Too tired to experiment, I settled for a chain Italian restaurant and settled down with my book. I couldn't concentrate, though, my eye constantly drawn to a fresh-faced Deliveroo guy wearing a cycle helmet which he never took off, who kept wandering in, and then out again, always empty-handed. Initially eager, he went through various stages of sagaciousness and then boredom, before eventually settling down in a corner, his helmet still strapped firmly to his chin.

His plight offered a perfect illustration of the social divides that have grown up in the last two decades, of the gap between those who ordered their Saturday night meal sitting on their sofa using an app, and the gig-economy 'slaves' expected to fetch it for them by bicycle. As I waited for my own meal to arrive I couldn't resist going over to talk to him.

He was Polish (I didn't ask him where he stood on watermelons with beer) and he was happy to share that he got paid £6 an hour come what may. As such, having to wait for this order wasn't a disaster for him, other than he also got paid £1 per job, so he was losing out on the possibility of maybe another pound that hour. I asked if people tipped, but he pulled a face. It turned out these were discretionary and, I deduced, meagre. People generally paid online for the delivery, so it wasn't as if he could benefit from loose change. If he was really lucky he might earn £10 an hour, more than the £7.05 national minimum wage for someone of his age, but barely, and not guaranteed (an hour spent waiting for a job would be below that rate). I asked him where he was headed, and the answer was the Marriott Hotel, a fifteen-minute ride away.

'Wouldn't it be cold by the time you get there?' I asked.

'Maybe,' he shrugged. Not his problem.

At that point, his order finally arrived, the kitchen staff full of apologies. I sensed they were empathetic to his plight and may even have been related to him, given some of the accents I heard coming from the kitchen. The moral here was, if you use one of these services, remember how lucky you are and for goodness sake, tip! Those of us who'd managed to find our own way to the restaurant to be served by a waiter, who presented us with our food direct from the kitchen and without a fifteen-minute cycle ride, tipped him (at least I hoped we did), so the Deliveroo guy who used his own muscle power in all weathers surely deserved one too?

I wandered back to my table, passing a group of five elegantly dressed young women, four of them wearing headscarves, politely giving presents to one of their number whose birthday it presumably was. Behind them, two other young women, about the same age, had recently come in, their long hair defiantly on show, along with a significant proportion of their breasts, which they appeared particularly keen to display. Both sets of young women existed in their own worlds and both had a perfect right to do so. They did, however, provide a contrast to each other.

Outside, things had livened up. It wasn't exactly Liverpool, but then again I hadn't expected it to be, although the two shared a common problem with homelessness. As early as 8:30 there was a man flat out on a broken-down cardboard box in the churchyard of the centrally located All Saints' Church. Elsewhere, tents were being erected in shop doorways.

My day was done, and I wandered back to my hotel. Along the way, roughly every third voice I heard carried an Eastern Europe accent. Earlier, I'd fancied an Indian meal but had struggled to find a suitable restaurant, certainly in the centre. It seemed the sub-continent was passé in immigration terms. Safely back at the hotel, I perused the tourist leaflets in the reception area. Eschewing an evocation to 'Discover Rutland' (Eric Idle had made Rutland impossible to take seriously), I did pick up a 'Guide to Northampton' for a little light reading before bed.

After a surreal breakfast, during which the man on reception, the one enquiring whether I'd prefer coffee or tea and the one vacuuming the carpet outside all appeared to be the same person, I plunged myself into the town. Town mark you, not city. Northampton has made repeated attempts to gain city status and been denied each time. It has a cathedral, but this belongs to the Catholic persuasion, so doesn't count. It also has the magnificent All Saints, whose churchyard had been used as a temporary bedroom the previous evening, bang in the centre, and this was where I headed.

Along the way, I also passed the Holy Sepulchre Church. Dating back to 1100, this was modelled on its namesake in Jerusalem and built by returning Crusaders, notably Simon de St Liz, the first Norman Earl of Northampton; although I doubt he actually wielded a trowel personally. Apparently, it is one of only four round churches in the world.

The weather forecasters predicted possible rain, so I took this as a sign not to bother with a coat. Like Atherstone with its hats and Hinckley with its hosiery, Northampton also once had its speciality, shoes, earning it the local moniker of 'Shoetown'. In fact, the guide I'd picked up the previous evening boasted that the town's Boot and Shoe Quarter (yes, really) enjoyed the 'highest density of boot and shoe factories and the greatest survival of buildings associated with the business', although it was non-specific as to where it was comparing itself to. Was this the greatest concentration in Northamptonshire, the East Midlands, England, Europe, the world, the universe?

Like the Holy Sepulchre, All Saints can also trace its antecedents back a long way, the eleventh century in fact, even if the current building replaced the 'Collegiate Church' that burned down during the Great Fire of Northampton of 1675, an event omitted from my school's history textbook. A sign fixed near to the entrance claimed the building was 'amongst the foremost examples of Seventeenth Century Church Architecture outside London'. It looked like they'd got stuck on title case when painting the sign.

I'm no expert on Seventeenth Century Church Architecture, but it came across as very fine. An inscription along the top of the building either side of a statue of Charles II proclaimed 'This statue was erected in memory of King Charles II who gave a thousand tun of timber towards the rebuilding of this church and to this town seven years of chimney money attracted within it.' Inside, I could confirm it was chimney money well spent. I was offered an order of service on the way in but I waved it away, preferring to sit and listen as the choir, resplendent in their scarlet robes, practised that day's hymns.

Driven by my guide, which was proving very informative, I headed back out into the town. My Long Buckby hostess Gilly had described Northampton succinctly as 'a shithole', so my expectations weren't high, but I was prepared to give it a go. Earlier that year, Northamptonshire County Council had effectively declared itself bankrupt, only the fourth council ever to do so. On top of that, a recent report had recommended its disbandment, the investigators involved stating that its problems were so deeply rooted it was impossible to rescue. In other words, things had got so bad the only option was to tear everything up and start again afresh. It wasn't promising.

The county's problems were blamed upon either poor management or the cumulative impact of ten years of cuts and austerity. It didn't matter really whose side you took or whose fault it was. Either way, the county was unsustainable in its current form. This wasn't a problem unique to Northamptonshire, and could perhaps have contributed to Gilly's perception of 'those in the south-east' living in some kind of separate world, even if the geographic reality was that many of those in the cities (sorry Northampton) of Liverpool and Stoke earlier on my travels might have regarded Northampton as sufficiently 'down south' to be alien. I remembered the BBC survey about Englishness published earlier on during this stage of my walk, which suggested that the further people live from London, the more they identify with their particular part of England.

I wondered what part of England Northamptonites associated with? The East Midlands? I doubted it. The East Midlands has always seemed to me to be the blandest of local appellations, neither one thing or another. At least the West Midlands has Birmingham to coalesce around, as well as their distinctive accent. It was difficult to come up with any words or phrases inimitably East Midlands-ish. Maybe Polish had replaced them?

I headed for the Cultural Quarter, but it appeared to be shut. The museum and art gallery was undergoing some refurbishment, which presented me with mixed feelings as the world's biggest shoe museum had been on offer. Quite reasonably, given the hour, the Royal Theatre was also closed. Royal Theatre take note, not the more usual Theatre Royal, and these days combined with an Opera House, no less. Instead I headed for 78 Derngate, a privately-run attraction I was assured would be open, passing the very grand nineteenth-century Guildhall along the way. An imposing Victorian Gothic edifice, this offered an almost ironic face given the town's difficulties. I would have liked to visit it, but, you've guessed it ...

78 Derngate is a modest affair, but quite possibly the jewel in the crown of the town's offerings. It was the only house in England remodelled by the Scottish designer and architect Charles Rennie Mackintosh and it represents a dazzling example of the period between Art Nouveau and Art Deco, with its Japanese screens and colourful, almost too colourful at times, decorations above stairs, and its evocative kitchen, complete with green checked tablecloth and range below stairs.

The remodelling was commissioned by the wonderfully named Joseph Bassett-Lowke to move into after his marriage in 1917 to a daughter of one of the town's leading shoe-makers. I was largely on my own and wandered around the narrow house modelling the blue plastic shoe protectors given to me by the volunteer on reception. They took shoes seriously in Northampton. Despite being busy training a young woman on how to work the till, this volunteer also found the time to give me a personal introduction to the house from outside, looking up at the back. Bassett-Lowke ran a factory making models, garden railways and that sort of thing, and during both wars he'd made miniature replicas of enemy shipping to ease identification for those patrolling the seas.

Back in Bassett-Lowke's day, Northampton would have been a typical county town of just under 90,000 people, with thriving industry and an independent mindset fuelled by a belief in non-conformity. A few years before Derngate's heyday, the town elected a radical reformer, and atheist no less, Charles Bradlaugh, to Parliament. Whatever Bradlaugh's merits, he was certainly a contrast to an earlier representative, Spencer Perceval (not Percival for all you pedants out there), who still holds the distinction of being the only British Prime Minister to be assassinated. So far.

Suitably uplifted, I wandered back into town, doing so via some splendid stone cenotaphs complete with stone flags. These were designed by Sir Edwin Lutyens, whose other commissions included Whitehall in London, Manchester, Glasgow, Delhi, Johannesburg, Hong Kong and Auckland, all of which placed Northampton in pretty elevated company, and probably said something about relative changes in circumstances. I noted that a run of redundant red telephone boxes had been left empty, which given earlier experiences in the walk surely represented a missed opportunity?

My guide informed me that the St. Giles Quarter of the city was named the country's 'Great British High Street in 2015', although with its customary lack of context, omitted to say who had given it this accolade. The *Sunday Times* probably. Nevertheless, I doubled back and headed there anyway. It was refreshing to see a series of independent boutiques selling a range of things (as well as actually being open). It's true there was a disproportionate number of coffee shops, but this was the case on most high streets I'd been down. At the top of the street, the railings outside the Church of St Giles displayed a row of old high-heeled women's shoes (although, given the times, there was nothing to say that they could only be worn by women), used as flower planters for Alpine flowers, a lovely and relevant touch. It was also refreshing to see that they hadn't been vandalised. I didn't check too closely how they were secured for fear of attracting suspicion, of either the criminal or sexual variety.

Alas, St Giles wasn't the main shopping drag in the town. That title belonged to Abington Street. If my respect for the town had been slowly inflating, Abington Street did a fair job in puncturing it. Even my guide was light on what Abington Street offered, focussing more on a couple of sculptures erected there, one showing a Cobblers Last, the other a tribute to the Northampton-born scientist Francis Crick, one of the discoverers of DNA; rather than the actual shops.

These shops were a fairly motley collection, with what were once fine facades now home to either discount stores or the occasional national chain. Those that were empty housed the more fortunate homeless dwellers, free to leave their tents up all day. Taken as a whole, it wasn't an elevating sight. Abington Street was, if anything, merely a fairly extreme example of many of the traditional high streets I'd seen on my walk. That day there'd been the news that even Poundland was struggling nationally. Any shops still able to make a living, plus some which were teetering on the edge, had consolidated into malls, seeking safety in numbers. I wandered into the open space of the Market Square, but it didn't offer much other than space.

As it was near lunchtime, I headed for the Albion microbrewery, taking in a detour to the River Nene first, where a widebeam boat was gliding gently past the large Carlsberg Brewery located on the waterfront. This was the first Carlsberg Brewery outside Denmark, taking over the site previously occupied by the merged Phipps and Co and Northampton Brewing Company, which itself had been taken over by Watney Mann in 1968.

I reached the Albion just in time to miss a brewery tour, so I was largely left alone in a traditionally furnished bar, except for some extravagantly dressed individuals who'd parked an elegant row of vintage scooters outside. They recommended the Phipps IPA, and it was a good call. Northampton's beer was always known for its high hop content, required to counteract the effect of all the tannin the local shoe workers came into contact with, but not, I felt, added in the overwhelming way favoured by so many modern 'craft breweries'.

The Albion has revived Northampton's old beer marques and had made a brilliant job of it. It was an absolute pleasure to sit in the bar and recover my wits, surrounded by old pub fittings and ancient pub games. These included Northamptonshire skittles, which was like bar billiards, except with nine skittles on a netted table, which needed to be knocked down using small solid discs called cheeses. Okay, the brewery is another nod to the past, but in a positive way, in that it isn't just a playground, but a working business, providing innovation, skills and employment. All in all, a good example of the resilience and an eye to the future needed to cope with changing times.

A second pint was extremely tempting, but would have required a little wander back to the hotel to rest my eyelids.

The weather outside, though, didn't look inviting: smoky-grey clouds tinged with darker rims, and of course I was missing a coat. What to do? My guide's logic was sending me towards Abington Park, but I didn't really want to go down Abington Street again, and I wanted to get wet even less.

I ventured uphill back towards All Saints when I heard a tuba, accompanied by a descant of shiny-sounding trumpets belting out what sounded like a melody of popular show hits. Where I'd stood a couple of hours before, staring up to read the inscription along the top of the church, now sat a whole brass band, the Virtuosi GUS Band, which their conductor told us in between numbers, was shortly to represent the county at the brass band finals in the Albert Hall in London. Stop to think about that for a moment.

They were brilliant, and brave. The conductor knew he was tempting fate, but he cued his band up anyway, and they launched into 'Singing in the Rain'. Sure enough, the drops started to fall and people began to cast around for shelter, but it was as if Mother Nature was just having a bit of fun, for just as the band came to the end of the song, the rain stopped, never to come back. I took a programme from a volunteer handing them out and discovered that I'd chanced upon the Northampton Music Festival.

The whole town was transformed, with people acting as if they were at Glastonbury, spilling out onto the streets, bravely defying the threatening grey skies, clutching Festival programmes in one hand, a coffee or a pint of beer in the other, wandering easily from venue to venue. A variety of genres was on offer, with the jazz stage actually in the courtyard of the Guildhall. This meant I was able to peek inside after all, even if it was only the recently refurbished courtyard, with its bronze statues to famous town worthies, of which there were a surprising number.

Even the previously empty Market Square was transformed, hosting the main stage along with a row of artisan food stalls. It only seemed polite to sample the free-range Scotch eggs while listening to a mixture of local bands providing both covers and original material. I was so contented I even wandered around the inevitable stalls of 'retro' goods. This was the eleventh year of the festival, which meant it had only started this century. I could only conclude it was a good thing. It brought people together and showed the town off a bit. It was impossible not to get caught up in the vibe, and I found myself having a number of conversations with people next to me throughout the afternoon, a cheeky kip having been wiped off the agenda. In fact, despite this supposedly being a day of rest, by the end of it I'd walked nearly as much as I did on a non-rest day. Still, it was worth it.

I'd enjoyed my day in Northampton, and that wasn't a sentence I'd expected to write. I supposed I'd been lucky, but I'd been enjoying myself before the music festival, and that had just added cream on top of the experience. Yes, Northampton was down, but it wasn't quite out. It had shown strength of character and was trying to re-define itself in a changing world, and good for it.

Only one experience spoiled things. As the evening approached, I could see that things in the Market Square were going to hot up. A fair bit had been drunk, and from the programme it was clear that the music was going to continue and get louder. I was not familiar with the oeuvre of The Jets, the final band on the list, but I had a suspicion they weren't going to cover Sinatra or Abba. After dinner, I therefore made the call to head back to the hotel and get my head down, ready for another day's diagonal walking the next morning.

Having left the centre, making my way up to the Polish delis, I was accosted by a tall man in his forties or fifties, dressed fairly respectably, with a generously proportioned tattooed woman on his arm.

'Excuse me mate,' he enquired, making me stop. 'Got any change?'

I wasn't that well-dressed myself. Perhaps it was the fact that I was holding a book that marked me out as a potential mug. I knew exactly where he was headed, and what he wanted money for. I'd just seen him and his companion come out of a pub.

All day, I'd been surrounded by individuals and families from Eastern Europe having a good time, spending the money I knew they worked hard to earn. Welcoming people, making the best of themselves. Polite. Exactly the kind of people I suspected this man would resent and label scroungers.

I knew who the real scrounger was.

9

Progress

Impressively, by 9am the next day, the music festival venues had been tidied away, along with nearly all the litter. Only the main stage remained up, and even that was clear of any random sleeping drunk or homeless person. Following a short stretch of walking along the Nene, and then past the lock that marked the end of the Grand Union Canal's Northampton branch, my umpteenth canal, I was back into the familiar territory of open countryside. The town had presented a last hurrah with a large office building housing the headquarters of Avon Cosmetics. Not the UK headquarters, the global headquarters. Northampton must have been made up when they got that.

Almost as impressive were the new buildings still being erected, which were going to house the relocated University of Northampton. It turned out that new building was to be a theme for the day. Where my maps indicated open countryside, I often found myself amongst fresh housing, and having to pick out footpaths preserved between brick walls. I'd bought older editions of the OS maps off eBay, but not that old. This was very recent development. New mini-villages tacked onto traditional old villages, the name retained, the character redefined. The development wasn't obtrusive, and don't get me wrong, I accept houses have to be built somewhere. It was a surprise as much as anything.

This housing had certainly gone up since my previous trip through the heart of England, and as such was a tangible sign of progress – desirable or not depending upon your viewpoint. Was I beginning to enter commuter land? Was all this housing to accommodate people catching the convenient nearby trains to London? In that sense, was I now beginning to leave the fringes of Middle England and into the derided 'south-east', or was this a sort of no man's land?

Normal service was eventually reached when I battled through a large field of the rape I thought, hoped, I'd finally left behind. I crossed the M1 once again, this time around Junction 15, with a bridleway and a fresh array of wind turbines waiting to greet me the other side. Despite my earlier shock at the rate of building, I was reminded how much of England's green and pleasant land is precisely that (and also how much of it was laid to rape), as I continued along my way.

As I was thinking this, I thought I sensed a mirage ahead. A strange shimmer, a hint of water. None was marked on the map, and neither was what it turned out to be: yet another massive solar farm. These wind and solar installations, slightly hidden away, a secret to anyone other than their owners and walkers, were a real feature of this part of the country. Fenced off, and presided over by CCTV, the panels silently did their job without fuss and, in this particular case, without sheep, lost or otherwise.

Sheep were about to feature again though. As I walked over the latest in a succession of stiles following the tops of a run of fields, I thought I could make out a four-wheel drive with its bonnet up. My first thought was they'd chosen an inconvenient place to break down, and my second was it was an even stranger place to have a shave, for the sound rending the air was that of an electric razor, albeit a bloody powerful one, but then again bushy beards were all the rage.

Shearers, and I didn't mean ex-England centre forwards. Sheep shearers, two of them, clipping sheep, yanking them out of a pen, turning them on their backs and trimming their coats off, starting at the tail and working their way up along their sides. Meanwhile, an older, less muscular man gathered up the fleeces and sewed them into a large bag. I stopped for a chat, and they offered me a go, but by the time I'd taken my rucksack off and put my camera down, they'd yanked the last two remaining sheep out of the pen and set to work. I don't think they really meant it, and besides, they probably wanted to get home. These sheep were only one year old and it was the first time they'd been sheared. Who could blame those recently shorn for bleating angrily at me as I made my way down the edge of the field and into Stoke Goldington?

As I entered the village, I realised it was clearly a day for rural crafts, as a pair of thatchers were wrapping up their day's work from the top of scaffolding embracing a delightful old cottage. I popped into the appropriately named Lamb pub, the village local. It was a Monday and I knew I would be visiting later as I wanted to watch England's first game in the World Cup amongst company. I could see they had a television, so I sought an answer to my second question – did they serve food on a Monday?

'Sorry, no. It's a Monday.' There was no challenging that kind of logic. I waited, sensing there might be more.

'A chip van comes around later,' the barman offered. He carried a general air of nonchalance, as if he was somehow one step removed from the problem. Chips were something, something hot, but I didn't want to miss any of the action eating them outside. 'They're not very good though,' the barman added.

My mind was made up by then. I'd seen a village shop a few doors away, maybe they still had some sandwiches for sale, and there was always the emergency pork pie I carried (and regularly replenished) in my rucksack. I'd be okay.

As it turned out, the chips looked rather good, and some kindly soul bought five portions for sharing. By then though, I was full to the brim with what we call at home 'yellow food', my own purchases combined with the crisps laid out by the pub. As such, I was content to pass on this communal activity, although I was happy joining in with everyone else in celebrating a 91st minute winner, a choice encouraged by several pints of Phipps IPA, which I'd acquired rather a taste for.

The next morning I'd left myself a short walk into Newport Pagnell, these days regarded as more or less a northern suburb of Milton Keynes (although I doubt many of the residents would thank me for that observation). I reached the town via some field walking, enlivened by a glimpse of Gayhurst House, a late-Elizabethan mansion whose sheep grazed alongside the footpath, albeit in a thankfully benign mood. Although the house has the usual illustrious history, along with the practically obligatory Capability Brown landscape, forty years ago it was converted into fourteen flats.

I approached Newport Pagnell itself across Bury Field Common. On first sight, this huge expanse of open land is just a large moorland, but on deeper inspection reveals itself as a historical time capsule, offering a mini-history of England, for it is a rare example of a medieval 'open field'. This was an area originally made available by the local Lord of the Manor to his tenants for farming. Initially ploughed using the ridge and furrow system, by the twelfth century it was used mainly for grazing, with cattle branded so everyone knew whose cow was whose. By the eighteenth century, although cattle still grazed parts of the land, it was also being used for horse racing.

Plans to break the land down into smaller plots during the following century were prevented by public protests, which in turn led to that most English of things, a committee, set up to safeguard the public's rights and privileges. Shortly after, though, parts of it were dug up as preparations for a railway, which never happened, and during the Second World War it became part of the 'Dig for Victory' efforts.

Finally, in 1969, the local council bought the land off the then Lord, who still technically owned it, providing him with a nice little £30,000 windfall.

It was a fitting end to this leg of the walk. Despite my concerns at the start, things had gone well. The rain had, more or less, stayed away, and the walking had been strenuous but very doable. I'd also achieved a couple of significant milestones, including reaching the centre of England, an enterprise which could have gone either way, and, perhaps as significantly, reaching my own milestone: halfway through the walk. I'd initially thought this was going to be at Newport Pagnell, but later calculations suggested it could have been closer to Long Buckby. By these calculations, for I was sad enough to record the count daily, I'd also completed over half a million steps, getting on for 250 miles.

As I still had a bit of time on my hands, I opted to explore Newport Pagnell a bit. There were a couple of things to see, including Tickford Bridge, which has the distinction of being the oldest iron bridge in the world still taking traffic, although when I later posted a picture of it on Facebook with this claim, someone pointed out that I'd omitted to include any traffic. Newport Pagnell is also the spiritual home to Aston Martin and the company still has a small workshop and showroom on the edge of town. Finally, it's the location of the country's last surviving vellum producer, vellum being the dried calf or goat skin that preceded paper as the medium of choice for writing (the Magna Carta is written on it), and remains the material every new Act of Parliament is recorded on. In fact, an attempt to go all modern and use paper in order to save money led to a rare move when the

Cabinet Office offered sufficient funds from its own budget for the practice to continue.

I was on my way to see what I could of these works (the answer was very little, it's all around the back, and all you can see is what looks like a very ordinary front door of a grand detached Victorian house) when I bumped into Barry, or more accurately Barry's mum, Madge. I'd been walking down Caldecot Street when I spotted a kangaroo on the loose. Well, it was tied down with wires, but it was definitely a kangaroo, about three feet high and made out of straw, secured to the top of a recently re-thatched half-timbered cottage, partially hidden by scaffolding. There was straw scattered everywhere on the ground (the thatchers had only recently completed their work) and Madge, a woman who I guessed was probably in her eighties, but sprightly and taking no nonsense from the three large dogs that were scaring the bejesus out of me, wasn't happy.

What did cheer her up was the fact that I found the kangaroo amusing and had paused to take a photo of it. It seemed it had become something of a local talking point. Madge's son, Barry, had spent most of his life in Australia and it was a homage to this portion of his life. A shouted conversation with Barry followed. Wearing shorts and perched on top of the scaffolding while he treated the higher timbers on his house, he waved a friendly paintbrush. It turned out the kangaroo might not be long for this world, apparently the council wasn't keen. When I asked why, Barry was unable to come up with a rationale beyond not having permission. In other words, they were taking umbrage at not being consulted first. His grown-up children had started a social media campaign to save it, and I offered to further his cause on Instagram. I explained what I was about and Madge asked if Barry would get a free copy of the book if he featured in it. There were no flies on her, but the answer was no.

Before leaving, I had one more task to fulfil before going home for a rest and to plan the next stage. Just over thirty years before, I'd been part of a syndicate that had built a house for an exhibition run by the Milton Keynes Development Corporation called Energy World, highlighting innovations in energy efficiency in homebuilding.

This was the sort of thing the Development Corporation used to do, trying stuff out almost for the sake of it. They were great to us, a bunch of idealistic twenty-somethings armed with nothing except a plan. That plan was to showcase a building system pioneered by the German architect Walter Segal, with the aim of showing that anyone could build a house, and to provide the basis for a business which we would go on to run. We were given weekend access to a rambling old house on the edge of town due for demolition, for we were only going to build at weekends. Indeed, our proposition was that it was possible to build our house in only twelve weekends, so, naturally, we only started to build it twelve weekends before the start of the exhibition. In our defence, we were young.

We recruited a gang of architecture students prepared to commit to twelve weekends of on-site practical training and got going. My role was to help drum up the sponsorship needed to get free stuff, of which, I recall, we got a fair bit, largely due to my partner-in-crime's persuasive telephone skills. When I first drew my diagonal line through England, it had passed through a number of places significant in my life. I'd already visited my old alma mater at Keele, and this was another of those places. I wanted to see how the house had got on. I knew it was still there because I could see it on Google Maps, and had even tracked down its address and written to the current occupiers, who in turn had agreed to meet with me, which proved that Royal Mail still served some parts of the country.

I'd originally thought I'd just take a bus from Newport Pagnell, as Milton Keynes itself was off my route by around five miles, outside the informal two-to-three-mile buffer zone I'd set myself either side of the line. Heavy rucksack notwithstanding, though, I could see that there was a way to walk it, taking in not just a stretch of the Grand Union Canal, but also a walk through a park, then on through the centre of the city and then some of its housing. It would be a chance to revisit the grand experiment of Milton Keynes (still a town, but trying to become a city, watch out Northampton) and also walk a stretch of the towpath beside a canal that had been part of my original route nearly twenty years before.

I set off, not quite knowing what I'd discover. Milton Keynes might not technically be on my diagonal line, but this excursion was in the overall spirit of the walk. The towpath was fairly busy, mainly with dog walkers, while the water itself enjoyed a steady flow of both hire boats and retired people in their own craft, most of whom were accompanied by dogs. Dogs were a big thing, and it was one of these that next caught my attention.

The water wasn't only home to boats, but also a family of swans, including an important-looking and, it turned out, belligerent cob, or Daddy Swan. I'd noticed them gliding by, the cob on the lookout, and also clocked a lone walker with his dog joining the towpath from a sloping track to the left. I was about fifty yards on, when suddenly there was an explosion of noise, water splashing, swans honking, a dog barking madly. Maybe the dog had gone for one of the cygnets? Looking around, I could see it was the opposite, the cob had gone for the dog, much to the latter's general surprise, for he'd just gone for a curious look. It was a case of an incident of the curious dog on the towpath.

The dog retreated, presumably in shock, while the cob smugly rejoined his family, mission accomplished. I shouted something out along of the lines of 'That showed him!' to the dog's owner, and he came over. It was time for an encounter. The dog owner was called Martin. The dog was called Jessie, but don't expect me to tell you the breed, I know as much about types of dogs as I do types of cars. I get lost after Aston Martins. My new friend had lived in Milton Keynes for thirty-four years, so old he predated Energy World, which he remembered.

I asked him what he thought about the town. He started by getting the concrete cows out of the way. These objects d'art had for ages been the first point of reference for most of the population when the name of the town came up. They were now housed in the town's museum (don't ask, it was closed), although I had earlier seen an homage in someone's back garden: a set of concrete sheep. That done, I asked him what kept him there.

'This,' he replied, spreading an arm over the canal, 'the open spaces, the quiet.'

I pointed out the irony that what kept him in arguably the country's most innovative, forward-thinking town, was the bit getting on for 200 years old.

He acknowledged this, but went on to eulogise the cycleways that still criss-crossed the town and the parks, one of which, Campbell Park, I was about to walk through. In Martin's view, the town had almost become a victim of its own success, building in ever greater concentrations, resulting in narrower roads, especially in the centre, where parking was now a problem. I wondered if this wasn't true everywhere, and we agreed that in this respect, maybe Milton Keynes had 'joined the club', become just another town. I asked him whether there was a sense of community, but he didn't think so. He was ambivalent, although his wife was from the Philippines, and one of the reasons they'd stayed was because there was a strong Filipino community.

I left the canal and entered the park, which rose up above the water offering views of the surrounding area, and was peppered with regular artworks. As I climbed, I began to regret my decision to forego the bus, but at the same time I didn't, as the walking both cleared my mind and gave me space to think. Milton Keynes had, remarkably (something that had shocked both Martin and me) recently celebrated the fiftieth anniversary of its founding. It had always been an optimistic place where almost anything went, on the basis that if you don't try, you won't find out – at least to my perception, anyway. I remembered going there on a Geography field trip from school in the mid-1970s, when the town was an experiment in action, a live Sim City, although, of course, computer games didn't exist then – computers still ran off perforated ribbons of paper.

I remembered thinking then that what the place needed was a football club to help pull it together, give a sense of shared community. Well it had one now, although in a very Milton Keynes way it had co-opted one from someone else, Wimbledon, and renamed the club the Milton Keynes Dons. It also benefitted from great transport links, the railway into London providing many with access to their workplace, not just from the town but from the surrounding area, as I'd discovered on my walk. It also had its 'H' and 'V' road grid system, the 'H' standing for Horizontal and the 'V', you've got it, for Vertical. This was great when it worked, but the endless subdivisions within it could also convert what was, on the surface at least, the highly logical, into the highly infuriating, resulting in a number of 'roads to nowhere'. Ah well, you win a few, you lose a few. Very Milton Keynes.

Was a lot of the housing relentlessly the same? In parts yes, but often not. Again, they'd experimented, and as with all experiments involving the aesthetic, some of it worked, some of it didn't. Milton Keynes was very much a glass half full or empty sort of place. Views on it were often a reflection of the view-holder as much as an assessment of the town. Crucially, it had provided a place for hundreds of thousands to live, many of its early settlers people desperately in need of somewhere better to live. It had also taken some of the strain off the London suburbs.

It had vision, something sorely lacking in more modern times, times crying out for a visionary approach to a huge problem: housing. Whilst in other parts of the world, notably China, whole cities were being constructed with the future in mind, connected cities which recognised that the future of work probably didn't involve commuting to an office every day, we were adding new estates onto old villages, apologising as we went. And for those who say we don't have the space to do this, I advise a diagonal walk through England. If we have space for wind farms spread over miles, we have space for new towns.

What is lacking nowadays, and maybe existed to a greater degree in the 1960s and 70s, is a belief in the future, something the conversations I'd had suggested was in short supply. We need a bit less looking back to a golden past – one actually cluttered with global conflicts, food rationing, digging for victory and one industry towns providing jobs for life but at subsistence wages. If England is to progress as a country, surely it needs to look forward, to adopt just some of the vision Milton Keynes once offered, and to some extent still does. The town could very easily have become a modern slum. It hadn't, and this was to its credit. It believed the future was a good place to be, and had done its part in helping create it.

My mental meanderings were brought to an abrupt halt on entering the town centre. Perhaps it was another sign of Milton Keynes maturing, but like most of the other reasonably sized places I'd been, it had its problem with the homeless. A tent city, okay, more of a small hamlet, was pitched under an underpass. People were also panhandling just a few tens of yards from the shiny shopping centre, which was slightly less shiny than I'd remembered it. The decline of retail had hit here too.

In fact, the centre gave off a sense of being slightly shabby. Grass was growing through cracks in parts of the pavement, signs proclaiming the optimism of 'Midsummer Boulevard' (a boulevard! In England!) had gone wonky and showed signs of rust. The Point, a red girder pyramid construction, the apogee of nightlife and a cinema complex when we were building our house over thirty years before, was now a little seedy, home to a casino. I read later that there were plans to demolish it and start again. The once new had become old and needed refreshing. Even new towns have a lifecycle.

One thing did remain, however: the good walking and cycling routes. I was able to walk out from the centre down to the area of Shenley Church End, where the Energy World was staged. The housing estates had bedded in. Children were cycling around and playing in the various parks on what was a balmy early summer's evening. It felt safe, as clean as any suburb can hope to be and ordered. It was also easy to find my destination, partly because I started to remember where I was, partly because of the logic of the road system. All the roads where the exhibition used to be were named after famous scientists.

'Our' house was now occupied by David and his wife Mayumi, along with their teenage son, and they were extremely welcoming, keen to learn more about the house's genesis. Coincidently, they'd moved there from Northampton, and had regarded the move as a definite upgrade. We chatted over coffee and they gave me a tour of the house and its garden. It had changed, of course it had. Previous owners had altered some of what my erstwhile architect colleague might regard as its purity, but we had built a house for an exhibition, whereas for subsequent owners it was their home.

Certain key features remained, including some of the exposed beams of the timber frame construction and a stained-glass window we'd commissioned from a local artist. Some of the rooms had been knocked together into one, but that was fair enough. I'd probably have done the same. A garage had been added (being very eco, we'd looked down on the notion of a car) and some dormer windows added to make the, admittedly small, bedrooms a bit bigger. The house itself was still recognisable, however, and visiting it had been well worthwhile.

I asked David and Mayumi what they liked about living there, and they referred to a sense of it being safe for their son to cycle around in, as well as the access to green space. They also appreciated the quiet, waking up to birdsong. What did they think about Milton Keynes in general? They loved it. Again, the access to places to go, to exist as a family, appealed. In many ways they echoed many of the points that Martin raised on the towpath. Mayumi was of Japanese origin and worked in one of the Japanese companies that had located there. For her there was the benefit of a strong Japanese community for them to lock into. I knew that the site had been developed around a central grass area with a courtyard intended to act as a communal gathering spot. It turned out this had been only a partial success. Maybe it didn't matter what you did to the English, they would only mingle and talk to their neighbours if they absolutely had to, or in times of extreme adversity.

A Scot by origin, David had initially been wary of moving to somewhere that labelled itself a 'new town', a term he associated with less successful places like Cumbernauld. He'd been pleasantly surprised by Milton Keynes, and you can't really argue with that. For me, it felt good to have been part of what I regarded as the success story of the town. Built to accommodate a quarter of a million people, it had achieved its target. More to the point, people enjoyed living there. I was struck however that, while still vibrant, it was no longer 'new' as in a 'new town'. Perhaps it's a mistake to use the prefix 'New' on anything, like 'New Pence', 'New Labour' or 'New York'? It had matured.

I'd booked a home stay in an Eco House that night in the mistaken belief that it would be on the site of the old Energy World. In fact, it was over half an hour's drive away, so David generously drove me there. My new host, Marcus, was a housing support officer (he wasn't quite sure of his title, it kept changing). The home he was sharing with me (and I marvelled at how I'd been welcomed into three different people's homes on this leg of the trip) was new, showing that Milton Keynes continued to experiment. As I've said though, sometimes experiments work, sometimes they fail, and the houses had all suffered from a design fault needing reconstructive surgery after residents moved in.

They looked like houses from the future, made from pods, themselves constructed from what looked like plastic panelling (it was probably some eco-friendly material, recycled from old trainers), which some people had labelled Legoland. The brainchild of the then Deputy Prime Minister John Prescott (I'll let that thought settle a while), these were pre-fabricated houses which in theory could be erected in twenty-four hours. Sounded familiar. Designed by the world-renowned architect Richard Rogers, the houses had suffered from problems with their tilted (I'd like to say diagonal) roofs, where a funnel sat to pump air, as well as from the seals on the windows.

As we gazed out onto his beautifully landscaped tropical garden, Marcus assured me that while it had all been very traumatic at the time things were okay now. He too was happy living in Milton Keynes, and we enjoyed chatting into the late evening. I slept well, avoiding dreams of killer cows, disgruntled farmers and wind farms, and was especially glad not to summon up visions of rape plants. It was time go home again, I needed a break.

Stage 4

Newport
Pagnell

to

Dagenham

78.9 miles
180,015 steps

10

Hot in Beds

Newport Pagnell was pretty much as I'd left it, with few outward signs of the strange goings on that had been taking place in my absence. Not only had the good weather earlier in the walk matured into a fully-fledged heatwave so intense that proudly manicured lawns had turned into dustbowls, but the country had discovered a calm and dignified leader, offering hope and dignity.

His name was Gareth Southgate, and he was the coach of the English football team in the World Cup in Russia. As if the heatwave wasn't enough of an aberration, during the few weeks I'd been away the nation's football team had done rather well, reaching the semi-finals of the tournament. Although a football fan, like most older English people I'd developed a sense of detached scepticism towards the national team. I'd lost the habit of investing hope, instead regarding premature and often humiliating exit from major tournaments as the norm.

This tournament bucked that trend. Out of the blue, the English team, mostly young and diverse, with backstories of struggle, suddenly offered a symbol of hope. They presented a suggestion, even if it was the merest chink, that maybe a baton was being handed on. That they and their peer group could be defined by the future rather than someone else's past. A common refrain used amongst them was that they were 'making their own history', that they were interested solely in what they could achieve now. The contrast between this attitude and the older talking heads 'back in the studio', obsessed as they were with references to each achievement being the greatest since God was a lad, only became starker as the tournament wore on. During interviews the players remained unconcerned with what had been. This was their time.

Once the team met its perhaps inevitable defeat, even the pundits were happy to admit that, for a time at least, the team had offered a refreshing contrast to the shambles that politics offered back home. And shambles it was, dressed up as farce. After months of negotiations with the EU, the government had finally conceded what most people had realised some time before: that the dreams of a sovereign independent, free-trading, UK were just that – dreams, of the pipe variety.

This reality was revealed following an all-day session at the Prime Minister's country retreat at Chequers, during which she presented a plan to pursue a strategy towards the EU that was so diluted from the Brexiteers' original intent that it was almost homeopathic. This resulted in the resignation of the Minister for Exiting the EU, which told you most of what you needed to know, along with that of the Foreign Secretary and all-round clown Boris Johnson. One left on a point of principle, the other to illustrate his lack of any principles, other than the principle of his own ambition.

At the same time, a movement for a second vote on the final terms of any agreement, a so-called 'People's Vote' was gathering pace. No one knew what was going to happen. Whatever the outcome only one thing was certain: a large proportion of the country was going to feel betrayed by 'the system'. But while our political leaders thrashed around and failed to lead, we'd been given the example of a thoughtful, considered and dignified alternative way of doing things in the national football team and their intelligent coach. Whoever thought things would come to this – football offering a role model?

The continuing heatwave meant that anyone could be a weather forecaster, so I'd planned accordingly. Shorter distances for each day, and a mid-leg stay with yet another cousin where Annette could join me and we could engage in a game of swap the laundry. For the sake of prudence, I'd also packed wet weather gear. It was light if bulky and provided insurance against a sudden thunderstorm. Also, shorter distances offered some 'wriggle room' if I got caught out and needed to take shelter for a while.

I passed over Newport Pagnell's Tickford Bridge, still devoid of much traffic, and headed left, before reaching an unkempt entrance to a bridleway on the edge of a field. My timing was good, as a kaleidoscopic peloton of brightly attired and behelmeted cyclists was hurtling towards me. For a moment it was a case of me or them. I reckoned I could have done some damage by swinging my rucksack out into the road, but their superior numbers would probably have triumphed. This rise in the popularity of cycling had definitely been a feature of the previous two decades, encouraged in part by Olympic triumphs, with velodrome success usually triggering a gold rush of medals since the poor showing in the 1996 games.

As if to jerk me back into reality, as I picked up the familiar rhythm of field-side walking a pair of game birds flew out of the hedgerow and nearly knocked me off my feet. The landing would have been brittle, as the crops, green and supple last time I'd been out, were now golden and ready for harvesting, at least to my untutored eye. The soil looked more like a limestone pavement, cracked and tessellated after a long period without rain. These were deep fissures, wide enough to swallow a clumsily dropped pen or, heaven-forfend, a phone, into the depths of Hades. All this despite the fact that the school holidays had yet to start. For the younger portion of the population the starting gun on summer was still resting in its holster.

As a result of these desert-like conditions, the route was easier to follow, if a little tricky to actually walk, as I needed to retain half an eye on the ground to avoid tripping on the concrete-like ruts. Within a couple of hours, I found myself on the Milton Keynes Boundary Walk: the border between the aspirant city's administrative boundary and Bedfordshire, something that offered both opportunity and threat in equal proportions.

My route by-passed Salford (no, not that one) and, on approaching Aspley Hall, become less defined. The reason

Preparing the ground: filming the video introduction for the website with local students.

Another Place: Anthony Gormley's iron men installation on Crosby beach. A great way to end the first day of the walk.

A narrowboat in the revamped Albert Dock, Liverpool.

Memorial to the Parachute Regiment at the Alrewas National Armed Forces Arboretum

There's still a few of the old bottlekilns left in Stoke, but it hardly justified a 'Cultural Quarter'

Salt extraction remains an active industry around Middlewich

Interesting uses for old phone boxes: a defibrilator, a library and a children's art gallery

THE OLD WHARF HOUSE

THE OLD VICARAGE

THE OLD RECTORY

THE OLD POST OFFICE

Old Village Hall

THE OLD NEWSAGENTS

THE OLD HABERDASHERY

THE OLD DAIRY

The Old Coach House

Old Bakery Cottage

THE OLD BAKEHOUSE

OLD POST HOUSE 32 NO PARKING

We English do like harking back to the past

Bollox
to
Brexit

www.bolloxtobrexit.com

LEAVE

Which way? Outward signs of a national debate were rare. Note the signpost also indicates a Euroroute.

North Downs Way

North Downs Way
Cuxton 4½ miles

E2

for this soon became clear. Paddocks. Horses meant money, with that money spent on sparkling new fences provided for the horses' benefit, not walkers. Waymarkers mysteriously disappeared or were swallowed up in undergrowth, and I was forced into regular consultation of my Pathwatch app to keep out of trouble. A narrow path eventually brought me up and over the M1 yet again (near Junction 13 for those keeping track), after which I was reacquainted with my nemesis: rape plants. Rather than the vibrant green vine-like growth from previous legs of the walk, this was dry and defeated, honey brown and demanding to be harvested and put out of its misery. Its power to annoy was gone. It was a victory of sorts, if a Pyrrhic one. In the distance, I could see the first combine harvester of the trek at work, throwing up a cloud of dust behind it.

My diary must have had 'day for sudden "bejesus" surprises' in it, and somehow I'd missed it. A muntjac deer leapt from the undergrowth less than two yards in front of me and dived into a field of ripening barley, barking his discontent at being disturbed. I didn't understand what he was saying, and it was equally unlikely it would be familiar with some of the language emanating from my mouth as I pressed on. Tired, hot and distinctly sweaty, my focus switched to the last few hundred yards to the Airbnb waiting for me at Aspley Guise, now firmly in Bedfordshire. Naturally, this sat at the top of the village's only hill.

Showered and refreshed, I wandered into the village to eat. Aspley Guise is a pretty place, with a good pub, an Indian and Thai restaurant (that's Indian and Thai, not two separate establishments), and even a hotel. The pub got my vote, largely on account of the range of hand pumps on display by the bar. I took a table and made to place my order. The waitress was delightful, but repetitive, as the answer to every question I posed her ('Which beers do you have?', 'What's the special?', 'Can you tell me the soup of the day?') was, 'I can find out for you.' Maybe I'm old fashioned, but … well, you can fill in the rest.

The food was good and received an endorsement of sorts from a Frenchman sitting next to me, who was walking a dining companion through the menu. He'd been before and knew this would be quicker than involving the waitress.

'It's good,' he replied to one enquiry, 'but done how the English do it,' he qualified, before adding magnanimously, 'but that's fine.'

The quality of everyday dining is something else that's improved since our narrowboat adventures. Back then, the mere act of getting a table was an achievement, never mind actually having food delivered to it.

My bedroom's curtains were backlit by the sun when I woke the next day, so I enjoyed a quick breakfast chatting with my hostess Anne, as I was keen to take advantage of the relatively cooler earlier hours. She and her husband Jock had lived in the village most of their married lives and raised their family there. They liked its intimacy and freedom for their children to enjoy the countryside, but lamented the growth of housing in the area. I felt a bit guilty raising the plans I'd read about for 20,000 new homes in their part of central Bedfordshire.

They were also unhappy about the vast new warehouses being built around them, especially near Milton Keynes.

The department store John Lewis had recently expanded its distribution centre outside the town, and it wasn't alone, due to the proximity to the motorway. It was a refrain I'd heard before, notably in Stoke, with warehouses the size of old factories coming into an area, blighting the landscape but employing only a fraction of the people the old manufacturing plants had.

Back on the footpath, the surprises kept on coming. On entering woodland I was ambushed by three large Labradors, as surprised to meet me as I was them. Even with my limited knowledge of dogs, I knew that Labradors were supposed to be softies. But theory and practice don't always come together, and it took my heart a few minutes to calm down. The attitude of their owner, that the whole episode was in some way amusing, wasn't one I shared. This surprise was trumped by a better one a minute later, when I spotted a family of foxes on the path ahead, seemingly oblivious to both my presence, and that of three killer dogs within a hundred yards.

I was now on the edge of the Woburn Estate, home of the Duke of Bedford, known more for his Safari Park than any other significant achievements. On the way, on the edge of Ridgmont, I passed through my first harvested fields, where the exposed earth revealed patterns that resembled not so much crazy, as stark raving mad, paving. On the horizon, it was possible to spot one of the huge warehouses Anne had alluded to. This belonged to Amazon, and was a facility which had attracted a, shall we say, mixed press over the years.

The route now followed the Greensand Ridge Walk, parts of which were designated the John Bunyan Trail.

The former is a forty-mile walk named after the greenish iron mineral found in the local sandstone that forms the ridge, although none of that was visible during my time on it. The John Bunyan Trail is named after the author of *The Pilgrim's Progress*, who is associated with the area. This device of naming trails after famous local personages is a common one, although despite the various associations I had with my diagonal route I doubted anyone would ever call it the Nick Corble Way.

The early eighteenth-century Segenhoe Manor was just visible in the distance and was followed by the former parish church of All Saints, now abandoned, but not forgotten, as it is maintained by the local council as an ancient monument. Originally built in the twelfth century, the church underwent major alterations in the 1820s, including a new tower. Despite these, it was superseded by the church in nearby Ridgmont. Ironically, a notice on the board of its replacement, which I'd passed earlier, suggested that, due to falling attendances, it too was in danger of being decommissioned despite recent investment of its own.

Between these two churches, I'd stopped for a water break by a randomly placed park bench on the side of a field. Controversially, it lacked the near obligatory small brass plaque dedicating the seat along the lines of 'Uncle Bert, who loved this view'. The view across the field had now become commonplace, mile upon mile of ripe laden crops interspersed with occasional woodland, both ancient and cultivated, offering welcome shade. Given Bedfordshire's reputation for flatness, there were also a surprising number of short, sharp, climbs. By the side of one field I spotted a sturdy ladder propped up against a tree, a plastic chair that looked like it had been liberated from a village hall, wedged precariously at the top. I posted a picture of it on Instagram and discovered that this was a perch for shooting deer and not a tennis umpire's training stool.

On entering Brook End, I was greeted by that most quintessentially English and unchanging thing, a cricket pitch. Given the extreme weather, it looked more like one of the recently harvested fields, although the groundkeeper had made a valiant attempt to retain some vestige of luxuriance in the middle. I then came across the second most quintessential English village sight, a pub, the Green Man, where I was able to take off my rucksack and engage in an 'encounter' with the lady behind the bar, who was intrigued by my walk and as keen to ply me with water (with ice!) as she was beer. Both were welcome, as was the delicious meze platter.

It was good to rest under a parasol and consult the map. This showed Brook End to be part of Eversholt, although it might have been more accurately called Evershalt. As well as Brook End, within a mile there was a Water End, New Water End, Wilts End Farm, Church End, Higher Road End, Lower Road End, Hills End, Potters End, Lower Berry End and Tyrells End. All these stood on the edge of the Woburn Estate, with the Greensand Ridge Walk actually passing through the estate. Although avoiding entrance fees by referencing a public footpath is one of walking's particular pleasures, I had to pass on this occasion as my diagonal was pulling me like a magnet to the east, towards a metalled path unfortunately exposed to the blazing midday sun.

This was followed in turn by a series of satisfyingly diagonal paths through golden wheat, with another pit stop at Brick Pits Spinney. Originally, this would have been a pit where clay would have been dug in order to fire bricks, often to order for a specific commission. Once enough clay had been dug, it would be filled, often with rubbish, capped with soil and left. Bedfordshire had historically been a brick-making centre. The Amazon depot seen earlier was on the site of the old Ridgmont brick works.

In complete contrast, the result at Black Pits was a wildlife haven, and I paused to take on more water, the ice sadly history by this stage, and to take in my surroundings. In the distance I could see the blue top of a motorway sign, the road itself invisible and inaudible, while closer to I spotted another muntjac as well as smaller wildlife, lazy butterflies, curious insects and noisy birds. Other than the motorway and the telegraph poles through the field ahead, I wondered if this scene had changed much over the centuries. Of course it had. Nothing stands still, not even the countryside, which had endured seismic changes such as the clearing of the forests, the introduction of the four-field system, enclosures and the coming of the canals and railways. Even muntjac deer were a twentieth-century introduction.

Indeed, not even the countryside was immune from Brexit. One of the most visible signs of change following our leaving the EU, it emerged,[17] would be on the countryside. Freed from the constraints of the Common Agricultural

---

17 Source: The Ramblers. *Walk Magazine* Autumn 2018. Also, *The Economist* 1 September 2018 'A New Furrow'

Policy, a greater emphasis on countryside stewardship rather than production for its own sake was being promised. This wasn't a particularly new idea, but at least it was something positive, although I wasn't holding my breath.

As the thirsty insects began to take more than a friendly interest in the sweat seeping out of me, I clambered up and set off again. As always, the last two miles of the day became elastic, stretching and stretching, usually uphill. Ahead lay Toddington, like its predecessors on the walk, Keele, Watford and Newport Pagnell, more familiar perhaps as a motorway service station than a place in its own right. It turned out to be a spread-out village clustered around a large green, or more accurately, brown, where there was the requisite war memorial and preserved village pump, as well as a church, a library, some shops and, I was pleased to see, a choice of no fewer than six pubs. Having taken in the village I was ready for a shower, but the pub I'd booked to stay in was shut. I did another perambulation reasoning my hosts might be on a school run, only to find things unchanged.

Spotting someone in the car park I asked if she was anything involved with the pub.

'No, I'm trying to get in. I'm a guest,' she replied in an unmistakeable Irish lilt.

She was called Siobhán and was over in England for a funeral, taking the opportunity to call in on some clients of the small business she ran at home running up prototypes of electronic gizmos (she lost me at this point). As we shared a predicament, we also shared conversation, and it came as no surprise when the subject of Brexit came up.

Siobhán had been trying to get the measure from her customers of what Brexit might mean for her business. She, they and all of us didn't have an answer for that one. It was her view that the larger companies like Microsoft were in an advanced state of planning for any scenario and that ultimately their businesses would survive. She was pragmatic and thought her business would survive too. She would find other suppliers and customers, but the work required to do so for her was disproportionate. Critically, she lamented the lost opportunities. How there'd be less interaction with customers amongst innovative hubs such as Cambridge, where she'd been earlier that day. This, in turn, would lead to a loss in creativity, for all parties.

Besides, Siobhán always enjoyed coming to England, and indeed being amongst the English, but opportunities to do so would, inevitably, be constrained in the future. This wasn't something tangible, but was real nevertheless. She was exasperated but fatalistic. She was also very tolerant, staying with me for three-quarters of an hour before the pub reopened, despite the fountains of sweat still pouring off me. Then again, a bit like the government, she lacked an alternative option.

None of Toddington's six pubs served food, so Indian it was. Until near the end of my meal, I was the only customer; the only sitting customer, that is. It was fascinating to watch the takeaway trade come and go, most of them displaying the confidence of regulars. Some telephone callers were advised their meal would be ready in ten minutes, others in three-quarters of an hour. It was impossible to know whether this was because of the complexity of their order or their familiarity with the staff. On the other hand, it could just be a game the order taker played to pass away the hours.

One customer came in personally, placed his order, and instructed it to be brought over to the pub across the road when it was ready. This may have been because he intended to eat it there, or because he didn't like the Kingfisher or Cobra on offer at the restaurant, a swift pint of which appeared to be de rigueur for many of the men who came to collect orders. As I waited for my bill a short man of early retirement age came in and, refusing the menu, said he'd have the chicken dish he'd had the previous week. Somehow, the order taker was supposed to have remembered this.

'Chicken Madras?' the man with the pad suggested.

'No, you know, the Chicken …'

'Swarma?'

'No, not that one, Chicken …'

'Pasanda?'

'No, Chicken …'

This one could run all night, but I was invested enough in it to take it to its conclusion.

'Rohani?'

'No …'

'Jalfrezhi!' the order taker exclaimed, convinced he'd arrived at the answer. He was to be disappointed.

'Nope … Chicken …'

'Biryani?' was suggested, only to be dismissed.

'Pasanda?'

'No. Vindaloo. That was it, Vindaloo.'

How neither of them had started there it was difficult to imagine. The order was placed and I left.

The cacophonous rendering of Toddington's church bells, directly outside my open window woke me up the next morning. This meant only one thing: one of my ear plugs had fallen out overnight, ear plugs and an eye mask having become an essential part of my kit. It was time to leave my slightly seedy hotel and exit via the fag-end strewn fire escape, leaving the keys on the bedside cabinet as I'd been instructed. Naturally no breakfast was on offer, so I headed for the delightful Bistro 24, a local coffee shop, surviving in the absence of a Costa. No sooner had I settled down with my order than the shop immediately began to fill with whatever the collective noun is for young mums (a concern? an indulgence?). To a woman wearing sunglasses propped in elegant hair, they'd dropped their children off at school on what was the last day of term, although I got the impression this was a regular Friday morning breakfast ritual.

Seeing it was going to be their last gathering for six weeks, most appeared determined to bank that many weeks' worth of chatter in advance. I tried to tune in to their conversations, but the noise level was too loud and too high pitched, punctuated with laughter and the screams of pre-school age children. Instead, I tried to lose myself in a copy of the local paper, *The Herald and Post*, helpfully left on the table. Here I discovered that the local MP was currently sitting as an independent, pending investigations into alleged sexual misconduct, and that the nearby airport at Luton was celebrating its eightieth birthday. The paper proudly described the airport as the country's fifth biggest, which came across as a bit of a backhanded boast. The front-page story was about an eighty-four-year-old man (he was even older than the airport) beating off an intruder using a billiard cue.

I left as the last full English breakfast was being served. Ah. The full English. Something that remained unchanging, despite the health police. The young mums looked okay on it, maybe it was okay to indulge just once a week, or maybe they were fortifying themselves for the weeks ahead?

Next up, before heading out of the village, was the local baker, for an advance purchase of lunch (a cheese and pickle roll and a tuna salad roll – they were only small). The elderly woman behind the counter quizzed me on where I was going, having spotted the rucksack. When I replied Luton, she pulled a face likely to curdle the cheese in my roll.

Back amongst the fields, the eponymous service station lay tucked away in the valley to my left, identifiable by the Corgi-model tops of the lorries parked up there. After a couple of miles of farm track I turned left, towards my diagonal and also the motorway, onto a byway. Technically more than a footpath but less than a road, byways are defined as 'a right of way along which it is legal to travel by any mode … excluding "mechanically propelled vehicles".' The track was enclosed with high hedges, with tracts of blue-flowered wild borage growing along the side.

I once again crossed the M1 and followed another byway down the side of an industrial estate and a track that looped around the very northern edge of Luton, or more accurately Leagrave, once a village in its own right, but now swallowed up by Luton. The sun had gone in and it had become very muggy, almost threatening rain but in a childlike way, pretending to threaten, without really being menacing at all. Was the curse of school holidays going to hit? Having sat out the hot days in examination halls, longingly gazing out the windows, were the hopes of the nation's youth of long hot halcyon days about to be doused?

Having hauled myself up to the top of an unexpectedly steep hill (the map clearly marked a water tower, so I should have anticipated it), I headed south, into dense housing and down an alleyway, towards the heart of Luton. One of the houses to my right was still displaying a flag of St George, presumably a leftover from the World Cup, or perhaps just a general expression of patriotism, it was impossible to know. It was odd, this assertion of 'Englishness' through the use of this particular flag. As recently as the 1980s, England fans had been happy to express their allegiance by brandishing Union Jacks (or, more correctly, Union Flags). Look at pictures from the 1966 World Cup Final and that's what you see.

Widespread adoption of the St. George's Cross probably dates from the 1996 European Championship. Held in England (prompting the chart-topping 'Football's Coming Home', which had enjoyed a resurgence during the English team's Russian success), this tournament had taken place shortly after the Scots and the Welsh had been granted their own Parliaments. English football fans rallied around the Three Lions, even if few could say what they represented. Most would probably be shocked to discover they were derived from the coat of arms of the Plantagenets, who had last ruled the kingdom in 1154. How very English.

Outside football, the flying of the St George's Cross has become something, well, almost un-English or, at worst, a tad, you know, neo-fascist. Again, how very English for it to become un-English to fly your own flag. I'd read[18] there was also a connection between Englishness and the Brexit referendum, with 73 per cent of those identifying themselves as primarily English voting to Leave, against the 66 per cent of those who defined themselves as primarily British voting to Remain. I gave this particular flag-flyer the benefit of the doubt and walked on.

The alleyway morphed into a tree-lined path taking me down towards Leagrave Common. I was on a mission to find the source of the River Lea, which was due to become a regular companion over the next phase of my walk, in much the same way as canals had been earlier in the trek. Sometimes called 'London's second river', the Lea flows into the capital from the north, where it becomes a navigation, that is a river that is 'canalised' and channelled, both to allow boats to pass down it unhindered and, in the Lea's case, as a way of supplying water. South of Hertford, where it becomes a navigation, it tends to be known as the Lee. A river so good they named it twice. Often forgotten, the river achieved something of a renaissance in recognition following the restoration work carried out on it where it passed the site of the 2012 Olympics.

It was difficult to imagine the river's importance to London standing by its source. Unsurprisingly, it had dried

18   Source: BBC. See: https://www.bbc.co.uk/news/uk-44306737

up. Even the barred grating near the sign proclaiming the spot as the river's source was dry. It turned out this wasn't even some kind of natural spring, rather where rain run-off from nearby roads supplemented the river. There hadn't been much of that in recent weeks. Instead, before me lay a collection of tall grasses, willow and stinging nettles all sitting in a slight depression. Impressively green it's true, but hardly a bubbling spring. This was deemed to be the main one of five springs feeding the river, known collectively as Well Head, with the other main source a few hundred yards to the west at Sundon Brook. I checked this out, and could see some water actually flowing, albeit impeded a bit by the cliché of discarded shopping trolleys.

I walked back to the supposed source along a series of scorched playing fields where a council employee was marking out a cricket pitch with white paint. A quartet of freshly emancipated schoolboys kicked a football around behind him in defiance, in true 'jumpers for goalposts' fashion. I remembered from a previous walk that there was an art installation featuring a number of brass hats on stalks nearby, a tribute to Luton's history as a maker of straw hats (and the origin of the local football team's nickname of 'The Hatters'). It was nowhere to be found, or maybe I was just too tired and hot to be bothered to find it. I asked a couple of locals and they professed ignorance of it, and when one talked of it in the past tense I took this as my cue to stop looking and unpack the by-now horribly tepid contents of my Toddington-purchased lunch.

Revived, I followed the river as it picked up speed, and decided to follow it as far as I could before it disappeared under Luton. A well-marked Riverside Walk made this easy, even if the track was paved and hard on the feet, especially to feet bound up to avoid blisters. The track took me through Limbury Meads, a County Wildlife Site, where I duly spotted some wildlife: a green and crimson woodpecker. For centuries prone to flooding, this area has been converted into a pleasant walking route into the town centre, where I didn't know what to expect. It was true the town didn't have the brightest of reputations, but I tried to maintain a positive mindset.

As I got closer to the centre the housing started to become larger, better tended pre-war, semi-detached and detached homes all exuding an almost affluent air. I walked through Wardown Park, an area developed at the beginning of the twentieth century, following the council's purchase of land previously owned by a local solicitor. Given the size of the park, soliciting had clearly paid well back then. The park has a lake, fed by the Lea, and was popular on this sweltering day, both with parents and young children, although not teenagers playing football. We knew where they were. The park received a spruce-up during its centenary, perhaps offering another sign of hope for the town?

Was Luton going to be another Northampton? Somewhere that defied its reputation, both locally and nationally? They were both medium-sized towns, sharing a population around the 200,000 mark, both trying to find their place in a changing world. It was time to find out.

Although initial impressions had been positive, these took a blow when I did a little research before diving into the town itself. A completely unscientific online poll[19] rated Luton the third worst place to live in the UK, behind Hull and Dover. As one critic said: 'Thank God there's three motorway junctions, two railway stations and an airport that can be used for a swift exit.' On reading this, I recalled the information board in Leagrave which told how the River Lea once formed the boundary between the Saxon lands of Mercia and Danelaw to the east, leaving Luton standing on the border between Christendom and Heathenism. It wasn't promising.

My hotel was on a corner of the Arndale Centre, which in turn sat on the edge of the main square with its ornamental fountain, which parents where encouraging young children to use to cool off, possibly in lieu of a bath. On leaving the mall, I went up the first street I could see, opposite the imposing 1930s Town Hall with its clock tower and two-tonne bell. Note to self: secure earplugs properly tonight. This building replaced the original Town Hall, burnt down by disgruntled ex-servicemen on Peace Day 1919, which must have punctured celebrations a little.

The street, Wellington Street, ran uphill and I was able to spot Romanian, Polish, Turkish, Greek (not next door to each other) and Thai establishments along a short run, as well as an 'International Store' run by someone spreading

---

19 Source: *The Sun* (I did say it was unscientific). See: https://www.thesun.co.uk/fabulous/5240287/ilivehere-englands-10-worst-places-to-live-in-2017/

their bets. Luton has one of the most diverse make-ups in the country. It's one of only three British towns outside London with a non-white majority (the other two are Leicester and Slough). Although the figure for those who described themselves as white was around 55 per cent in the 2011 census, calculations based on these figures suggest the level has dropped below half since then.

These figures are not as straightforward as they might appear though. Of those identifying as white many originate from other EU countries, notably those on the eastern edges of the Union, and it was certainly my experience that these were much more prominent than those with darker skin tones. I also noticed a large proportion of children of mixed parentage, making me wonder if skin colour, ethnic origin and country of birth were all just statistical devices. They were simply people. It's worth noting that 81 per cent of Luton's residents define themselves as British, even if their origins may have been elsewhere.

What does all this tell us? Probably that Luton is a microcosm, or an extreme example of trends seen elsewhere. A symbol of change, and the uncertainty, and sometimes hostility, that can bring. Despite the high level of residents from other European countries, Luton had voted decisively in favour of Brexit, 56 per cent against the national average of 52 per cent. One explanation that's been offered for this is that many of those from ethnic minorities voted against the 'newcomers' taking their jobs, thereby parroting the alarum calls of the Far Right used against themselves. Indeed, the town's leading UKIP politician, who came to England from Pakistan twenty-nine years ago, has expressed discontent with what he regards as uncontrolled immigration from Eastern Europe.

Luton also has a reputation as a home for extremism, of both the Jihadist and Far Right varieties. The standard bearer of the Far Right, the English Defence League (which, it is worth noting, has displaced the British National Party at number one in the neo-fascist charts, a small but significant difference), was formed in Luton. Likewise, extremist Islamic groups and terrorists have originated in the town. I kept half an eye out for evidence of this, for graffiti or antagonism, but I searched in vain. All I could see were people trying to cope, with the heat, and with their lot in general.

A release of a sort was offered at the top of Wellington Street, where a so-proclaimed 'Adult Store' stood on the main road. A sign on the front of the store spoke of a 'discreet side entrance'. After wondering if I'd led a sheltered life and missed something, I realised what was meant and took a peek, as it were. The side entrance may have been discrete, but it wasn't as 'discreet' as promised, a large red sign next to number 24a in white lettering a foot high announcing a doorway for the 'Adult Shop'. A small sticker in the corner warned people to 'mind the step', presumably easily missed when looking around to see if anyone saw you going in.

Back where the street met the main drag a number of drunks were already in evidence, even though it was only five in the afternoon, albeit on a Friday. Maybe they were celebrating the start of the school holidays, or possibly hiding from the thought of them? I walked up this thoroughfare. Although pedestrianised to make it more accessible, it was pretty desperate, full of third-rate shops and gambling emporia. I sensed any retailers with any pride had decamped to the Arndale Centre. This looked reasonably clean and drunk-free, so I wandered in.

The first thing I noticed was that two doors down from a Poundland stood a Luton Town FC store. It wasn't busy. Mindful of having to eat sooner rather than later, I followed the signs for the 'Feast Street', passing a poster for the Luton Foodbank on the way. I was too hungry to indulge in irony. An Ann Summers store stood unembarrassed opposite a River Island. The people of Luton appeared obsessed with sex. No discreet side entrance here. Both Marks and Spencer and Debenhams sat unobtrusively in the corner of the Mall, as if not quite sure how they'd got to be amongst such company.

Feast Street turned out to be a disappointment. A KFC, a 'Cake Box' and a place specialising in toast? Toast? Maybe it was toasties, I didn't hang around to look. Not really a feast. Not really a street. A billboard back on the spine of the mall invited people to visit 'LoveLuton.org.uk'. It came across not so much as a request but more of a plea, and I wondered how many hits the site received. It struck me that this symbolised a difference between Northampton and Luton. Whereas the former had a sense of people caring for it, Luton had more the air of somewhere people were passing through, but had somehow got stuck there. Okay, I'd been lucky in Northampton, catching it on a day of civic pride, but I could only feel as I saw.

Later, I checked out the LoveLuton site, which promoted the town as a creative space, stressing its hat-making origins. The former was hardly a novel strategy, every medium-sized town had hit upon the idea of promoting itself as a hub of creativity, even Hinckley earlier on the walk. The whole 'Hat District' approach was an echo of Stoke's attempt to promote its 'Ceramics Trail'. One was focussed on the future, the other on the past, but I wasn't sure either of them was hitting the mark. Okay, I was only passing through, but then again, as the old adage has it, you don't get a second chance to make a first impression.

Eons ago, back in the coffee shop in Toddington, when I'd been reading the *Herald and Post* I'd come across a letter to the Editor. I love letters to the Editor, they often tell you more than any article about a town. This one highlighted how Luton was trying to revive itself with a new shopping centre, and how something like a new House of Fraser might do the trick. It looked like someone hadn't been checking their memos. First, hello, high street retail was dying and second, hello again, House of Fraser had just announced a halving of its store portfolio – it was too busy closing stores to think about opening new ones.

Towns like Luton, and it was still a town, even if it was also a Unitary Authority, like Stoke (a city) and Milton Keynes (not a city), were going to have to find a new way to give themselves purpose other than as a shopping destination. Maybe it was as a creative centre after all, but my message would be, make it obvious rather than implicit. Even the art installation at the source of the Lea had disappeared. The closest I came to seeing something eye-catching was some murals in the Arndale promoting ... you've guessed it, the importance of a good hat.

Back in my room, I browsed the internet to see if I'd missed something. I hadn't. Meanwhile, the clock on the

Town Hall struck the hour (I was going to have to close the window, not even ear plugs were going to be able to stand up to that). It was time to eat. In the absence of any alternative, I plumped for the Wetherspoons just over the square from the hotel named, appropriately enough perhaps, St George Square. I was, and remain, a fan of a 'Spoons, the way they renovate old buildings (this one, The White House, had been a nineteenth-century brewery) and use old photos and other homages to the locale in their decoration. I also loved the (possibly apocryphal) story behind the name, Wetherspoon being the surname of the Geography teacher at his school who'd told the founder Tim Martin (a big supporter of Brexit) that he'd never amount to anything. Finally, I loved the value for money. Less than £7.50 (okay, £7.49) for fish and chips and a pint. Unbeatable.

My belly full and throat lubricated, I went for one final stroll to confirm I hadn't missed anything. All I saw was the by-now depressingly familiar sight of homeless people bedding down for the night in shop doorways. I had a quick chat with a security guard closing the doors of the Arndale, presumably before anyone took up residence, although sleeping outdoors was probably preferable to indoors given the heat, and headed for my own berth ten floors up overlooking a flat roof and a threatening clock tower.

The next morning, I grabbed what I could from the bunfight of a buffet breakfast laid out for the tour groups passing through. I really wanted to know where they'd been and where they were headed, but they were mostly American and didn't leave any time between mouthfuls for talking. Instead, I got on my way. The Lea re-emerged above the main high street, with my route marked now as the Upper Lea Valley Walk. I passed the university, once again the only part of the town that appeared to have had any serious investment in recent years and, having passed under a roundabout, checked Pathwatch to make sure I was on the right road.

I was, and it took me alongside a long office building belonging to the car manufacturer Vauxhall. Vauxhall opened the largest car plant in Britain here in 1907 and went on to make Churchill Tanks during the Second World War, something that made the town a target for Hitler's Luftwaffe. The town weathered the 1930s depression rather well, driven mainly by manufacturing, and it was, as we know, around then that the airport opened. The heyday of the town lasted until the 1970s, with the Arndale Centre opening in 1972, and although the Centre was revamped in the 1990s that was a long time ago to have had a heyday.

These days the Vauxhall plant on the edge of town employs 900 people, a shadow of its peak of 30,000, with a focus on commercial rather than passenger vehicles, which is appropriate given that two types of Vauxhall van, the Bedford and the Luton, were named after the area. It was still a mechanically propelled vehicle, of the type that could not be used on a byway, but only just. I was to see this plant, but I hadn't intended to. Fooled by signs showing a cycling and walking route out of the town where no one but the very brave would attempt to either cycle or walk, I'd got lost. Apparently there was more than one route out of Luton, excluding those suggested by the contributor to the 'worst place to live' website.

As well as being fooled by the cycleway signs, I'd been put off by the high cliff face alongside the dual carriageway I was now walking up. Surely I wasn't expected to climb that? Yes, I was. I ducked into some woods and emerged on the other side of the road. There, some overgrown wooden steps pulled me up the cliff and beside some tall fencing. Just then, with only a couple of seconds warning, the loud, yet familiar sound of a jet engine rattled my senses. It was John Lennon Airport all over again.

I was on the perimeter of Luton's airport, where no sane man dares to tread. I'd been expecting it, but not this suddenly. When I'd planned my route the airport had been a bit of an obstacle. Well, more than a bit: the diagonal went right through the runway. As luck would have it, there was also a footpath running alongside the perimeter, which I was walking along now. It stood on the edge of a high embankment, with the runway itself sitting on another above me to the left. What started out as a hacking-through-the-undergrowth path soon emerged onto a field edge, lined not just with stinging nettles, but also an unusual red and yellow berry, some of which had turned to black, which I later found out was probably viburnum.

Luton liked to call itself London Luton Airport, in a perhaps rather desperate attempt to gain some borrowed credibility. Still, at least it had resisted naming itself after a local celebrity.

Eric Morecambe Airport, anyone?

11

Herts is Where The Home is

Bedfordshire held a final surprise. Near the end of the airport perimeter fence, and still within range of a sudden jet engine blast, stood Someries Castle. This dates back to the fifteenth century and claims to be Bedfordshire's oldest surviving brick building, although 'surviving' may be stretching a point. What stood before me, near the entrance to a working farm, was clearly a ruin, albeit one in pretty reasonable nick. It stood two stories high, and although it lacked a floor, it was still possible to see the remains of a spiral staircase, the octagonal turrets and some arched windows. The latter included an angled 'squint', which once allowed ladies of the house to view Mass.

The building's brick construction was unusual as the material was only just being used at the time when it was built, and it must have been an article of faith to have used it exclusively, as well as expensive. They'd even incorporated a diamond pattern using different coloured bricks. It was impressive, both for its structure, and for being unexpected, and in this sense was an uplifting way of leaving the county after some mixed experiences.

I was now into Hertfordshire: home turf. Hertfordshire was where I'd been born and spent the first twenty years of my life. It also explained my Watford fixation. The diagonal didn't cut through my home town of St Albans, but it did come close. As chance would have it, in another one of the strange coincidences that had closed the decision to undertake the walk, it passed within a few yards of the house we'd rented for two years after leaving St. Albans back in the 1980s, in a place called Blackmore End. This lay slightly north of the city, and yes, St Albans is a city, with its own cathedral and everything. Sorry about that Northampton and Milton Keynes. Just around the corner lived yet another cousin, and it was here that I'd arranged to spend the night and rendezvous with my clean clothes, as well as Annette of course.

The planes arriving into and leaving Eric Morecambe, sorry, London Luton Airport, continued to make their presence felt, and later that afternoon my cousin bemoaned plans to increase the number of flights. They didn't seem too bad to me, but then again, I'd seen and heard them at source, so it was all relative. The footpath signs in Hertfordshire were exemplary, indicating not only the right direction but also destination, distance and even a designated number for the footpath. They were also clear, uncluttered by vegetation and all present and correct. Staffordshire's footpath people needed to come to Hertfordshire on a Learning Day.

Having crossed the border, I wandered into a small village called Peter's Green, where I ordered what was fast becoming my standard drinks order – a pint of bitter shandy and a pint of tap water, with a splash of ice if that's okay with you, barman.

'Any particular bitter, sir?'

I surveyed the pumps. They were all McMullens, the local brew. Whichever I chose it was going to be a taste of childhood, well, not exactly childhood, but you get the drift. 'Country, I think,' I replied, and watched as he drew the amber fluid into a straight glass. I was going to enjoy this, even if prudence demanded a quantity of lemonade.

Suitably refreshed, my route followed what felt like an ancient drover's lane, flanked with trees, which in turn offered welcome shade. Judging by the regular puddles of white feathers, it also acted as some kind of 'Killing Fields' for local pigeons. This emerged onto the lane where my family's rented home stood, so I decided to take a look. I'd written to the current occupiers, but received no reply, despite my assurances in the letter that I wasn't a madman or scammer. I didn't judge them for not wanting to engage, that was their choice after all, but when I arrived another possible explanation revealed itself. It looked the same from the outside, but decidedly quiet inside. There was no sign of furniture and no evidence of habitation on the drive or front garden. Okay, most houses in the close looked quiet, it was a hot and sultry day after all, but this one didn't even have any of the top windows open. Maybe my letter still sat on the doormat, as the house looked deserted.

Back on the road, there was no getting away from the fact that this was an affluent area. Some of the houses that had been built since I'd lived there made what had been our perfectly acceptable, detached four-bedroomed house, look like a peasant's hovel. They weren't the norm though. It was as if they'd been grafted onto the rootstock of the local community, shortly after which their new owners had decided to install electric gates to keep that community out.

Before linking up with my cousin Robert and his wife Denise, I paused at the fringes of a golf course under the welcome shade of a large oak. The fairways looked brown and parched, of course, but the greens were, well, green. A deep, vivid, emerald green. I got out my pad and jotted some notes, watching two women finish off a hole as I did so. As they walked off, one remarked to the other, 'How very English, a man propped up under a tree writing poetry.' If only she'd known I was writing about her.

It was a late start the next morning after an extremely convivial evening, and Denise led me to a shortcut alongside the golf course which headed into the nearby village of Wheathampstead. Along the way, a crop of shrivelled peas, or at least they looked like peas, occupied a large field, after which it was time to get re-acquainted with an old friend: the River Lea. It looked in good shape, verdant on its banks with reeds and low trees, with a steady flow, the surface reflecting the blue of the sky with the few white clouds taking on the appearance of a low mist.

Wheathampstead itself looked a fairly self-sufficient place, not that much changed from when it used to my nearest village. There were still shops either side of the river, a large pub, a church and a school, as well as coffee and cake stops, as this was clearly a popular place for visitors also. Not far out of St. Albans, it was easy to see the village's attractions, and I didn't dare look in the estate agent's window to check out house prices. The river flowed under a bridge and was a feature of the village, with a small quay.

The Lea was no longer navigable here, but one theory has it that the village was originally established by invaders from Belgium who came up the river from the Thames. A plaque on the bridge, part of the Wheathampstead Heritage Trail, stated that in the 1940s a circus elephant was brought there to drink and damaged the quay: a pretty random fact to offer the passing traveller. During my brief stay it was popular with anglers, young and old, which was more in tune with the other fact on the plaque which stated that Izaak Walton had mentioned the river in his seminal work *The Compleat Angler*.

A riverside path took me out of the village, with the river itself hidden to the right, but still trackable from the tall sedge and yellow flag iris growing on its banks. Families emerged clutching picnics, and a few young children were enjoying paddling in the clean water. I walked for a couple of miles and, on finding solitude, and a convenient bench, stopped to rest and take on some fluids. There was a slight breeze, but as temperatures were forecast to threaten 35°C that day, plus the fact that I'd had a late start, I was being sensible. I sat to let nature envelop me, with the swoops of grey wagtails particularly impressive. It was then that I heard it. One long whistle, followed by four short ones, the familiar call of the red kite, reminiscent of home. Having just said goodbye to Annette a couple of hours earlier, I felt a slight pull towards home comforts. No one had forced me to do this trek, to spend these precious summer days walking on my own and sleeping in sometimes quite dodgy hotels. It was something I'd chosen to do and I was glad I had. The experience had already surpassed my expectations: the places, the people, the history, all had made the occasional discomfort, and gallons of sweat, worthwhile.

The next landmark was another golf course, that belonging to Brocket Hall. Now a hotel, the Hall has the distinction of having been home to two Prime Ministers, the Lords Melbourne, confidant to the young Queen Victoria, and Palmerston. Fun fact: the latter was the only Prime Minister to die in office (so far), supposedly from a fever, although another theory suggests his demise followed an encounter with a maid on a billiard table. Not my sort of encounter you understand. More recently, the Hall was owned by the Lords of Brocket, the current one inheriting from his grandfather when he was only fifteen and subsequently going off the rails a bit, his career encompassing the ignominy of appearing as a contestant on *I'm A Celebrity Get Me Out of Here!*. This followed a short stay at Her Majesty's pleasure after an incident involving Ferraris and an insurance company.

The footpath ran right through the golf course, which had all the appearance of the desert having migrated to Hertfordshire. Climate change was a thing sure, but this was ridiculous. It was difficult to see where the sand in the bunkers ended and the grass began. The greens, though, had been suitably watered and nurtured, acting like tiny oases dotted around the sparse landscape, emerald jewels scattered randomly on a beach. The path then led onto Lemsford Mill, which appropriately enough housed the offices from which the Ramblers' Holidays company operated. I stopped at a pub, the Sun, for the usual pints, where sleeveless vests, shorts and red faces were very à la mode. It was difficult not to notice that the accents being bandied about were now decidedly more north London, with the liberal substitution of 'sir' with 'mate' and 'chief'. Basically, it had become more 'gor blimey' – know what I mean?

A challengingly low bridge under the A1(M) brought me into Stanborough Park, which was heaving with families enjoying the water, adventure park and weather. Young children were patrolling the Lea with nets, much to the disenchantment of the local ducks and moorhens. I was very tempted to join them as my feet were, by then, very sore; and the little toe on my right foot was giving me gyp. I suspected a blister, but didn't really dare to find out. On exiting the park, a decision needed to be made as to how far to follow my route round the south of Welwyn Garden City, where my next hotel awaited. One way or another, these miles would have to be done, but my bed was nearer the centre and could be struck for at any point. Dodgy toe notwithstanding, I pressed on a bit longer and managed to make it to the most southerly point of the town before admitting defeat.

My berth for the night was in another pub, where the process of checking in took forever, with the barman using what looked like an old Sinclair XL to find my booking. The room, when I eventually got there, was fine, and again had its own fan, but it was noisy. The pub's clientele had clearly been drinking for a while, and were equally clearly content in the knowledge that their children were safe on the handy play equipment, which it appeared required constant shrieking to operate. After making myself human again, I opted to head into town to see what it could offer. Before then, however, I was delighted to see that the blister on my right foot had gone through the cycle of forming, bursting and exposing red raw skin without needing my intervention, the latter stages presumably having taken place during the final couple of miles around the edge of the town.

Town. Yes, not city. Welwyn Garden City is a town, with the 'city' an affectation provided by the town's founders. Not simply a town, it is also a 'new town', and I was keen to compare and contrast with Milton Keynes. Whereas Milton Keynes had just celebrated its fiftieth anniversary, Welwyn Garden City was gearing up for its centenary. Apparently, the inhabitants of both towns prefer use initials, MK for Milton Keynes, and WGC for you know where. Knowledgeable in all things building-related, my previous night's hosts Robert and Denise had highlighted how the standard of housing in WGC was much higher than in MK, and my first impressions confirmed this. Whereas MK had experimented with different styles on the principle that it might stumble across something that worked, WGC's planners had opted for a more consistent approach, with a clear preference for bricks and mortar.

Furthermore, WGC's streets were much more open, almost boulevards in the truest sense, with wide verges, pavements and front gardens, as well as the liberal application of random open spaces. It was easy to see where the 'garden city' part of the town's name came from. As with MK, a lot of WGC's housing was constructed around the same time, but somehow the latter's came across as more permanent. It was easier to see these houses still standing in another fifty years than MK's, with the suspicion being that many of the more modern town's will end up making way for fresh waves of development. Although both new towns, and both the product of pioneers out to create their own version of a new suburban Utopia (WGC had, somewhat optimistically, been advertised as 'an opportunity to live in the sun'), they'd turned out very different. If nothing else, MK ended up being five times bigger than WGC, and was still growing. WGC operated on a much smaller scale all round and was probably better for it.

I headed out to Handside Avenue to find the first house in the town to be occupied, back in the 1920s. It stood at number 43 and has a modest blue plaque (rectangular, not circular) announcing the fact. It was actually fairly nondescript, mainly because it looked like it had been built side-on, presenting a large white wall with two windows and a steeply pitched roof. I couldn't tell if the building to its side was part of the house or part of a separate run of cottages. Earlier, a run of Dutch-style houses had run down the street and I'd hoped number 43 would be one of these, but it wasn't.

From there, I headed into the heart of the town, the Howard Centre, named after Sir Ebenezer Howard, the driving force behind the New Towns movement. A large commemorative medallion set into the ground near the shopping centre proclaimed: 'His vision and practical idealism affected town planning throughout the world.' That wasn't something that could be said of many people, nor necessarily an accolade many people would seek. Having said that, my travels suggested we lived in a time when many towns were going to have to reinvent themselves if they were to remain relevant and sustainable, and perhaps a few more with Ebenezer Howard's vision and practical idealism wouldn't be such a bad idea.

The centre came as a very pleasant surprise. A fountain spouting blue water (I think it was something to do with the NHS celebrating seventy years) stood sentinel over a long tongue of green called The Parkway separating two roads, both lined with shops. Whisper it quietly, but these shops were also thriving, with remarkably few of the charity shops and fast food joints that characterised other medium-sized town's retail centres. The only boarded-up unit belonged to the deceased post office, possibly the victim of no WiFi. For once, there was no sign of homeless people either.

This hadn't been the founders' vision. Their idea was to have one large store which sold everything, a bit like GUM in Moscow – a Stalinist approach when old Uncle Joe was still working his way up (and, at the same time, through) the Politburo. This resulted in the creation of Welwyn Stores, a local monopoly on, well, everything. Not surprisingly, this didn't go down too well with those who'd fled the big smoke to live in the sunshine, but the store held on for some time, despite being supplemented along the way. In 1984 it was finally taken over by the John Lewis Partnership, allowing the good middle-class folk of WGC to breathe a collective sigh of relief. The centre also has a good selection of places to eat, mostly the sorts of chains that have shunned Luton. I ended up watching the conclusion to the Open Golf Championship in the very pleasant Two Willows pub. Golf had become a theme of this leg of the walk, although even in Scotland where the Open was being played, the fairways looked decidedly straw-like.

I woke early the next day. I'd shut the windows to keep out the still bubbling noise outside when I'd got back to my room, but the fan hadn't proved a reasonable substitute for fresh air. Still drowsy, I indulged in a little bit of Radio 4, the news something I usually body-swerved, preferring instead to let my own observations form my thoughts rather than those of crisis-hungry journalists or supine politicians. As the voices rattled away in the background I could see that the sun was already out and the sky was preparing itself for another blistering day. An early start would be prudent, I just needed to get my limbs to work.

From what I could tell, the Brexit soap opera was coming to some kind of a head. The Prime Minister had finally set out her stall, and even though her proposals didn't satisfy anyone, that was irrelevant, as they were all that was possible given the parliamentary arithmetic. Armed with this set of proposals, notwithstanding the fact that they satisfied no one, she and her ministers were now going to embark on what was ludicrously labelled a 'charm offensive' to sell them to the leaders in other European capitals. At the same time, talk of an 'accidental No Deal Brexit' was being warmed up, whether as a negotiating tactic or as a very real possibility, it was difficult to know.

Meanwhile, in a related story, the head of Amazon UK

was warning of possible civil unrest should a 'No Deal' come about. Maybe what was really needed was for him to combine with the heads of Starbucks and Apple to set out a real dystopian future, one lacking iPhones, iced lattes and, well, everything else (which was Amazon's place in the system) to get people to wake up? If anyone wanted a glimpse of what that might look like, I'm sure they could get BT to lay on a demonstration. Just press '1' for 'Normal service'.

In the absence of this, there remained little sense that the population at large was that troubled by Brexit. No one on my travels was raising the subject spontaneously, it was almost as if the whole thing was some kind of abstract exercise. This contrasted wildly with Paul Theroux's experience when he'd undertaken his coastal tour of Britain for *The Kingdom By The Sea* in 1983, when a similar national crisis of identity, the Falklands War, had raged. Then, the war had been a regular topic of conversation. His American accent may have been a factor, though, with many of those he came into contact with taking the opportunity to rant against the neutral, almost censorious, position his home country had adopted towards the UK and the war.

I slowly got going, but as I was donning my boots and doing a final check round, another story caught my ear. This was introduced as 'a success story of the last twenty years', so naturally my ears pricked up. It concerned recycling, a much greater emphasis on the use and re-use of scarce resources having been a feature of the century so far. Unfortunately, the nub of the story was how a study had shown that a significant proportion of plastic set aside for recycling was being sent abroad and used as landfill. Even the success stories were, quite literally, rubbish. No wonder trust in our leaders was so low.

Despite the eventual early start, by 8am I was lathered. Still, by this stage I was used to walking around in my own personal sauna. The early clear blue skies persisted, with only the odd vapour trail spoiling their perfection, offering no barrier to a fierce, direct sun. I was going to have to pace myself. Reacquainted with the Lea, after a mile or so my walk diverted south along a track, temporarily leaving the Lea Valley Walk behind. Inconsiderately, nature just didn't follow my diagonal. Meanwhile, a baby deer was having a whale of a time flattening a field of oats, the first time I'd come across this crop.

A lovely long shaded track, Hornbeam Lane, followed, not dissimilar to that I'd encountered just after the Herts border, and it was easy to imagine this as an ancient right of way, perhaps used to drive cattle to Smithfield, or possibly geese, their feet dipped in tar to help them make the journey, to be sold at Christmas. On crossing a road, the path became paved with black bricks and acquired a sand track to one side. At the top of a hill sat Warrenwood Manor and Stud. Of course, horses. What do horses mean? Money!

The track regained its former state shortly after, and I enjoyed a number of brief encounters. Folk were friendly here, with my Diagonal Walking T-shirt exciting some interest and the distribution of some cards. By the time I reached Newgate Street, I was beginning to hallucinate about a coffee and a slice of something sweet, breakfast having been a hurried affair. It was around 10:45 and a sign on a local restaurant said they were open from 10:30 Tuesday to Friday. It was Monday. There was nothing for it but to press on for Goffs Oak and an early lunch. A few cumulous clouds began to gather tentatively in the sky, but not enough to threaten to stifle any of the continuing heat.

Goffs Oak did not disappoint. At least, The Goffs Oak, a pub, didn't disappoint; with a fine vegan salad (why not?) and the statutory shandy and multiple pints of water, as custom now dictated. On closer inspection, Goffs Oak didn't have much to recommend it: a garage, a shop or two, a war memorial, church and a post office, which at least put it one up on WGC. Perhaps the place's greatest claim to fame is as the place where the little girl who would become Victoria Beckham grew up. It might not have much to offer, but it hardly justified spending the rest of your life looking like your face had been slapped with a wet fish.

A little bit outside the village stood a gated community complete with the requisite complement of Range Rovers and BMWs. This was followed by the Adath Yisrael Jewish Cemetery, a last resting place for a Jewish congregation based in Edgware. The cemetery banned both flowers and women at internments, as was their faith, although to me a good funeral needs both flowers and women.

Not long after, the housing quality went up yet another notch with impressive large dwellings complete with fountains and triple garages. If the area outside Wheathampstead was posh, this was decidedly genteel (if not gentile). Another gated community was being built, Halstead Grange. I looked it up later and found that it consisted of fourteen luxury five-bed houses with classical frontages (Doric columns to you and me), and a starting price of £1.6 million. McMansions in other words.

Despite the early start, the afternoon had passed its adolescence and was considering a midlife crisis, so it was a good job that I'd planned a little luxury of my own for the evening's stop, justified because it was directly on my route. Or so I'd thought. It was in fact a good mile off it, which by the end of a day's walking was always a mile too much, and when I eventually tracked down its large iron gates they turned out to be locked. And padlocked. With a note. The note advised using the Lieutenant Ellis entrance. This was about as much use to me as telling me to use the Mr Spock entrance, I had no idea where it was, and neither did my phone.

I nominated an important looking man at a nearby campsite wearing a name badge to be my saviour, and he delivered. He told me where to head for which was, naturally, the way I'd come, and advised that there'd be a way 'into the estate' from there. So it was that, an hour or so later than hoped, I found the reception to my four-star business hotel. I may have been hot and a little bit fed up, but at least I wasn't in the room behind reception where a speed-awareness course was taking place. I tried to imagine the scene when they'd each arrived for their course that morning and found the gate padlocked, and the dilemma of either putting their foot down to arrive in time or to be late.

The hotel was in a grand old house called Theobalds Park, which had once been owned by the splendidly named Sir Hedworth Meux, an Admiral of the Fleet during the First

World War, and later Equerry to Edward VII and George V. Old Hedworth was actually born Hedworth Lambton, the second son of the 2nd Earl of Durham. He changed his name to Meux in order to inherit a substantial fortune from Valerie, Lady Meux, on her death in 1910, she having been left a fortune herself on the death of her husband Sir Henry Brent Meux in 1900. Hedworth went on to live in the house until his own death in 1929.

It wasn't quite on a par with being home to two Prime Ministers, but it would do. In fact, closer inspection revealed that before the current house was built the grounds had been the country estate of James I, before becoming a Georgian family home. The current building was home to a military riding school during the Second World War. Who'd have thought horses had still been important to the war effort then? To that list, it could now add hosting Diagonal Walking for the night. I followed my instructions to the annexe, or cheap seats as I suspected the rooms there were known, only to find that they were located right next to the padlocked gate. Of course.

During a quick explore of the grounds, I discovered that Lieutenant Ellis was the pilot of a B-24 bomber who guided his laden and stricken aircraft away from the nearby town of Cheshunt in 1944, information that humbled my earlier annoyance. Dinner at the bar called. The menu wasn't too exciting, but there were a couple of 'Dish of the Day' options that offered some hope. Stupidly, I enquired, experience having taught me nothing.

'Can you tell me your salad of the day?'

'I'm afraid I don't know, I haven't been told.'

'Do you think you could ask?' A pause. Maybe it was conversations like this that turned people to Deliveroo?

'Yes, I could ask.'

'Well, would you, then?'

A look of surprise filled the waitress's face like a blush. In the end I ate a burger. It gave me indigestion all night.

12

Higham Dry

The Met Office was now advising people to stay indoors as temperatures threatened to break records, but that wasn't an option for me. My legs were feeling it a bit after a week's walking. I hadn't planned a break into my schedule on this part of the walk mainly because neither of the obvious choices, Luton or WGC, seemed to demand an extra day. Sticking with my new strategy, I got up early and had breakfast as soon as the restaurant opened. Thankfully it was self-service, which at least meant I didn't have to ask what the egg of the day was.

Once walking, a clear landmark appeared on the horizon: the distinctive towers of Canary Wharf, shrouded in a low-lying haze and covered in a cobweb of cranes. Like buses, you can wait all day for a landmark and then get two in a matter of minutes. In my case, the second one was the M25, which I crossed via a footbridge, the path's more ancient rights presumably trumping those of the upstart motorway.

As was now perfectly normal, the sun was shining brightly and I found myself beside water again, this time the intriguingly named Turkey Brook, heading east along the long-distance path called the London Loop. This is a 150-mile route which more or less follows the M25 and acts as a companion to the shorter Capital Ring, which describes a tighter circumnavigation around London. Annette and I had completed this latter route the year before and had been pleasantly surprised by how it managed to combine open spaces with interesting urban stretches, and this turned out to be true of the Loop also.

The path was wide and well defined, and yet another muntjac leapt out to greet me. I'd seen a lot of these on the walk, mostly in the early mornings. Otherwise, fellow users of the path tended to be either joggers or mothers with children. Although the M25 didn't act as a demarcation between urban and rural (the scenery was still open and pleasant), I was now unambiguously heading towards London, with my route cutting a line across its north-eastern corner.

Urbanity crept up on me. Stretches of walking amongst housing started to accumulate, without yet dominating. I went past Turkey Street, after which the brook was named (or maybe it was the other way around?); noticing empty and eerily quiet schools, where workmen were now chipping away at window frames and generally measuring things. Rail and tube lines also began to feature, with Turkey Brook now channelled and wearing a topcoat of algae underpinned by discarded baby buggies. Reeds and bulrushes by its side added a splash of colour to the otherwise colourless concrete at its edges.

The brook flowed into the Lea, which had been silently wending its way further south where it became navigable to boats. Like a newly married woman, it acknowledged this change in status with its new name, although the difference involved only a single letter. This new status was confirmed by Enfield Lock, where I stopped to watch a narrowboat go down. The owner, who was on his own and therefore obliged to use the slimy ladder inside to get back onto his boat, was hoping to get back onto the Grand Union Canal. He didn't give the impression of being too chuffed to be on this more urban route, although to me it looked idyllic, but perhaps I'd just been away from boats too long? The river is actually navigable for forty miles along this stretch, and as well as going past the Olympic Stadium offers a couple of routes onto the Regents Canal which, together with the Paddington Arm of the Grand Union, cuts an arc across the north of London.

After the lock, I repeated the error I'd made in Luton, slavishly following the signs for a designated cycle and walkway on the assumption they were taking me the right way. I was also probably lured on by the thought of staying with the Lee, whereas in fact my route should have been taking me down the eastern edge of the massive King George's Reservoir. In mitigation, I'd been looking for signs of this before realising that it nestled behind a high embankment that rendered it invisible. What I could see was a flood relief channel, which unsurprisingly looked decidedly low, with a fluorescent green growth on its surface and banks of rosebay willow herb and bamboo-like bushes lining its banks.

The reservoir is over a hundred years old, the King George in question being the fifth, and it marks the eastern edge of Enfield. It is complemented by another to its south, named after the slightly less famous William Girling, Chairman of the Metropolitan Water Board at the time. I was only really interested in the most northerly of these two reservoirs, known collectively as the Chingford Reservoirs, and a barely used footpath following its edge. Making progress required some occasional hacking at undergrowth, something I hadn't had to do for a while.

Whilst it was perfectly possible to pick a way along the path, I was, by now, openly defying the Met Office's warning about daring to go outside on a lovely day. Later, I noticed the cover of that day's *Sun* newspaper, never one for understatement, carried a warning triangle with the headline 'Hazard Warning', along with a skull and crossbones. The path was exposed and as it was around midday I was glad to be well supplied with water, as well as grateful for a gentle breeze at my back. Blackberries and elderberries, green earlier on this walk, had now ripened, and I found myself picking a few of the former to add some taste to the constant flow of otherwise tasteless liquid I was throwing down my throat.

A steep climb (which was bad) through woods (which were good) brought me into a fresh London Borough, Waltham Forest, before sending me rapidly downhill again, requiring baby footsteps such was its steepness and the weight of my rucksack on my back. Once again, I was taken by surprise by how open the land was, this being Chingford Plain, which even has a golf course. The London Loop, left behind at the reservoir, now re-joined my route and together we marched into the northern tip of Chingford.

The open spaces were largely down to the extent of another forest, that named after Epping, which was to be a defining feature of the next two and a half days of walking. This had been a royal hunting ground and I was about to come across evidence of this in the form of the Queen Elizabeth Hunting Lodge. A white-painted building (including the beams, which gave it a strangely un-Tudor-like appearance), it stood on a brick plinth and extended over three stories with a tiled pitched roof. Surprisingly, it was open, and better still it was free. I entered and was rewarded with a great view out over the forest, as well as more history than I could handle from information boards and a chatty guide.

Epping Forest is known as the 'People's Forest', a moniker it gained following a visit from Queen Victoria in 1882 in which she magnanimously declared how wonderful it was that she could dedicate the forest for the enjoyment of her people. It was, but somehow she omitted to mention how demonstrations against local landowners, who'd been slowly enclosing sections of the forest, had begun as early as 1799, and how it had taken until 1878 for the Epping Forest Act to be passed. Thus, the forest was placed under the care of the City of London Corporation and royal hunting rights ended.

I was grateful for these efforts, as the forest penetrates deeply into this section of London, greatly enhancing my route. I could have lingered at the lodge, but I had an appointment to keep and I needed to top up my water. I spotted a café called the Butler's Pantry and headed towards it as I had a fancy for a slice of cake, or failing that an ice cream. Although the pantry was far from bare, the queue to get served was long and I needed to get on my way, so instead I filled up my drinking bottle from the fruit-infused supply, drank that, and then re-filled the bottle, all in the time it took one family to place their lunch order.

My tanks topped up, I tripped, stumbled and staggered through the woods of Hatch Plain, a warren of paths beside the River Ching, which I used as my guide. The going was tricky due to the confusion of paths and the way that ruts had hardened into concrete, combining with tree roots to create a formidable obstacle course. At one point, a tree branch caught hold of my hat, bent back and flung itself out, performing a magic disappearing trick. I stopped and looked for my missing hat, essential protection for my near-bald head, but it was nowhere to be seen. I wandered in ever-widening circles, wondering just how powerful the branch's fling had been when it dawned on me that it might still be resting on the top of my rucksack. Anyone filming my cartoonish efforts would have captured YouTube gold.

Gordon Turpin, the Chair of the Highams Park Planning Group, was waiting for me at the other end of the woods. We'd communicated by email following some forward publicity on the walk, and he'd agreed to accompany me through the park and tell me a bit about the efforts of his group to bring it back to the centre of the local community. The park, along with its lake, were the remnants of a garden laid out by Humphrey Repton, the Capability Brown of his day, for the Walthamstow Manor of Highams. As is often the way, the park has had a succession of 'big houses' on it over the years. The most recent of these was built in 1768 and was subsequently acquired by a banker, John Harman, the man who commissioned Repton to create the park out of the surrounding forest. Incidentally, the house is now Woodford County High School for Girls.

As was often the way with these projects, penny-pinching wasn't on the agenda. Repton wasn't really in the game of adding the odd herbaceous border and painting a fence blue. No, nothing less than creating a lake would do, along with developing vistas, with the eye encouraged by the landscape to take in particular views. Later on, parcels of the estate were sold off for development, both for a suburb for artisans, and later on some housing aimed more at the middle classes. By 1936 only 28 acres of the original park remained, and a portion of this was sold to the council for public open space. This was added to the lake, which had already been sold to the good old Corporation of London in 1891 and subsequently opened to the public.

Later, the park was pressed into service for pre-fabricated buildings to house those displaced by the heavy bombing during the war. These pre-fabs remained in the park as late as 1961. The foundations of these buildings were clearly visible, exposed in the grass by the dryness of the summer. Gordon took me through the woods, where a highlight was a four-hundred-year-old pollarded hornbeam oak he described accurately as like something out of *Lord of the Rings*. On reaching the newly opened café in the park, we were joined by his colleague Martin, and together they were able to share with me some of the achievements their group had brought about.

They offered a heartening story of local involvement and regeneration driven from the bottom up, rather than imposed from above. Empowered by the 2012 Localism Act, which sought to bring local planning back to the people actually affected by decisions in their area, Gordon come together with others to develop a Neighbourhood Plan. Apparently this is something any local neighbourhood can do to help define what a local population actually wants from an area.

In their case, they had the resource of part of Epping Forest as well as the park and lake around which to coalesce. In total, fourteen sub-committees were formed covering areas such as sports and the arts and a plan was put together and approved. This then gave the Planning Group the status of a statutory consultative body; in other words, they had to be consulted before anything was done locally. Through admirable perseverance, they achieved clout. The group has blossomed, and created some local momentum which has seen a flowering of local creative talent, as well as more tangible benefits such as the creation of the park's café.

Just as importantly, the Group and its actions have brought people together. Martin told me how he regularly bumps into people he knows from his involvement in the Group. They also formed an amiable group called 'The Snedders'. Snedding is the art of stripping away the branches of a felled tree, and the group, who were tasked with doing some of the manual labour required to control the part of the forest under their remit, had adopted this as their nickname. The community had been brought together, not just in snedding, but also through arts, music and events such as a picnic in the park. Martin suggested that this greater sense of community has also encouraged others to set up local restaurants and food stores in the area, making it more vibrant, and in the long term, viable. Not just another dot on the map, as I put it to him.

The Highams Park story is an encouraging one and it was great to be told a bit about it. Martin interviewed me for his internet radio station HSpark Radio, and I in turn interviewed him for a podcast. Being more on the 'been there, done that' end of the spectrum, we mused on how what goes around tends to come around. We remembered the flourishing of the real ale and bread movements in the 1970s, and how these had echoes in the modern microbrewery and artisanal food movements, as well as trends towards vegetarianism and veganism. These were all examples of people taking the initiative, doing what they felt was right, rejecting the corporate machine. It was an interesting development in the internet age where, on the one hand, de facto monopolies such as Amazon and Google encouraged group-think, but at the same time offered opportunities to reach and create new audiences, like Martin was doing with his radio station. At the end of a long day, I found the Highams Park story uplifting, with an element of 'parable for our times' about it.

Our interviews over, Martin walked me through the forest, heading south on the outskirts of Walthamstow towards Leytonstone, where my final bed for this part of the journey awaited. First however, there were those final two elastic miles. These stretched through open land, a green (well, not that green) corridor separating Walthamstow from Wanstead, also a remnant of Epping Forest and one of those spaces that belie the idea of London as a mass of housing.

My hotel turned out to be more of a student dorm, although I was told I could upgrade to a room with a bathroom for a tenner, which I did, out of consideration for others as much as myself. Later, wandering through Walthamstow, it was clear that café society had yet to reach this part of London. Just as I was reconciling myself to choosing between another Indian meal or a picnic in my basic room, I chanced upon the King William IV pub. This turned out to be a real find. Not only did it serve local ales, but it was also able to provide a decent meal, all to an amazing soundtrack, although perhaps I should say playlist, rooted deep in my era: Roxy Music, Lou Reed, Bowie, The Human League, Talking Heads. I finished my meal just as 'Perfect Day' came on and took my empty glass up to the bar. Passing it over to the landlord I gave him a six-word review of 'Great beer, great food, great music.' In return, he gave me a look of thanks, or maybe it was one of shock, it was difficult to tell.

More classic East End accents were prominent on the streets as I weaved a way back to my room. That wasn't surprising, although in reality theirs was just one of a chorus of accents including Eastern European, Asian and Caribbean. Something worth celebrating I thought, although any good feeling it engendered was punctured when, back in my room, I made the mistake of catching up on the news. Apparently the freshly-minted Foreign Secretary was as willing as his predecessor to bend his principles in order to further his own career, and had been spending the day haranguing his counterparts in Europe, telling them that the Great British Public would blame them if the by-now growing possibility of a 'No Deal Brexit' came about. I doubted the Great British Public was that naïve. In the meantime, the vision forming in my head was of a collective giant Gallic shrug before our previous partners carried on with their business, leaving us high and dry.

My route continued the next day along the Centenary Way, a fifteen-mile route through the forest named after the centenary of the passing of the Epping Forest Act. I followed the line set out by occasional white-tipped poles. I wasn't sure these were to waymark the walk, but they were heading in the right direction. Along the way I had an encounter with two women walking their dog as we stared at a scene of devastation on the other side of the road near Wanstead Flats.

One of them was from Toxteth and we shared our experiences. They were interested to know that I'd gone to look at the £1 houses and we discussed how the experiment was progressing. We then got onto the desolation opposite and they related how there'd been a major fire which had taken three days to get under control. The firefighters had only just prevented it reaching a petrol station, and the road in front of us had been closed throughout. Opposite, everything above the ground was very black, underpinned with a mass of grey ash. Incredibly, the paths had survived, so thankfully I was okay to proceed. Closer up, a few green shoots could be seen through the blackened bracken, no doubt encouraged by the tsunami of water used to quench the fire.

Wanstead Flats constitutes the southern edge of the seemingly endless Epping Forest, which on that day looked more like Epping Wasteland. I stopped to write some notes and take some photos when I sensed myself being approached by a man, probably in his thirties, with clothes so dirty it looked as if he'd slept in the scalded ruins of the scrub (maybe he had). He was moving quickly, mumbling as he went, and I suddenly realised how vulnerable I was. With my iPhone on display and camera round my neck I must have been a tempting target. A rush of blood infused my head and I quickly moved away, well, as quickly as my load and legs would allow. I'm sure he could have taken me out if he wanted, but I suspected he was being more opportunist than that. As I half-ran, half-stumbled away he shouted at me in what sounded like Russian, slightly slurred, as if he'd been drinking. He may only have wanted to bum a cigarette off me, but I wasn't going to take any chances.

It took a few minutes for my heart rate to get back to normal. I felt safer in open ground, but the incident offered a reminder to stay on my wits. As if to add to the feeling of near-disaster, crows gathered around me, cawing loudly. The nearest human beings were around a quarter of a mile away, young lads bravely playing football in the heat. Back to normal, I noticed strange U-shaped bits of metal about thirty inches high dotted around the common. These turned out to be tethering posts for the barrage balloons which had encircled the East End of London to deter low-flying aircraft during the war, a reminder perhaps of what can happen when nation states stop working together.

Over to my left stood a large lake, much shallower than normal judging by the stain-like marks around its rim, the water having receded like a middle-aged man's hairline. I walked through the long grass, aiming for the edge of the forest, keen now to sample the variety of streetlife, when an attractive young black woman jogged past me wearing headphones the size of small salad bowls. She was singing at the top of her voice, dancing as she jogged, which isn't easy, not that I've ever tried. Her complete lack of inhibition lightened my otherwise-darkening mood.

The Centenary Walk had been perfect for my needs, but it was time to head east again and regain the diagonal. I left Epping Forest at Manor Park, and was greeted by an eclectic range of shops selling, in turn, hi-vis clothing, Islamic Books and a 98p shop, a cheeky competitor to Poundland. Unlike many other places on my walk, the retail scene here was thriving, less with recognised chain stores and more through small independents. Romford Road was particularly exotic, and enlivened by a magnificent and ornate bronze-brick Carnegie Library. Now no longer a public library, it has become an arts space and a focus for community and creative endeavour, which was good to see.

Although predominately an area occupied by Muslims (I passed the UK headquarters of the Pakistan Muslim League (N), the political party, which as I passed by was in the process of losing a general election in that country), a vibrant, amplified service was taking place at the Celestial Church of Christ nearby. I then passed under the North

Circular Road, London's true boundary according to Gordon from Highams Park, rather than the M25. I was now leaving the London Borough of Newham and passing into Dagenham and Redbridge, with its distinctly unloved River Roding and mini tower blocks. Two office workers with NHS lanyards emerged from one of them and lit up cigarettes.

The environment was getting more built up now, and the Redbridge Library proved a convenient stop to take on and discharge liquid, sitting opposite the monolithic grey Kenneth More Theatre. I paused for a moment to reflect on immortality. I just about remembered the actor Kenneth More for his role as Douglas Bader in the World War Two classic *Reach for the Sky*, but I wondered how many residents of Redbridge and Dagenham did. Maybe it didn't matter, at least there was a theatre.

As I was contemplating this a small man with a tired look and only two bottom teeth (both of them tobacco yellow) greeted me: 'All right Jim?'

I looked behind me. There was no one there.

'You're Jim ain't yer? Police officer down Canary Wharf way?'

I disabused him, at the same time feeling a tiny bit sorry for Jim, wherever he was, if he looked as I did at that moment.

'Fifty years I've been in this manor,' the man declared. 'Never forget a face.'

He was having nothing of my denial, perhaps reasoning I was working undercover, but luckily at that moment he was himself approached by an older man wearing a white vest and a dirty blue cap, who wanted to buy a cigarette off him. My new friend gave him one and waved away any suggestion of payment, receiving a fist bump in return.

I felt a momentary twinge of remorse at my reaction to the man on Wanstead Flats, but remained convinced I'd done the prudent thing. My Russian had been decidedly more menacing.

Along Green Lane, east of Ilford, I passed a stall selling mangoes. Just that. Mangoes, by the box and sorted according to variety and country of origin. There must have been around thirty different types and I wondered where the stallholder sourced them. Fruit and veg stalls were popular in this neck of the woods, or perhaps I should say manor, the wares always immaculately laid out. Some of the vegetables were new to me, with enough colours and shapes to keep Esther Rantzen in innuendoes for months. Meanwhile, over the road a takeaway offered 'Fish and Shish' in a wonderful example of multiculturalism.

As the shops petered out a long line of identical houses replaced them, probably pre-war, all with bay fronts. They'd avoided the curse of being broken down into flats, although without exception the front gardens had been sacrificed to take cars. I regained my diagonal at Goodmayes, where I headed due south at a Millennium Clock, inscribed with the opening lines of Genesis, and no, I don't mean 'Follow You, Follow Me'. As I headed down this new road the housing became more varied, with purpose-built flats, some bungalows and roads off with suffixes such as 'Drive' or 'Gardens' – all quite suburban. The buildings looked newer, suggesting this had been fresh housing after the war, filling in gaps left from the bombing. A garlanded tuk-tuk sat in front of one, the flowers made of plastic. Was it a wedding vehicle, a bit of fun, or used to deliver curries? There was an advertisement for Kingfisher beer on it, so I guessed the latter. It was then, just as I was concluding that this was clearly a more affluent area, that a rat scuttled past my feet.

Welcome shade presented itself in the form of a tree-lined boulevard which brought me into Becontree on the edge of Dagenham, crossing my diagonal again as it went. The pavements presented heavy going, and the lack of seating meant it was difficult to get a proper rest anywhere. I'd resorted to sitting down at bus stops waving away the regular flow of red buses dutifully slowing down to pick me up. I could see how I might look – sweaty, tired, dusty and dry. The drivers were probably pleased I didn't want to get on, although I was sure they'd seen worse. By the time I saw the familiar sign for the Underground, I decided it was time to call it a day. The District Line was calling.

A train arrived, and I lifted off my rucksack and took a seat. Another section of the walk was complete. It had been a good one. The heat, and its impact on the landscape (as well as on my sweat glands) had been a defining feature, but there'd been more to it than that. The ripening crops, the beginning of harvesting and active wildlife had reminded me of some of the constants of the English countryside. Our fields and hedgerows still, to some extent at least, defined us. So too did our towns, even if these were having a tougher

236

time of things. I'd endured the Badlands of Luton, and experienced the surprise of WGC and parts of East London. I'd also experienced a number of encounters along the way, including the uplifting ones with Gordon and Martin.

The walking had also taken place at a time when the practicalities of Brexit started to come to a head. Most of the time, I'd been insulated from the headlines by my own priorities, not least keeping one foot moving in front of the other during what was turning out to be the hottest summer for at least forty years. Every now and then, the outside world had bubbled to the surface, generating a maelstrom of emotions, few of them positive. Whichever side of the Brexit divide one stood, what was happening wasn't pretty. In fact I was reminded of my conversation with Siobhán back in Toddington, when we'd agreed that the word 'ugly' was perhaps the best way to sum the whole process up, and that had been before it had escalated into another gear of hideousness.

The newspapers presented a story of a nation divided, but that hadn't been my experience. Like me, most people were wrapped up in their own day-to-day, their work, their family, surviving, thriving, getting ready for the school holidays. The subject was either a topic for behind closed doors or one people had become simply exasperated by. It had become impossible to know who to believe, who was credible, such were the starkly different scenarios being presented. It was little wonder that people, both in the UK and in Europe, were metaphorically throwing their hands up in despair. What was clear was that whatever happened a sizeable proportion of the population was going to be left angry and, perhaps, to use a word much favoured by some, betrayed. If the process was ugly, it was equally certain that the final outcome wasn't going to be pretty.

I picked up a discarded *Metro* newspaper and read the latest. The new Minister for Exiting the EU (was there ever a more cumbersome job title?) had effectively been side-lined by the Prime Minister, who was going to lead the Brexit process personally. Meanwhile, the minister's job had become one of contingency planning for a 'No Deal' scenario. There was talk of food shortages and use of the army. Welcome back to reality I thought.

Or maybe I'd just left it?

Stage 5

Dagenham
to
New
Romney

83.2 miles
189,374 steps

13

Gateway to
the South (East)

The school holiday weather curse had done its thing. Within days of the schools breaking up the heatwave ended. It had been replaced by Heatwave 2.0, which carried more of a north/south divide feel about it and was altogether more mercurial. The 'normal' English summer had returned, and sure enough, the day I picked up my route again something happened that hadn't happened to me for a very long time.

I was rained upon.

At first I was in denial and I stepped out onto the streets of Dagenham in the firm belief that this couldn't be happening, or that if it was it would surely stop. It didn't. For the first time since Liverpool, way back in April, I was obliged to don my wet weather gear. It wasn't exactly hammering it down but it was enough to guarantee a drowned rat impersonation if I didn't take preventative measures. The familiar problem of nowhere to sit, this time to don my waterproof trousers rather than take a drink, resurfaced, and I was back to finding the nearest bus shelter. Naturally, a bus came along just as I was fiddling with the fly area, making it look as if I'd used the shelter for other purposes.

Back walking, it occurred to me that whatever I did, I was destined to carry out my diagonal walk in a lather of sweat. Where the blistering sun used to create a sauna, I was now experiencing more of a Turkish bath of my own making.

Having stretched the hood of my cagoule over the brim of my hat, I was able to take in my surroundings through a screen of falling droplets of rain. The streets were understandably empty, and I needed to watch out for passing buses and trucks keen to levitate the gathering pools of water around blocked drains and send them in my direction. There was little to distinguish the neighbourhood. Only an unexpected date palm in the front garden of one house, its leaves decidedly droopy, provided any interest.

For many people of my generation, Dagenham is synonymous with car building, much like Halewood outside Liverpool had been earlier on the walk, and Luton after it. Like Halewood, Dagenham had been the site of a major Ford plant. In Dagenham's case it still is, even if much diminished. In its heyday in the early fifties, Ford Dagenham employed over 40,000 workers. It was also notorious for the stranglehold the unions exerted over management, to the extent that they'd even resisted equal pay for women. This became a cause célèbre, later dramatised in the film *Made In*

Dagenham. Car production ceased in 2002, and these days the plant produces only engines, employing just over 3,000. Quite what the future holds for this rump in a post-Brexit England, in an industry that relies on just-in-time delivery across Europe, it was impossible to know.

The landscape was alleviated by a large expanse of open land to my right. This was the Beam Parklands, an open space primarily offering flood protection, although in so doing it also provides a wildlife sanctuary and bit of greenery for the locals. An information sign boasted it could hold water equivalent to 180 Olympic swimming pools, an Olympic swimming pool one of those measures used widely to describe a volume of water, but which no one can really comprehend. Unfortunately for me, the parklands were balanced by a stretch of dual carriageway on my other side, where the danger from passing puddles was suddenly multiplied.

By the time I reached the outskirts of the appropriately named Rainham, I was ready for my lunch, and I stopped off at Jack's Café, where I opted for a jacket potato before plunging back into the rain, my route now heading south with all the determination of a swallow at the approach of winter. Passing Ingrebourne Hill – in reality more of a hillock, but I could see how that didn't carry the same ring – I was now back on a section of the London Loop, leading me into the attractive heart of Rainham. There was a kind of compactness and village-like feel here, with a church, shops, station and even a clock tower doubling as a World War I memorial and a focal point. It was easy to imagine a time when Rainham existed in its own right, rather than as part of London, especially as I headed further south, under the A13, and into Rainham Marshes.

If Beam Park could manage 180 Olympic swimming pools, I couldn't imagine how many Rainham Marshes might hold. These separated the village from the Thames, which was going to be my next major landmark, and once defined the area economically. Initially, the area acted as a floodplain, but over time, Rainham, like Formby earlier on the walk, became a final dumping ground for human waste, making it a centre for market gardening, as well as the raising of livestock. There are still some cows grazing there today.

Later, wharves along the Thames once helped supply local chemical and fertiliser factories. One of these was Murex Limited, once Rainham's biggest employer. Murex took raw materials from Africa and South America and extracted rare metals such as vanadium and the wonderfully named molybdenum. The fleeces of sheep still grazing during that time turned black from the pollution arising from the site's furnaces. I was pleased to see that the site wasn't yet another redundant plant. The rice company Tilda now uses it to sort, mill and package rice from Italy, Canada, India, Thailand and Uruguay.

An asphalt path took me through the marshes, offering alternative routes, and thereby pulling me off the London Loop for a while. Streams criss-crossed vigorously growing shoulder-high reeds, brambles, elder and stinging nettles. Of more interest were the thousands of tiny, less than thumbnail-sized snails, some with brown shells and others, even smaller, with more of a vanilla-coloured shell with a chocolate swirl through them. Following a posting on

Facebook, it was suggested that these were white-lipped snails. It never failed to amaze me how much other people knew about wildlife, or maybe they just enjoyed more ready access to the internet?

Rainham Marshes also hosted rifle ranges used to train British soldiers as late as the 1960s, and also had another military connection. For a while, rusting metal signs had directed me towards some 'concrete barges', but by the time I actually reached the Thames the last thing I'd been expecting were actual barges. Made of concrete. Stupidly, I'd imaged either a work of art or barges once used to transport concrete. Not barges made of concrete.

These were abandoned lighters, sixteen of them. Scattered around like beached whales. Amazingly, these boats were lighter than the water they displaced, and were made of ferro-concrete, that is, concrete reinforced with iron, a cheap material at the time. That time was during the last war, when five hundred of these beasts were built, mainly to transport water and fuel, playing a significant part in the D-Day landings. Most found a final resting place in the English Channel, but these were dumped here in 1953 and sunk on the shore to beef up the flood defences. These days, they are popular with wintering rock and water pipits.

As I left the barges behind, a briny tang filled the air, albeit one balanced by a distinct whiff from the massive, and thankfully invisible, landfill site inland. I supposed it was as good a place as any for landfill, and was probably preferable to sheep-defacing furnaces. Apparently, the site can accept up to 1.5 million tonnes of waste a year, and no, I've no idea of how many Olympic swimming pools that represents.

The rain was still falling, more heavily now, but at least I was walking beside the Thames rather than a dual carriageway, and my progress was counted down in regular 200m way-markers. The water was murky olive in colour and was moving quite fast, even if there was little traffic on it. In the distance, I could make out the spindly, slightly humpbacked, Dartford Crossing, which I needed to cross the next day, with a towering chimney on its far shore. The last mile or so of the walk followed the line of an old sea wall. The practice of building a sea wall to protect land from the effect of salt was apparently known as 'inning', a phrase, along with Paul Theroux's 'embayed' that did what it said on the can. The current sea wall can be dated back as recently as the 1980s, so flooding was clearly still an issue, which made sense when I stopped to think of it.

Eventually, I reached the other destination point highlighted on the rusty signs, the RSPB centre at Purfleet. Up until then, the only wildlife I'd seen were ducks, perhaps because it was such lovely weather for them, but I supposed a body as venerable as the RSPB knew what they were doing. Maybe a concrete barge or two for passing pipits? Over the previous hour the rain had stepped up a gear, and for what seemed like the first time in months (and it probably was), I actually felt cold. I was more interested in a chuffing coffee than seeing choughs, and if it could be accompanied by cake, then so much the better.

The centre duly delivered, a wonderful Americano and an unusual zucchini and lime sponge. I cradled the cup as a small puddle of rainwater formed underneath me, reasoning the café's staff were probably used to it. Glass cabinets offered all sorts of binoculars, binocular holders and binocular stands for sale, more variations of binocular-related merchandise than anyone could reasonably think possible. Suitably refreshed, I wandered towards the door to explore the reserve, but it looked intimidatingly big, wet, and decidedly barge-free. I've never been much of a twitcher. I appreciate bird life, but not enough to undertake additional mileage after a long day, only to take inadequate photos of them. Besides, I was a binocular-free zone.

A sign outside the Centre invited visitors to donate the number of steps people had done that day, which they were accumulating to illustrate the distance a swallow travels in a year. I offered mine, by then around the 25,000 mark and thought they'd be pleased, but it turned out they'd stopped collecting them the day before.

My hotel stood a mere five minutes away, and the thought of a warm shower had become intoxicating. So I crossed a welcome footbridge over a muddy inlet and headed slightly uphill into the Royal Hotel. The only hotel in town, the Royal Hotel was so-named because it was allegedly frequented by the Prince of Wales, later Edward VII. What he got up to there is probably best left unasked. Clean, warmed and fed, that evening I went for a light stroll. The rain having finally stopped, the skies had parted to reveal a strange yellowy-orange thing sinking into the horizon. Purfleet didn't take a lot of exploring. There was some history, including an old Magazine Building, and I'm not talking about last week's *Radio Times*. This long, virtually windowless oblong was built in the mid-eighteenth century and was used to store gunpowder and ordnance for the army until as recently as 1950. In its day, it held 10,400 barrels of gunpowder, that's 460 tonnes of the stuff; goodness knows how many Olympic swimming pools.

It was difficult to imagine, but the riverfront was once a tourist destination and popular ferry point. Then again, it was difficult to imagine how Butlins holiday camps were once seen as the apogee of family fun. In the distance to my right, the twinkling light at the top of Canary Wharf Tower could be seen, and in the other direction, the Dartford Crossing was now much more prominent. I wandered along the promenade, an attempt to spruce the place up a bit, and it was clear there was now more traffic on the water; possibly because of the tides. The sunset was actually rather glorious, so I lingered and took a few photographs on my phone for the Instagram account.

The next day began much sunnier, and I decided to reassess Purfleet with an open mind. Overnight, I'd read a review of the place on the internet which described it as a 'home for chavs, druggies and jobless layabouts'. Whilst that might have been laying it on a bit thick, the place clearly had an image problem. A report in that day's *Thurrock Gazette* described an attempt to rename it as Purfleet-on-Thames, which carried more than a whiff of desperation about it. Kingston or Richmond it wasn't. Earlier in the year, plans for a £1 billion regeneration scheme including a new town centre, a medical centre, parks, a cinema and a revamped railway station had been announced. Inevitably, the scheme also included plans for a creative quarter, with a film and TV studio facility. I'd heard it all before on a number of occasions along the walk, but good luck to them all the same. Without ambition, we are nothing, and this was nothing if not ambitious.

There were echoes of the Thames Gateway, an earlier, similarly ambitious, project to regenerate the area along the route of the HS1, the high-speed rail route from the Channel Tunnel into London. This included not only Purfleet, but Thurrock and, south of the river, the towns of Dartford and Gravesend, both along my diagonal route. Labelled the largest regeneration project in North West Europe (a wonderfully precise definition, with more than a whiff of the marketing department behind it), the scheme was set up to redevelop both marshland (I'd seen plenty of that), farmland and brownfield sites, the latter nothing to do with human waste, thankfully. The jury was still out on its success.

The path through Purfleet weaved amongst new housing, although whether this was a result of the Thames Gateway initiative I couldn't tell, as well as threading through commercial parks populated with all-too-familiar large grey soulless boxes with long articulated lorries parked outside.

I followed the roads along a series of roundabouts to the Lakeside shopping centre. A huge development of more than 2.5 million square feet (take it from me, that's a lot, especially if you end up walking three quarters of the way round it trying to find a bus station), this opened in 1990, before the whole Thames Gateway thing. It took me over an hour to get there, only to discover it was shut. It opened at

10 am. As my bus was at 10:05 I took a rain check, almost literally, as it turned out. Yes, a bus, because, for the second time on the walk I was obliged to use public transport to negotiate a major river. First the Mersey, now the Thames.

My diagonal line sat pretty much bang-on the Queen Elizabeth II Bridge, as the Dartford Crossing is properly known, and pedestrians were about as welcome there as recreational walkers were in Staffordshire. However, a bus, the X80, crossed the bridge for fifty pence more than the toll for a private car. It was just as well, as it avoided a long detour away from the diagonal (probably to the Blackwall foot tunnel to the west), or the use of a taxi or Uber, which seemed less in the spirit of things than a bus.

Rain was forecast, so I wanted to get swiftly on my way. Lakeside felt a bit intimidating. It was a cathedral, or more accurately, a theme park, requiring its own map. Besides, why would I want to go shopping? It would only add weight to my already cumbersome rucksack. Bizarrely, the X80 linked Lakeside with its rival south of the river, the equally massive Bluewater shopping centre in Kent. I couldn't imagine the logic in this. Was it so people could comparison shop? What was certain, was that passage between the two was the main purpose for most people on the bus, as I was required to press the request button to get the driver to stop on the other side, where, somewhat disconcertingly, he asked me where the bus stop actually was.

Crossing the river had felt a bit like my own private Rubicon. Being from 'the south', the Thames is iconic to me, a wide, vibrant artery, busy with river traffic as the bus crossed over it. It was also iconic for the walk, as from the other side I would be entering the route's final county: Kent. I'd started in Lancashire, passed through Cheshire, struggled through Staffordshire, passed in and out of Warwickshire and Leicestershire, cut straight through Northamptonshire, skimmed Buckinghamshire, endured Bedfordshire, gone home in Hertfordshire and enjoyed Essex. I'd also passed through the unitary authorities of Stoke on Trent, Luton and Milton Keynes, and the London boroughs of Enfield, Waltham Forest, Barking and Dagenham, Havering and Thurrock. And now I'd arrived in Kent. It should have felt like an accomplishment, but it actually felt more of a let-down. My time on the road wasn't so much edging towards the end, it was dashing madly, like a demented lemming.

As my dad used to say, 'If you can't take a joke, you shouldn't have joined.' So, reconciled that it was an emotion of my own making, and in fact a positive one, I pressed on into Dartford, or more accurately, Stone and Swanscombe via Greenhithe. I was now walking along the southern shore of the Thames, heading east, out to sea; although the water was still very much an estuary here. There was still a bit further to go before I saw the sea again.

After passing through a business park, a stretch of pleasant riverside walking followed. New flats have been built overlooking the surprisingly busy river, their bins out for collection. I couldn't help but notice that the bin designated for rubbish unsuitable for recycling was green. What kind of idiot bureaucrat came up with that, I wondered? Surely, the one thing everyone can agree on when it comes to waste is that green is the one colour associated with recycling? The promised rain began an hour early. I had a telephone interview scheduled with the local paper, so I found a nearby bench to begin the dreaded waterproof trousers and cagoule-donning routine. For the first time on the walk, I was having to tog up for a second consecutive day.

Later, having headed inland at Swanscombe, I came across that rare thing, a closed footpath. Luckily, the authorities offered a helpful alternative on a clearly marked map, so the only frustration was having to track back the way I'd come, which meant repeating a short hill. Diversion safely negotiated, I stopped for a coffee and a leak in a local leisure centre and passed to the west of Ebbsfleet International railway station. Opened in 2007 as a Channel Tunnel station, this was a visible output of the Thames Gateway initiative, as well as a highly tangible link to the rest of Europe.

The Ebbsfleet name was initially rejected by the operators of the Channel Tunnel, it being a seventeenth-century construct. Was it only in England that a seventeenth-century construct could be seen as *parvenu*? The name stuck however and, as I was about to find out, to gain traction. As if from nowhere, a massive housing development appeared: Ebbsfleet Garden City. Another Garden City! One so young it hadn't celebrated any anniversaries, and was actually being built, now, before my eyes. Numerous developers were busy building houses of different designs and sizes on an area called Castle Hill.

This was a project to build 15,000 homes, as well as supporting infrastructure, on previously unused land, including one of the many disused chalk quarries in the area. Nearby Swanscombe had been the first place in the world to make Portland Cement on a commercial scale, using the plentiful local chalk. There were even plans to use old tunnels dug through the quarries to link residents in the new Garden City with, you've guessed it, the Bluewater shopping centre. Part of the planned infrastructure, a school, was already in place, and I could see that some of the homes were already occupied. The development was billed as where 'London meets the Garden of England', with a lot of emphasis placed upon the station and the jobs clustering around it. The obvious question was how secure these jobs might be post-Brexit, which given Kent's high level of support (59 per cent) for leaving the EU, may, in theory at least, have posed a dilemma for some.

All this development had had the effect of applying a giant eraser to the local footpaths, and following what I thought was the route on the map I hit a dead end at the bottom of the old quarry. For the second time inside an hour, I was retracing my steps uphill, eventually finding what I presumed to be my path just after a new roundabout. Trudging back up the hill on the hidden footpath, I gained spectacular views out over the lake at the bottom of the quarry, destined to become a local leisure resource for those living in the new houses.

As with Milton Keynes and WGC, it would be interesting to return at some point to see how the whole thing bedded in. More building work revealed itself to my left as I walked along a ridgetop path. For the next few hundred yards it felt as if I'd wandered onto the set of the old TV series *The Prisoner*, as CCTV cameras followed my every move, mounted on high telegraph poles, a bullhorn attached to each pole. With every step, I expected to be suddenly shouted at, with no obvious means to reply. I gave a little wave to the cameras, but instantly regretted it. Convinced my features were now being analysed by face recognition software I pressed on.

The path petered out, leading into my first overgrown footpath since before London. Luckily this was only for a hundred yards or so, although enough to adhere sufficient seeds to satisfy Kew Gardens to my damp trousers. Some steps appeared and I rose up them willingly, only to be confronted with the mega-busy three-lane A2. The map showed a footpath on the other side, but closer inspection revealed that there wasn't actually a bridge connecting where I was to where I wanted to be. Unlike its contemporary over the M25, this footpath had lost out to the more modern route.

There was, however, a pavement on the side of the road which led up to a footbridge half a mile to the west, and there was no other option but to take it, accompanied by the roar of traffic and, it goes without saying (but I'll say it anyway), an absolute humdinger of a downpour – just as I was out in the open with nowhere to take shelter. On reaching the other side, I started to retrace my steps. Looking at the map, there was, in theory at least, a route taking me to my final destination for the day. The problem was, there was a short stretch through woods lacking a marked footpath. Although I suspected I could probably blag it, it seemed a shame to take this just because I was fed up, to say nothing of spoiling the integrity of my mission to stick to footpaths and other rights of way.

Instead, I picked up my path, a mere six lanes of traffic away, checking first to see if there was an underpass. There wasn't. This was clearly an unpopular route, and I only just caught the Kent County Council footpath sign sending me across a recently harvested open field. I hadn't walked through fields for a while and I was glad I'd resisted the temptation to take the shortcut, a decision further vindicated by the fact that the rain stopped miraculously, and all of a sudden, totally out of character, the sun made a brief appearance.

Immediately before me stood a Kentish oast house, my first but, I was sure, not my last, of these. Converted into a home, the building sported the characteristic tiled pyramid, complete with a pointed metal cowl vane on top, which would have turned in the wind to bring air in when the buildings were used to dry hops. As I crossed the field, a stray horse, white and emaciated, was wandering amongst the hedgerow. I wondered if anyone knew it was there. Seconds later, I stepped over a dead fox, a buzz of flies around its fanged mouth.

On the other side of the field, my route followed roads, the second of which, Sandy Lane, took me into the delightfully named Bean where I was due to spend the night. I later found out there's also a place called Grain in Kent. I don't know if they're related. If the scorched banks and trees and remnants of rusty old springs lining Sandy Lane were anything to go by, it appeared the main recreational activity around Bean was the torching of old mattresses. On entering the village I got directions to my B&B from the local shop and, finding the key left for me, let myself in to an empty house.

I conducted my ritual shower and got changed. The local pub didn't serve food, so, having missed out on the delights of Lakeside, I decided to opt for the choice offered by its rival and bus buddy, Bluewater. I whistled up a taxi and waited. Meanwhile, Kim turned up. She was the B&B's housekeeper, although her precise status remained uncertain throughout my stay. She was keen to know about my walk, so I told her. Although I'd mentioned it only in passing, she picked up on the Brexit angle, one of the very few people I met prepared to discuss it. She asked me where I stood, so I told her and asked her how she'd voted. On revealing she was a Leaver (something which, as we know, put her in the substantial majority in Kent), I asked her why she'd voted the way she had.

'Largely because of the things I heard from guests who come here,' she told me. I'd have loved to have delved deeper, but unfortunately, a text on my phone told me my taxi was looking for me. There was just time to ask her if she'd vote the same way again, given everything that had happened since.

She was clear. 'Yes.'

I asked if there was any reason why.

'I think I'd have to stick with my original position,' she replied.

As I put my shoes on, I suspected she wasn't alone in this. She didn't strike me as clear on her stance – she was eager to know more about my side of the argument (or, at least, I interpreted her questions as this) – but felt she and the country had made a decision, and should therefore stick with it, almost despite any consequences. I was sure we could have talked for longer, but I had an appointment with a shopping centre. It was only a couple of miles down the road, but the clouds had started to gather again, and I wasn't confident of avoiding another soaking. Besides, I'd done enough trekking for the day.

If the high streets of England are wondering where all their trade has gone, I can tell them. Laid out in a triangle on yet another old quarry, Bluewater sits in its own dip in the firmament, like a partially hidden El Dorado. It has every conceivable retail outlet, and then some. It also has a cinema and a whole room devoted to trampolines and climbing walls. What isn't there to like, if you are that way inclined? It's impressive, even if I was left a little cold. As with Lakeside, it all felt a bit overwhelming. Perhaps I was too habituated to the solitary life on the road? Anyway, as we've already established, I wasn't in the market for more stuff to carry, although I was very much in the market for stuffing my belly. It was still early, though, around four. I didn't want to eat that early and wake up in the middle of the night in a deserted B&B feeling hungry, so I went for a wander.

My overriding impression was of hordes of bored children running around. Although the school holidays were only three weeks old these children were clearly bored witless, trampolines or no trampolines. Strangely enough, this observation coincided with my reading an article about the length of school holidays – and if you're a teacher or schoolchild, you might want to look away now.

The article suggested that school holidays are just too darned long. It described a phenomenon called 'learning loss' or 'unlearning', with pupils forgetting much of what they learn at the end of an academic year and having to spend the start of the following one catching up. The article also highlighted how long school holidays fuel social disparity, with better-off parents able to afford to give extra tutoring for their children, or access to other learning (musical instruments, sports, or just job placements), not so available to the less well off. It was a thought-provoking argument, and I recalled the conversation I'd had with Jacqui back in Liverpool about the inadequacies of the current schooling system, and how, like many other parts of 'the system' it could allow itself to get stuck in traditional mindsets. We did tradition well in England, and while this wasn't necessarily a bad thing, it wasn't always the best template for the future.

I ended up having a perfectly acceptable meal before locating the taxi rank. Just as I did so the threatened storm clouds gathered over the top of the complex. That day, it had been announced that the assets of the dying House of Fraser department store chain, one of whose stores was one of the three anchors in the complex, had been bought by the budget sports retailer Sports Direct. Perhaps the weather was trying to say something.

14

From Bean to Fruit

Two more guests turned up in the B&B overnight. They were Dutch cyclists, a couple touring the south-east of England on two wheels. They'd booked into the B&B at the last minute and like me had been defeated by the rain. We exchanged pleasantries, and they were kind enough to express sufficient interest in my walk to request a card. I duly obliged.

My breakfast finished, I felt as if Kim and I had some unfinished business, and I asked if she'd consent to be interviewed for a podcast. My interest had been piqued the previous day when she'd said her views on Brexit were informed by comments she'd heard from guests. This might be an opportunity to plug into the mindset of a whole group of people (namely those who B&B in Kent), rather than tuning into individuals one at a time.

She wasn't keen, but shared some of what she'd picked up from her guests anyway. She told me how they often spoke of job losses and barriers to trade put down to EU legislation, and when I asked if she could remember any specific examples she mentioned the steel and sugar industries. She was firmly of the view that we could survive on our own.

I listened to what she said. After all, this was part of the point of my walk, to listen. Kim admitted she was speaking from the heart, she didn't have any real evidence to support her views, and agreed that the Referendum campaign itself had been a disgrace. Once again, she pressed me on my view. She really did come across as genuinely interested in hearing the opposing argument. Her reward was a fifteen-minute rant. Sorry, I mean a fifteen-minute intelligent articulation of the issues, possibly a little more grounded in fact than sentiment. Neither of us was right or wrong, we each had our own view, and we each held it as tight as a child in peril, so we agreed to differ. Somewhat embarrassed with myself, I paid up and left.

Bean is a compact little village, with a doctor's surgery, community hall, foodless pub, school and a recycling point, which is probably just as well as it's part of Dartford. After the storms overnight it was sunny again, but not the scorching sweat-inducing heat of earlier in the year, which came as a relief. It looked like the waterproofs could stay stashed away. On finding the footpath out of the village I immediately came across a man wearing a short haircut, a camouflage shirt and very dark sunglasses. Oh, and he was also toting a gun. A friend in a similar get up joined him, although this one looked older and possibly friendlier. I decided to break the ice.

'What you after?'

'Anything, really,' he replied, with a shrug of the shoulders.

'I'd better get going quick then!'

'You're all right. We don't do that any more now. It's illegal,' he joked. At least, I think he was joking.

I set off down the footpath, which narrowed as it headed downhill, as if it wanted to demonstrate the concept of the vanishing point, accompanied by the soundtrack of *Saturday Night in Basra* from the ridge above. Wide views opened out over North Kent, incorporating pylons, wind turbines, fields and distant villages. A long, satisfyingly diagonal path opened out over a field of defeated, but not yet harvested, rape. I registered a small victory.

Nash Street marked the point at which my route was joined by the Wealdway, an 83-mile-long path through the Weald of Kent and Sussex, linking Gravesend in the north with Sussex on the southern coast. The path became a bridleway at this point and appropriately enough I met two women on horses. We stopped to exchange stories, but it was difficult to really engage in conversation with them so high up, looking down on me. Besides, one of the horses was preoccupied with stripping the hedge and its rider with stopping it. It was a classic Encounter of the First Kind.

The weather was such a contrast to the previous day that I treated myself to my traditional pint of shandy and pint of water at the Railway Inn at Sole Street, where there was also a rather fine five-lane, floodlit petanque court. Maybe it was something to do with being so close to France. I enquired as to whether they were serving food, but it was a foolish question, proffered more in hope that expectation. Instead, I took my pints out into the garden and snaffled the chicken pasty I'd bought in the local shop moments before in anticipation of their response.

Back on the path, violet-blue chicory lined the hedgerow, along with what looked and smelled like wild oregano. The recently shorn fields revealed sharp flints and the landscape became hilly, with electricity pylons stretching out in all directions like a deranged spider's web. Standing at the top of a ridge, I could see a faint splash of blue in the distance that looked on first impression like a horse box, but turned out to be a bouncy castle, a fact revealed by the shrieks of the children on it. I decided to sit for a while and just enjoy the view and my situation, while also making a mental note to check when my last eye test had been.

The rucksack off my back, it was good to feel the sun on my face. Feathery clouds set off a deep blue sky threaded with plane vapour trails. It felt good to just be in the moment, rather than simply following a line on a map. How lucky was I to be able to enjoy these views and to undertake this walk? The view, the mood and my feet (apart from a blister on one of my little toes) were all at one with the world. After a few minutes luxuriating in all this I stirred myself. If I stayed any longer I was in danger of writing a haiku.

I might have waited longer if I'd known what was in store: a steep chalky-white path down through a meadow so sheer I practically broke out into an undignified run. As there was only a barbed-wire fence to break my fall, this wasn't exactly optimal. Undaunted, I made it without ripping myself to shreds and paused to regather my wits. I wasn't the only one in a good mood. Overhead, a small light aircraft was performing aerobatic manoeuvres. I was joined by a man walking his dog and we both looked up. As this was Kent, there was a distinct possibility that the plane was a Spitfire. It wasn't, but it was good to imagine for a while that it might have been. To my unsophisticated ear the dog walker's accent still sounded rather 'London', a sort of Danny Dyer-lite.

From here I headed due south again, through over-ripe wheat fields, the path clearly marked but undulating. I left the Wealdway at Great Buckland to head east in order to regain my diagonal. When planning my route, I'd tried to use long-distance paths wherever they were practicable, on the basis that they were harder to get lost on. Other options were available, but it felt perverse to follow these merely to stick a few hundred yards closer to the diagonal. Mine was a pragmatic rather than dogmatic route.

For a few hundred yards this meant following the North Downs Way, but it was to be a brief visit. It turned out to be enough to take me up perhaps the steepest, most knee-grinding bit of track I'd encountered during the entire walk, and in the end I wasn't sorry to leave it. North Downs? North Ups Way more like. Inevitably, this was followed by a steep downward path, through a spinney along a footpath through a private estate. I knew it was a private estate because a sign told me. It was also keen to tell passing walkers that the estate was doing all it could to maintain the path and make it conducive to the local wildlife. Good for them, I thought, and thanks for the heads-up.

It then became clear why I was being channelled so effectively, and why they were so keen to make things perfect for the local wildlife. Dozens of lively game birds, blissfully unaware of the date. The eleventh of August. The next day men in Barbour jackets and carrying hardware that would have put the two men at the beginning of the day into delights would be able slaughter wildfowl without sanction. Although officially the start of the shooting season for red grouse, the 'Glorious Twelfth' is widely accepted as the start of the shooting season generally. I felt blessed to have arrived a day early, if a little sorry for my little birdy-chums. On the other hand, given the noise they were making, perhaps like the chickens in the Aardman film *Chicken Run*, they were actually planning their escape? I hoped so.

Another ascent followed, with mature beech trees clinging to the hillside as if they were concerned about sliding down. This brought me out onto woods with a view of my destination, as well as a series of yet more worked-out chalk quarries along with the North Downs to the north-east. High hedges then lined the final path into Snodland.

Yes, Snodland. Only one letter off being mucus-tastic. If Bean was (as it were) a great name, Snodland definitely trumped it. As I approached the end of the lane excited, imploring, male voices could be heard: the unmistakeable sound of a football match in progress. The start of another season, that for football. This was the Saturday in August once labelled 'The Big Kick Off', although these days, due to the demands of television, it was more of a 'Medium-Sized Kick Off'.

My bed for the night was at an Airbnb owned by a high-octane actress called Gilda. Terrific fun to be with, Gilda's energy was at the same time revitalising and exhausting after a hard day's walking. I eventually managed to get away and grab a shower, and after catching up with myself went for a wander around Snodland, as was now part of my routine. Not quite a town (the locals call it a village), Snodland wasn't short of Co-ops. It already had two, but had evidently decided this wasn't enough, so it was building another. This was in the car park of an old pub which, amongst about a million other pieces of information, Gilda told me locals had campaigned to be converted into a gastropub. Alas, their lobbying fell on deaf ears.

I assumed the new Co-op was going to consolidate the other two, but wondered what would replace the sites they left behind. Based on current evidence, it was likely to be esoteric. There was already a Tricky Dave's Discount Store, a shop called Petaholics and A 'n' D's Bargain Food, which I dodged. Other than that, there was the usual collection of hair salons, male and female, betting shops and, of course, a bespoke tailor. Because Snodlandites take their tailoring seriously.

In truth, Snodland wasn't too bad a place. It has a mix of housing, with some historic buildings including an old fire station converted into a museum (it was shut), and even its own water company. It also has a clock tower. This was erected in memory of Charles Townsend Hook by his mother and sisters, upon his death in 1877. The Hooks owned a paper mill in Snodland from the middle of the nineteenth century, eventually producing over 5,000 tonnes of paper a year, which was a thousand-fold increase from when the family took it over. This was symptomatic of wider growth. Over the twenty years from 1861 the village trebled in size, its growth aided in part by the railway.

The clock tower remains an impressive red and white brick rectangular edifice with a cockerel weather vane on top and arched entrances at the bottom on each face. Its position was probably once quite important, but these days it's crammed in a corner between two modern houses, a matter of less than six feet from the front door of one of them. Their own personal campanile. I hoped it didn't strike the hour.

The gastropub gambit having failed, I investigated the local pubs. This being Saturday night, I probably should have anticipated that none of them served food. As in Toddington earlier in the walk, there was nothing for it but to revert to the old standby, the local Indian, the Agra. As I was a singleton, they sat me in the corner opposite the fridge and hoped I'd behave. As I perused the menu (there was a minimum charge of £8.50 for 'dinning' in the restaurant), I noticed that the fridge was well stocked with Mateus Rosé and catering-sized packs of After Eight. I was going to be all right.

Snodland was okay, it just lacked a dimension. By nine in the evening it was deserted, even the fast food shops, which had been heaving earlier in the evening, were packing up. Given the prominence of the Co-ops, I called in on one to pick up some plasters. It was busy here, mainly with people buying ready meals. I empathised. Snodland was caught in the trap of having nowhere to go at night, which in turn drove the demand for at-home dinning. It was a Huntsman's Chicken and egg dilemma.

The weather forecast for the next day was revised upward overnight. I could only assume the forecasters had looked out of the window and rushed to their computers, as it was gloriously sunny. Rather than encasing myself in Gore-Tex, I was debating whether to zip off the bottom half off my convertible trousers. I decided against it, there was a limit to how much you could thumb your nose at the weather gods. I got going early to make the most of it, passing through the placid Leybourne Lakes, created from old gravel pits, where a group I'd assumed to be anglers (although these are usually solitary beasts) turned out to be scuba divers, all wearing wetsuits as if they were about to search for a dead body.

The recent rain had tickled nature back into action, and there were little tufts of emerald amongst the otherwise scorched grass. My route channelled me down a narrow path by the side of the railway line, where buddleia was growing triffid-like, enough to require sudden spread-eagling against the fence to dodge urgent cyclists coming the other way. To my right, a huge paper mill was in the process of being decommissioned, a euphemism for demolished. This was the site of the former Aylesford Newsprint, or Aylesford Paper Mills. At one time, this produced newsprint for *The Times*, *Mirror* and *Observer* and produced a totally recycled product, making it the largest paper recycling plant in Europe.

The business was once a significant employer locally and was the victim of both a decline in newspaper readership and overcapacity in the industry. A large new plant in Norfolk owned by investors with deeper pockets finally did for the facility. In the end, it was a victim of both market and social forces, and although exchange rate fluctuations with the Euro had complicated matters, for once no one was pointing the finger at the EU for the demise of an iconic employer. Plans to build houses on the site had recently been rejected, with the council holding out for a more mixed-use solution. For now, the site existed as a mess of twisted, skeletal, metal bars and giant boulders of concrete. The back of the building was ripped off, as if caught in a tornado, exposing the interior. It was all very post-apocalyptic.

A large block on the map outside Aylesford suggested another factory, but this one had been already replaced by housing: the Ashlin Estate, where a brand new four-bedroom colonial-style detached house could be had for between £450,000 and £500,000. These looked out over the road onto an inter-war development of semis, which had three bedrooms and cost roughly £100,000 less, where presumably newsprint workers and their families once lived. The two developments graphically summarised different phases in Aylesford's history, with the owners of the new houses much more likely to commute into London on the rail line than earn a living locally.

Remembering my visit to the National Memorial Arboretum earlier in the walk, and the nation's reawakening of empathy for the armed forces, I took a short detour to look at the Royal British Legion Village. This was founded just after the First World War to take soldiers discharged from the nearby hospital. These days, it also acts as the HQ for the Poppy Appeal, and includes a social enterprise which, amongst other things, makes road signs.

The site provided a surreal experience. It was like wandering around the Keele University campus all over again. There was even a baronial pile, Preston Hall, which had been the original hospital, with a good reputation for also treating TB. On the village site itself, there were blocks of flats in halls named after prominent people, again like Keele, although there were considerably more cars here. It was a quiet and contemplative place, and I again reflected on the rise of Help for Heroes and other charities. The English weren't a callous people. Compassion and respect for those who serve in the armed forces wasn't a new phenomenon. We'd just grown complacent, assuming those needing help would be looked after by the state. It had just taken a dubious, divisive, war to wake us up. At the risk of sounding obsessed, I wondered whether Brexit would have a similar effect, acting as a form of shock therapy taking us into a fresh place. The only problem was, no one could predict whether that place would be better or worse.

When I'd first started planning the walk, a paucity of convenient crossing places had suggested the River Medway was going to be a problem. In the end, it was to be no Mersey or Thames, the crossing achieved in under a minute (yes, I did time it), without the aid of a bus, walking over an old bridge that led into the pretty village of Aylesford, a quite distinct entity from its namesake on the other side of the river.

Just before crossing, I spotted something on the ground. It was a brightly coloured rock, about the size of a goose egg. A crude picture was painted on it, a red and black affair a bit like a Tasmanian Devil, coupled with some writing. This spelled out 'Love on the Rocks' and instructed the finder to visit a Facebook page. I did, but I knew what was coming. I'd picked up one of these on a local walk earlier in the year. It was part of a trend for placing decorated stones as a form of treasure hunt for the social media age. Finders were encouraged to take a photo, post it on Facebook and place their find elsewhere for someone else to find. I put the stone back where I'd found it, but was reminded that I'd been carrying my stone, which belonged to the 'Wokingham Rocks' chapter, in my rucksack for days now. Much smaller, about the size of a child's thumb, it had got lost at the bottom of a pocket snuggling up to handbag-sized bottles of antibacterial gel and sun cream, as well as a mini First Aid kit.

Having crossed the Medway without incident I set about exploring the village. It was picturesque, with half-timbered houses, a tea room (shut) and what looked like some alms houses, where an inscription identified them as the Old Brassey Hospital. My curiosity sated, if not my thirst, I made for the north shore of the Medway, which was going to guide me into Maidstone. Initially, this followed a relatively recently laid asphalt path popular with cyclists. I once again detected the hand of the cycling lobby: as on the Liverpool Loop, there was a dearth of benches to sit on. I eventually found a wall by the edge of the river, which was low and muddy, to take on refreshment and water.

A couple of miles further on, there was no doubt about it. There was rain on the air, something confirmed by a glance at the water's surface. I ignored it hoping it would go away, and after a few minutes, to my complete astonishment, it did. The next landmark was Allington Lock, which acted as a limit to navigation. Controlling the river's flow were some large metal sluices, installed in 1937 by the Medway Lower Navigation Company and the River Medway Catchment Board. This explained the low water earlier. After the lock the banks began to be populated with rivercraft, with a fine array of Dutch barges and old sailing craft attracting much attention. A sign on the last of these announced the vessel as the Dutch barge *Emanuelle*, a 110-foot-long boat which carried cattle food and cereals right up until 1984. It looked in good shape. Out on the water, a pleasure boat and two canoeists drifted gently by.

The walk from the lock into Maidstone was part of a River Park created as a millennium project, and as I carried on along it the rain, like an old car on a cold day, kept trying to splutter into life, but failed to take hold. About a mile before Maidstone, I saw two men throwing a thick yellow cord into the river, something heavy on the end giving it momentum. I asked what they were up to.

'Magnafishing,' I was told. Stupid of me really.

This involved tossing an ice-hockey-puck-sized magnet out into the water and dragging it back on an attached rope to see what it might pick up. They described how a friend of theirs had found a nineteenth-century gun, as well as a hand grenade. It must have been fun pulling that out of the water. Military premises once lined the riverbank they explained, so it stood to reason there might be some ordnance in the river. Because soldiers with nothing better to do often throw their weaponry into the nearest river.

Meanwhile, my guy had 'caught' something, and a small crowd gathered as he gently hauled his line back to the shore. We all waited patiently until, like a big fish, it fell off the magnet just as it reached the edge. An involuntary sigh went up.

'No problem,' our magnafisher reassured us, dropping his magnet back in and then hauling half a child's scooter, covered in green slime, up onto the bank. Well, it was one way of spending a Sunday afternoon I supposed. I walked on, wondering if the magnet ever hit an unsuspecting fish on the head, thereby truly putting the 'fishing' into 'magnafishing'.

Aficionados of the Maidstone canoe club added a splash of colour to the otherwise sludge-brown of the river outside Maidstone, along with a dark blue latticed metal railway bridge next to the Powerhub Business Centre. Once a munitions factory (were the magnafishers in the wrong spot?), the Powerhub offered office space for local businesses, but looked decidedly unloved and uninspiring. Later reading suggested that the much sought-after technology companies preferred to locate in business parks out of town. Towards the end of the last century, the Sharps toffee factory, said to be the biggest toffee factory in the world (well, it had to be somewhere) had been in the centre, providing many jobs. How things change.

Maidstone is Kent's county town, so if it wasn't doing well the whole county was likely to be in trouble. Luckily, it looked like it was. The walk up from the river took me through a relatively new Fremlin shopping centre, opened in 2006 and built on the site of an old brewery of the same name, another large town centre business now gone. It was a Sunday, and the shops were busy, and indeed Wikipedia carried the claim that the Fremlin was one of the top five shopping centres in the south-east of England by yield. This sounded impressive, but meant little to me. True, it has a House of Fraser as an anchor store, but this one hadn't been on the list of stores originally earmarked for closure.

The architecture in the heart of the town was varied, with some redevelopment taking place, including the promise of a history trail. Earl Street offered a selection of chain restaurants Luton could only dream of, and later that evening I ate in one of these, having wandered around to take in the sights. These included a plaque to Andrew Broughton, who was Clerk of the Court at the High Court of Justice during the trial of King Charles I, which didn't end happily for the royal personage. Upon the Restoration he was exempted from the general pardon and lived the final quarter century of his life in exile in Switzerland. The plaque listed him as 'Mayor and Regicide', which as CVs go is certainly impressive.

The town was also the birthplace of the nineteenth-century art critic, essayist and philosopher William Hazlitt, after whom the town's theatre is named. His plaque was affixed to the front of an 'Ask' restaurant and was more modest, describing him simply as 'Essayist and Critic', stating that he was born 'near here' with a lovely touch of vagueness. Behind the post box possibly.

I chose my eating place well, other than having my ears and most of my other sensibilities assaulted by one of those men who don't appreciate just how loud their voice is. Maybe he couldn't do anything about that, but football songs? Seriously? I needed to move as far away as possible, where I sat next to a family of three I'd seen earlier. I presumed they'd left; whereas there'd merely had the same problem. As I passed the top of Earl Street on the way back to my billet I passed the Deliveroo posse, and weaving my way back through the town it struck me that Maidstone was missing something. Homeless people. The first town of any size I'd been to other than WGC where this had been so. They must be doing something right.

Funnily enough, the main headline on the BBC the next day was a plan to end rough sleeping. This was due to be announced by the Communities Secretary, the aptly named James Brokenshire. Seriously, you couldn't make this stuff up. Give him any job but Communities Secretary. I got on my way. I was due to meet up with my younger sister, Sue. She was going to walk with me for two days and I needed to make our meeting point outside of town.

Although we made our rendezvous without mishap, Sue was keen to find a loo. I could see she was going to need breaking in to the ways of diagonal walking. Within minutes, we were back into open countryside, following footpaths that took us through small Kentish villages such as Otham and Langley Heath, with their half-timbered houses (except with tan-coloured walls rather than the more traditional white) as well as converted oast houses to die for, although there was often very little else in these places, not even a pub or a school. Or even a church. Sue remarked how it was exactly these scenes that people probably conjured up when imagining a typical English village, although I had seen equally iconic sights elsewhere, notably in what I'd labelled Middle England.

It didn't take long before it became clear what the area did have. Fruit. And lots of it. Our first encounter with commercial cultivation was a nursery specialising in trees. We couldn't work out what they were, so we asked a man sitting on a hay bale about thirty yards away.

'Dick holes!' he yelled back.

It had been a perfectly civil question. Perhaps we'd misheard him.

'Dick holes!' he repeated.

I smiled benignly. A later sign revealed them to be Farm Trees. How he got to Dick Holes from there we didn't know.

Farm trees are grown to provide firewood, fence posts or even raw material for furniture, and typically involve the use of hazel, chestnut or ash trees. What we'd seen were rows of saplings being reared for later planting. A long-term business if ever there was one. A profusion of hedgerow fruits, sloes, blackberries and elderberries followed before we hit pay dirt. First, a series of polytunnels, under which rows of strawberries, still being grown in pots, stood at waist height, still bearing fruit. Second, and more significantly for half our party, there was a portaloo. Some people are just born lucky. Reassuringly, beside the portaloo there was a water trough with taps, together with a sign saying 'Now Wash Your Hands' translated into seven other languages using a variety of scripts.

We were now firmly in the Garden of England. Although only a third of the way into the county from east to west, we were also firmly in Kentish Man or Maid territory. This was in contrast to Men or Maid of Kent territory, with the Kentish Man or Maid used to designate those born west of the Medway and Men or Maid of Kent for those born east of the river. There, I hope that's clear, and no, I'm afraid there's no provision for those confused about their gender.

The strawberries we could see were labelled as sustainable, which meant they were grown to minimise their impact on water usage (there were thin-tubed irrigation systems along the rows) as well as on the environment, through minimal use of chemicals. Strawberries are synonymous with Wimbledon of course, and apparently they've served only sustainable strawberries since 2012. Top fact. Sue couldn't resist trying one, spotting only after she swallowed it that there was a notice next to it which included the word 'Bioscience', which is rarely a good thing. We wondered whether she'd undergo some kind of transformation overnight, like Violet Beauregarde from Willy Wonka.

We continued on the footpaths, dipping in and out of further polytunnel nurseries and lines of fruit trees, or more accurately bushes, being trained to espalier along wires stretching down the hillsides, like French grape vines. Along the way, we bumped into various people, although none of them were that keen to engage with us. Smiling was on offer, but not any exchange of words. Initially dismissing this as unfriendliness, it took us a ridiculous amount of time to clock that they couldn't speak English. These were the pickers, by and large practically invisible, lost in the acres and acres of fruit. Only on one occasion did we spot them in a group, and even then they were at least a hundred yards away, huddled in a cluster like refugees. One or two had drifted towards the point where our footpath sent us through some trees attempting to get a signal on their phones. We offered a friendly greeting, but received only suspicious looks in return. The obvious question about who would do this work in a post-Brexit world was left unstated.

As the day went on, as well as strawberries, we saw raspberries, loganberries, blueberries, blackberries, blackcurrants, redcurrants, red apples, green apples, crab apples, plums, pears and cherries being cultivated. And hops of course. It was Kent after all. It was cultivation on an industrial scale, enough to make a Waitrose buyer's mouth water. Even a prison we passed had its own market garden.

For once, the weather forecasters had got things right, even if the expected rain did come a little earlier than promised. Luckily, we were passing a children's playground at the time and could take shelter under a climbing frame, before reverting to the more traditional 'hide under a big tree' method when the shower, for shower it was, gained momentum.

Our route led us onto the hundred-plus-mile Greensand Way, which follows a ridge of greensand rock east to west across Surrey and Kent, and is not to be confused with the Greensand Ridge Walk I'd followed earlier in Bedfordshire. Walking along the top of the ridge, we were regularly rewarded with wide open views, so much so that we became almost blasé about them. The paths were easy to follow, although there was the occasional hiccup, which Pathwatch was able to extricate us from. The local landowners maintained the paths well and welcomed walkers, even if not all welcomed dogs. One sign we passed announced 'Your dog could be shot if found amongst sheep,' although it was unclear whether the sheep actually packed heat.

The Greensand Way took us to Liverton Street, just outside Platt's Heath, where we'd arranged to meet up with Sue's husband, my brother-in-law, Tim, who was driving us back to their house for the night. Just before we got there, we passed an abandoned orchard. It seemed no longer fit for modern purpose, superceded by lines of apple bushes presumably much easier to pick, possibly by machine, which might be one response to any future manpower shortage. We also passed a recently ploughed field, its soil ruby red. A grubbed-up strawberry patch or tunnel, we reasoned; sustainable no longer it appeared.

Taken together, these offered a fitting end to a fruit-themed day.

15

Back to the Sea

We hoped the weather forecasters were on a roll, as they were predicting good weather all day, with highs of around 26°C and eleven hours of sunshine. We should have known better. Even though the day started well it soon clouded over, and at one point even threatened to rain. This was my second day's walking with Sue and, once reunited with the point where we'd left off the previous day, we said our goodbyes to Tim and slipped into a hedge with all the ease of Lucy, Edmund, Peter and Susan disappearing into Narnia.

We were immediately rewarded with a fantastic view south-west over the Weald of Kent beyond the wonderfully named Grafty Green. In the distance we could see what looked like oases. Earlier on the walk I'd have had them down as solar arrays, but here in Kent they were polytunnels, acres of them. We wandered through the equally well-named Broughton Malherbe, a small hamlet with a big church, still staying with the Greensand Way and now on a determinedly south-east trajectory, bringing me ever closer to my end point. Just outside Egerton, we walked beside the magnificent white-fronted Georgian façade of Egerton House, a nine-bedroomed, four-bathroomed, six-receptioned pile dating back to medieval times. A lottery winner's dream, and better still it was for sale, a snip at only £1.5 million. This included over ten acres of land, some of which we'd just got lost on.

Acres of blush red apples covered the hillside, drawing the eye into yet another great view of the Weald below. Crab apples were planted in between the apple bushes, presumably for efficiency, or possibly for a companion planting benefit, I didn't know. What I did know was that as we approached the rear of Egerton's church, Sue managed to spot a patch of alpine strawberries on the ground beneath us. We gathered a handful together and put them in our mouths. Sue hadn't transformed into a giant strawberry overnight and had adopted a devil-may-care attitude. Expecting ultra-sweet lusciousness, we were disappointed. They turned out dry and tasteless. Perhaps they weren't ready yet, or simply not meant to be eaten? We turned our attention to the church. Another big one, and dating back to the thirteenth century, it reminded us both of somewhere, Norfolk as it turned out.

In Egerton itself, we were to be treated to the full House of Fraser retail experience. Not the Sports Direct version, but a small village shop and post office run by a tall lady in a flowing purple gown called Fraser. Neither a Maid of Kent or a Kentish Maid, she described herself as a transplanted Welshie. The shop was for sale, and there was an effort to get the community to buy it by purchasing shares so it could continue. As I was familiar with this model from the community purchase of the pub where we used to live, we got into conversation. It was on sale for £550,000, but as the village only has three-hundred households this meant that on average every household would need to buy three to four £500 shares to make the deal work. It looked like a tall order. The village itself, meanwhile, looked well maintained, with a range of architectural styles on display, from the modern to the local red brick with plain tile roofing, including Yeoman Houses and Kentish Barns along the way.

Fraser was a mine of information and indomitably upbeat. I asked about how the area gained the wealth to justify such a large church. Sheep, she replied, which explained the Norfolk comparison. It wasn't just industries that came and went, but also how rural areas earned their keep. Once it was sheep, now it was fruit, although as the day went on it became clear that the fruit theme was weakening, in favour of ... sheep. Fraser also explained the difference between the Low Weald, which consisted mainly of clay, and the High Weald, which consisted of a mix of clay and ironstone. The Weald is a name given to a stretch of land that stretches from the marshes of Kent to the New Forest in Hampshire. This was to be a full Encounter of the Third Kind, namely when someone approached me (I was wearing a Diagonal Walking T-shirt), conducted under the protection of the Glebe Oak outside Fraser's shop on the other side of the road. We swapped stories and took pictures of each other, and before the day was out, Fraser had featured us on her store's Facebook page.

If fruit had dominated Sue's first day of Diagonal Walking, the second was to be defined by the Weald. Oast houses kept popping up, including a beautiful one set up for weddings at Elvey Farm. The grass was definitely greening now, and sheep could safely graze once more. We entered the village of Pluckley just as lunchtime was approaching, and I could feel a pint of shandy coming on, even if the cloud cover didn't justify a pint of water as well. On entering the Black Horse, which claims to be the most haunted pub in Kent (it was unclear whether this was seen as an asset), out of a mix of politeness and curiosity I asked if they did any food. I could have just gone a good ploughman's. It was a naïve enquiry: their kitchen was undergoing refurbishment.

So it was that we sat outside with our drinks and the sandwiches we'd brought with us just in case. While waiting for the drinks, I'd perused the pictures inside the pub. One featured the damage done by a V1 strike in 1944, a useful reminder of how close we now were to the coast. Others majored on shots taken during the filming of *The Darling Buds of May*, an early 1990s TV series based upon the books by H.E. Bates. The series portrayed a sort of bucolic rural idyll with David Jason as Pa Larkin, a countryside chancer. The book, and series, were set in Kent, with the Black Horse featuring as the Hare and Hounds. As a location, it was perfect, or perhaps I should say 'perfick'. Very little had probably changed between the time the books were written in the late fifties and when the TV series was filmed, or indeed now.

Houses in and around Pluckley sported an arched window effect, something attributable to the Dering family, who acquired the parish in the fifteenth century and introduced the style on all their buildings during Victorian times. Imagine having the power to impose an architectural style. Ever since early on in the walk, I'd been collecting photos of houses named 'The Old Something'. I'd got lots of Old Bakeries, Old Post Offices and Old Rectories, but in Pluckley I managed to grab the rare 'The Old Newsagent'. What was next I wondered, the 'The Old Cyber Café'?

The Black Horse's claim to be the most haunted pub in Kent wasn't an idle one. Pluckley has a claim to be the most haunted village in England. It was awarded this title by no less an authority than the Guinness Book of Records way back in 1989, which registered no fewer than twelve ghosts, not bad for somewhere with a population of around a thousand. My favourite was the Watercress Woman, who was supposed to sit by Pluckley Bridge smoking her pipe, drinking gin and selling watercress she gathered from the stream. An unusual combination in itself, the woman in question went that one step further and spontaneously combusted due to her gin-soaked state.

Needless to say, we saw no evidence of the supernatural and picked up our path, now heading due south, losing the Greensand Way in a quest to regain the diagonal, which had drifted away from us. The sun was an occasional visitor, but a reluctant one, popping out for a few seconds before popping back in again.

The fields contained more livestock here, some cattle, but mainly sheep. Outside the appropriately named Lambden, we needed to scrabble through a hedge on our hands and knees into a field of white woolly things. They weren't happy. Bleating as if their life depended upon it, they gathered around us in protest. Normally, sheep don't represent that much of a challenge, but when you're on their level on all fours, let me tell you, they can be a different proposition. We tried to shoo them away, but they were having none of it, and as we strode on regardless, a line of them gathered behind Sue, as if she was a sort of ovine Pied Piper. It wasn't until we reached the field edge that we realised we'd gone wrong. Either we'd got distracted by the sheep or they'd been trying to tell us something.

On the final stretch in we spotted a horse and Shetland pony tethered to a large metal spike on a grass verge, left without hay or water. The horse looked emaciated, and it was our guess, fairly or unfairly, that they'd been left there by Travellers. This is a practice known as illegal grazing or fly grazing, something now subject to the Control of Horses Act of 2015, and a particular problem in Kent. Whoever was responsible, it was a cruel practice and quite distressing.

As our time together was coming to an end, I recorded a podcast interview with Sue. A key feature of our chat was how, when walking, you gained a much deeper appreciation of the variety of each day and, I added, of each county. My mind went back to the reflections I'd been having on the ridge overlooking the bouncy castle a couple of days before. Maybe it was because the walk was coming towards its end that I was feeling so reflective, but it was reassuring to find out that others felt the same way too. Our two days together had been very different. It had been wonderful to be able to spend this quality time, usually so rationed, together.

The podcast complete, our path emerged onto a churchyard, where two women were playing with a power washer amongst the graves, while a solitary man tried to unravel a hose and an electricity extension cord. What they were up to was anyone's guess, but they greeted us cheerily and said we could join in if we wanted.

'With what?' we asked.

'Cleaning these chairs for the fête.'

First, there were no chairs in sight. Second, a large banner looking out onto the road announced the date of the fête as the end of September. It was August 14th. They clearly had a lot of chairs. Somewhere. We declined and wished them luck.

We emerged into Bethersden, a pretty village with a small run of shops (two beauty salons, one was required to keep up appearances in Bethersden) and a pub, as well as a butchers, complete with an ornamental butcher's bike outside. I went into the general store, as I felt a craving for chocolate coming on. A number of packets of Munchies were on the counter. I hadn't had a Munchie for years, so I said I'd take a pack.

'Oh, bless you,' the shopkeeper said, as if I was a repented sinner. 'I'm about to mark them down, they're only good until September.'

What was it with September for these people? Had we entered some kind of time warp? Had that hedge in Liverton Street been some kind of portal? 'Don't worry, they'll be long gone by then,' I reassured her.

'Oh, bless you,' she repeated.

I munched on my Munchies and Tim duly turned up on time. As we pulled out of the village, I noticed that the sign for the village fête was a recycled one. This year's fête was on the Bank Holiday. Even so, two weeks to clean some chairs?

Commitments elsewhere temporarily removed me from Kent, and when I returned to Bethersden shortly after the fête there was no sign of the chairs. As it happened, the Bank Holiday had been a washout, a sign that the English weather dial was now switched back to 'Normal'. The desert-like heat of the summer was only a memory now, and the evenings offered a hint of autumn, with dew-damp mornings and colder evenings. Lawns had regained much of their familiar green, even if closer inspection showed this coming as much from dandelion leaves as grass, and fields were being ploughed in readiness for fresh sowing.

Resisting the temptation to have the final two days of my walk blessed in the village shop, I took a short footpath through the heart of the village. At the other end of this I spotted a poster. This advertised the Bethersden Gardeners' Society (good use of the apostrophe, folks) Autumn Show that coming Saturday – all entries to Helen or Eleanor by Wednesday. Surnames were superfluous here. A raffle, plant exchange and refreshments were all on offer. Life in Bethersden was clearly one long social whirl. A few yards along the Ashford Road my route took me around the back of the village, where the last house before open fields had a cricket net in the garden. I'd seen tennis courts and even swimming pools, but never a private cricket net before.

About half an hour later I came across a breed of animal I'd not seen for a while: a miserable landowner. Grey-haired and probably in his late sixties, he was wearing a tatty blue jumper and a permanently annoyed expression. He was also riding a quad bike, and for a while I considered the possibility that this was to corral walkers across his land rather than livestock. I sensed an encounter was imminent, and it wasn't going to be pretty.

This was not a landowner who welcomed walkers. That much was evident from the broken stiles and lack of fingerposts and direction arrows, which was almost Staffordian in its distain. He watched me from a distance as I studied my map. I managed to keep the correct course for most of the passage across his land, but on the one occasion I got it wrong, he was on me in a puff of blue smoke and the gunning of the engine of his souped-up lawnmower.

'Chinese map you got there?' he bellowed, in a tone that didn't suggest easy banter.

'Unmarked footpath and no arrows,' I replied.

'Eh?'

I repeated my assessment of the problem.

'Why would you go that way?' he demanded, shaking his head.

Once again, I repeated my earlier diagnosis.

'Eh?' he repeated above the sound of his turbo-charged hairdryer.

It continued like this for two more exchanges. He either had a hearing or a cognitive impairment, it was difficult to be sure which. Perhaps both.

This was his opportunity to concoct the correct response, which would have gone something along the lines of: 'Yes, you're right. I've been meaning to get around to fixing those, thanks for reminding me, I'll get onto it this afternoon.'

Instead, I got: 'You've got a map haven't you?'.

It appeared the ethnicity of my map was now irrelevant. Despite umpteen opportunities to come up with a zinger of a response, this had been the best his diesel-deranged brain could manage. By this time, I'd spotted the gap in the hedge in the corner of the field so, taking a leaf out of cousin Simon's book, I thanked him loudly for his help, although I added, 'You miserable old git', as he spluttered away.

There was to be more to follow. A footpath across a field was planted to maize, and although it wasn't exactly as high as an elephant's eye, it was high enough. Memories of struggles through rape fields came to mind and I didn't have the fight left in me, so I took a detour along country lanes around Brissenden Green. This led to a long byway heading south-east through a forest of small beech and ash trees, following a rough track.

Unusually, the sign pointing down the track featured silhouettes of a four-by-four, a walker, a cyclist, a horse and, get this, a horse and carriage, the horse in full knee-in-the-air dressage mode. I initially thought nothing of it, pleased to be walking along a defined path where it looked impossible to get lost. As I went on however, the heavy shade thrown by the trees conjured up an eerie atmosphere, one which took on something of a children's fairy tale feel; without the gingerbread house, but retaining an option on a big bad wolf. I suddenly began to feel quite vulnerable, miles from anywhere, where the only sounds were creaking wood and birdsong.

It was as this feeling came over me that I realised that the strange silhouette on the byway sign represented a Traveller's carriage. If one of those came down the track with evil intent, I was in trouble. Barbed wire removed the option of a dash into the woods and besides, I'd seen those carriages in action and they were fast and manoeuvrable. A notice carrying the logos of both Kent Police and the County Council was pinned to a tree and announced 'Operation Freedown', reminding users that under the Road Traffic Act of 1988 all driving documents were required and that consequences would follow for transgressors.

I picked the pace up a bit and it was a relief when I made it to Hamstreet. There wasn't too much there for the casual visitor, it was true: a pub (shut) and a coffee shop, the Cosy Kettle (also shut). I ploughed on. The Old School House was now an Indian restaurant and there was a Church of the Good Shepherd, leaving no other option but to try the local village store and post office. Here the routine was for the woman standing by the till to shout 'post office' in a weary drone every time someone approached the weighing scales three metres to her right. It was almost Pavlovian. This happened three times in the minutes it took me to buy an apple and a Toffee Crisp. The apple later turned out to be rotten.

A walk across a field and through (and I mean through) some brambles, brought me to a bridge over the Royal Military Canal, which I was about to follow north-east, back to my diagonal. The product of an earlier rejection of the idea of a united Europe, the canal was built as a response to the Napoleonic threat. Initially, it had been thought that there was no need to defend Romney Marsh as a potential invasion point, as at the first sign of danger it could be easily flooded. Later investigations suggested that at least ten days' notice would be required to make this plan feasible, and then there was another thing. What if there was a false alarm and the marsh was flooded accidentally?

The prospect of a colossal bureaucratic foul-up was enough to convince the powers-that-were at the time to try something different. Something different turned out to be cutting a canal linking Seabrook near Folkestone, around the back of the marsh and on to the River Rother near Rye. The plan was to create embankments from the spoil that resulted from digging the canal, behind which soldiers could hide. Kinks were also incorporated into the canal, to ease raking fire at the enemy should they be mad enough to try to cross it. Mad enough because it was built nineteen metres wide and three metres deep – although it was doubtful that metres were the preferred unit of measurement at the time.

The then Prime Minister, William Pitt, was persuaded of the merits of the scheme, and in a reflection of his popularity locally, the canal became known as 'Mr Pitt's Ditch'. It was reasoned, with a very English pragmatism, that even if an invasion never took place, the canal would be a good way of draining the marshes. And so it proved. From its completion in 1809 to today, the canal carries water from the various drainage ditches in the vicinity (known charmingly as sewers) out to sea. Once the French threat was over, the canal was opened to navigation, but it never proved that popular and its commercial potential disappeared altogether with the coming of the railway, a tale familiar to any canal enthusiast.

As I walked along the raised banks of the waterway, my greatest threat looked like it might be coming from the sky rather than from across the Channel. The clouds had turned the sort of grey normally seen the morning after a barbeque: a light ash. The land was, as might be expected, distinctly flat, and the only wildlife I could spot were anglers lining the bank, doing what anglers do, namely not a lot. I left the canal and followed the Sedbrook Sewer, where a cob and pen were marshalling their five mature cygnets, each the colour of the sky overhead, along the narrow ditch. This emerged onto a newly ploughed field where, lulled by the impending end to a long day's walking, I promptly got lost. The ploughing had removed any obvious sign of the footpaths and once again, any signs had gone AWOL, adding an extra half an hour to the end of the day to sort myself out.

Luckily, a well-trodden path across my last field drew me into Newchurch – that and the tower of the eponymous church, which in fact dates back to the twelfth century, but was no doubt new at the time. I'd also been guided in by a limp RAF flag, light blue with the Union flag in the corner and the RAF roundel to the middle. I'd assumed this belonged to one of the locals, possibly a retired airman, but it was in fact the centrepiece of a memorial. Any frustration with the footpaths paled into insignificance as I read how the same fields I'd been walking had been an Advanced Landing Ground during the Second World War.

Amongst other things, they'd been used by planes providing cover for the Normandy landings. More remarkably to my mind, they'd also been used by planes whose role it was to intercept V1 Flying Bombs, or Doodlebugs. When they ran out of ammunition, the pilots would tip the bombs off balance using the ends of their wings. Such inconceivable courage. It would also have been in these skies, now grey, but then blue, that the Battle of Britain took place – a salutary reminder, along with the reasons behind the digging of the Royal Military Canal, of how badly things can turn out when relations between our island and the Continent beyond break down.

I was able to spend a little more time in Newchurch the next day, appreciating its ivy-clad old school house and its almost baronial village hall (the largest building in the village) and its leaning church tower. As with its counterpart in Pisa, its propensity to lean had become clear during construction, so the builders had done what builders tend to do – they botched it by carrying on building closer to the true, giving the tower a kink in the middle.

After a short stretch of lane walking, before long I was back out into open fields, where I encountered that curiosity, a pair of walkers – all the more unusual in that they were dog-free. We stopped and chatted, exchanging tales of long-distance paths completed and how often we got out to walk. They used to go out with walking groups, but the membership of these was aging, limiting them to an unsatisfying three miles – in their book hardly worth getting their boots on for. I wondered whether walking was a bit like church-going, an occupation dominated by those of more advanced years, destined to a slow decline. On the other hand, maybe they shared another characteristic in that it attracted those with more time, or need for companionship.

The old ploughed field problem reared its head again, but the local landowner had applied a simple solution, laying a thin layer of straw across the freshly exposed earth to mark the way, the first time I'd come across this. Simple, but effective. In theory, this day was to be a short one on account of the extra miles completed the day before – I'd originally intended to stop at Hamstreet, but had pressed on. In reality, progress was slow. Not only was I meeting more people, but I was also recording reflective podcasts and videos recognising the fact that this was to be my 39th and final day of walking.

Neither was I in the mood to rush things. Along with a day bag, I was carrying mixed emotions. The walk had dominated my summer – much more than I'd anticipated at the outset. The planning before a stage, its execution, the updating of social media during and afterwards, followed by renewed planning for the next stage, had pretty much become a full-time job.

I'd loved it all. The challenges, the ups and downs, the time to think and the opportunity to interact with others. The glorious weather had been a bonus; a pain at times, sure, but better than rain. I'd been challenged, occasionally frightened, frustrated at times and even annoyed and angry; but most of the time I'd been happy. Content. Fulfilled. Whether I'd achieved my goal of understanding my country any better as it stood on the cliff face of a 'brave new world'

was something I was still considering. I had found some …
peace, I supposed. Some understanding, a reconciliation.
More on this later, but for now, there was a walk to complete.

Next up was St Mary in the Marsh. In a day of 'lasts',
this was significant, as it marked the 85th and last of my
photocopied sheets from the Ordnance Survey maps that
had been my constant guide and companion. These maps,
along with our footpath system, really are a national treasure.
Only very rarely had I been misled by them, and when I had
it was always my own stupid fault, either through a misread,
or because I'd been too tight to buy the most up-to-date
map.

An unprepossessing sort of place, St Mary in the Marsh
has a pub, a bridge and a church. It does have one point of
interest, however. In a good example of the sort of serendipity
walking can bring, the churchyard was also home to the
grave of Edith Nesbit, author of, among other books, *The
Railway Children*. Finding it was easy once I adopted the
advice offered by Indiana Jones when searching for the Holy
Grail – seek the least obvious, the most humble. Like the
village itself, the grave was modest. It consisted of a carved
plank of wood attached to two wooden pillars, almost a stile,
which declared that the 'Poet and Author' was 'Resting',
although I was pretty sure she was dead.

Following another chatty encounter (where had all
these people been during the rest of the walk?), I promptly
got lost again. My most recent chatees, Phillipa and Sue,
came from New Romney and warned of a diversion just
outside town. They pointed out the direction they'd come,
and I foolishly followed it, despite the fact that it wasn't

the route I'd marked out for myself beforehand. Rectifying my mistake took twenty minutes, and brought me back to within twenty yards of where we'd been chatting. Oh well, it was just as well I wasn't in a rush.

As I'd discovered the day before, one advantage of the flat terrain in this area was the ability to use church towers as a beacon and a guide, and New Romney's proved just as effective as Newchurch's. That and the sewers brought me to my final field and signs of a lot of new housing being erected on the outskirts of the town, something Phillipa and Sue had commented on, and not in a positive way. My view was we have to build somewhere, and this looked as good a spot as anywhere. There was no sign of the promised diversion, and as I went through a gap in my final hedge I emerged onto the road. A sign announcing New Romney greeted me. This was it. A place that for months had existed only in theory now suddenly become a reality.

I walked down a residential road, which in turn led to the busier main road linking Romney with Hythe, although as it turned out, it wasn't the only transport artery with that claim. The road took me past a large Sainsbury's and into town, where I met up again with Annette for a spot of lunch. It felt appropriate to pause and take breath (as well as a coffee and a panini) before the final, final push.

New Romney is something of an oddity. If I'd been doing the walk eight hundred years before (unlikely, granted), I would have already reached my end point. A series of storms through the thirteenth century, culminating in the 'Great Storm' of 1287, led to such flooding that whole swathes of the south coast of England were effectively re-drawn – an

Ordnance Surveyor's nightmare. The towns most affected were Rye and New Romney. At the latter, the River Rother silted up completely, landlocking what had been a thriving port town. The storm deposited so much silt that even today buildings that existed before it have steps up to the modern land level. Unfortunately we missed the best example of this in the local church where, apparently, you can see evidence of the flood on the pillars inside. We went into the church, but got diverted by an art exhibition inside, and forgot to look.

New Romney is also one of the Cinque Ports. This is a loose confederation that traces its origins back to a Royal Charter of 1155. Through this, five towns on the south coast (the others are Hastings, Dover, Sandwich and nearby Hythe) were granted exemptions on various taxes (as well as gaining the income from collecting certain dues), all in return for maintaining a standing fleet against possible attack from nasty foreigners. Of course, the Great Storm of 1287 made New Romney's participation in this obligation a bit tricky, but the designation continues to have some resonance to the present day.

After a brief tour of the town, there was nothing for it but to take the long straight road into Littlestone, where the sea now meets the land. Initially, Annette set off with me, but when it became clear that the road was very long and very straight, we agreed a better plan was for her to fetch the car and meet me there, otherwise we'd be walking it both there and back. We were both comfortable with this decision. Annette was carrying a dodgy knee and I quite liked the idea of finishing the walk as I'd spent the vast majority of it: alone with my thoughts and the sound of my own footsteps.

My eyes were immediately taken by the sight of the immense Marsh Academy, a school with a sign proclaiming that it is 'Where Learning Comes First'. I tried to imagine the meeting where this slogan was devised. A few men (and they probably were men) gathered around a table. One of them decides to throw an idea into the ring, probably with a half-smile, just to get things moving. The others look at him as if he's a genius and the chairman announces 'Smashed it! Pub anyone?' Next door was the Marsh Leisure Centre, where presumably leisure comes first.

Other than the sound of seagulls overhead, there was no obvious sign that I was getting closer to the coast. In fact, the air was rent by another sound, that of a steam engine. I was passing a station on the miniature Romney, Hythe and Dymchurch Railway, linking these three towns along a 13½-mile track which provided the alternative transport option to Hythe. A fabulously eccentric, and entirely appropriately English, occurrence on the final mile of the walk, this line uses brightly coloured Thomas the Tank Engine style one-third full-size steam engine locomotives along this section of the Kent coast. Over the years it has been requisitioned by the army (they even built their own miniature armoured train), re-opened after the war by Laurel and Hardy, used to ferry schoolchildren to and from their place of learning and, after a series of owners, was adopted by the building magnate Sir William McAlpine. Now, perhaps inevitably, it is mainly a tourist attraction.

After the station, a small gap appeared at the end of the road: the coast. There were echoes of Formby when I got there and crossed the road to look out over the sea. Grand houses, a sense of tidiness and a long, wide beach. It differed from Formby in having no asparagus and, instead of pristine sand, the view here was one of pebbles, miles and miles of unremitting pebbles. These stretched to the stumpy twin towers of the Dungeness nuclear power station to the right (the south), and the white cliffs that marked Dover, the only one of the Cinque Ports that can realistically still call itself a port, to the left.

This wasn't actually New Romney, but Littlestone-on-Sea, a companion, naturally enough, to Greatstone-on-Sea. One theory for the names is that the entrance to the old New Romney harbour, reached via the River Rother, was always tricky to navigate. To make things easier two rocks, one larger than the other, were placed at either side of it. An alternative theory suggests that the effects of longshore drift mean that larger stones are deposited at one end of the beach, with smaller rocks found at the Littlestone end. From where I was standing it just looked like a long line of pebbles, too numerous to count.

I met up with Annette and we started to make our way north. A flock of white seagulls sat resting on one particular spot of the beach and took flight as we approached them. A few brave souls, young children and teenagers, were in the sea. Although the sun was shining, the sky was blue and the temperature was in the low twenties, from the expressions of the bathers the sea retained an ability to shock the system. Pockets of sea kale added a splash of green to the various hues of white and brown provided by the pebbles.

My target was marked on the map as a 'Tower', which sat conveniently exactly where my biro-drawn diagonal line hit the sea. A Victorian water tower, built in 1890 of red brick, with mock windows and a crenelated top, it was an appropriate landmark: quirky, privately owned (or so it appeared), revelling in its history and, to our eyes at least, decidedly in need of some TLC from the third floor up, despite looking very impressive from a distance. At least it wasn't leaning like the tower at Newchurch. Not yet, anyway. People were still living in it, and good luck to them, I wouldn't fancy living in something that might crumble around you at any moment. I wondered how they got it insured? Maybe they didn't. Also distinctly English was the small shed at its south-east corner, which needed a fresh lick of paint.

Climbing over the sea wall, I crunched onto the beach. After 932,000 steps, around 410 miles, 39 days walking, a herd of aggressive cows, a flock of clever sheep, numerous encounters and a lot of lost sweat, it was time to bring the walk to a close. Annette took some photos and I recorded some thoughts for a podcast, but the end needed to be marked somehow.

I remembered the start of the walk, when I'd decided against carrying a plastic bag of sand from one coast to the other, resolving to create my own traditions. Back then, I'd decided against carrying a pebble from Formby all the way to here, but in reality I had been carrying one for a good half of the journey, the painted one with 'Wokingham

Rocks' on it. I didn't just want to leave it where it would get lost amongst the ocean of pebbles on the beach. Instead I wanted the sea to take it, to move it, send it on a journey, allowing it to land where it saw fit. Maybe, in time someone else would find it. I hoped so, and that they'd pick it up and take it on their own journey.

But *Diagonal Walking* had always been about more than just the hike from one coast to another through the centre of England. It was also a journey of discovery, to test the state of the nation, or at least to arrive at some kind of understanding of it, and my conclusions on this will end this book. For now, all that remained was to take a short run-up and toss my painted rock into the sea, which I did as Annette looked on, filming the final moments with my phone.

A signpost where the Littlestone Road from New Romney meets the coast points towards various landmarks: the town centre, the miniature railway, Dungeness Lighthouse, the toilets. It also has one arm pointing out towards Romney's twin town of Ardres in France, its arrow pointing out over the sea to the horizon.

Ardres, like the rest of Europe, wasn't going to go away; and similarly, I sensed that the puzzle that was Brexit would retain its power to confuse for some time yet. The problems and challenges it represented weren't going to go away either, but neither were the opportunities. The only option remaining to me and my journey was to plunge in – not into the sea, but back into England.

So I turned my back on the waves and began walking once more, immersing myself again into the country, my country, and the future, whatever that might look like.

Afterword

It was always my intention that *Diagonal Walking* should be more than just another book about an old bloke on a long walk. Sometimes I referred to it as a 'project'. Another word that buzzed through my head was 'brand', the idea of creating something people could buy into, feel part of. Central to this was the concept of 'Walk With Me', through which I tried to get people to join in the journey – to follow and feel part of it, either in person or, more likely, through the various virtual channels I set up.

The model I had in mind when I started was crowdfunding, except instead of asking people to invest cash, I wanted them to invest their interest. Recognising people have different preferences as to how they engage online, this meant covering all the main bases. As such, as well as the usual social media suspects of Twitter, Facebook and Instagram, I also taught myself how to make and upload podcasts and videos. All these were designed to complement, and be channelled through, a website (www.diagonalwalking.co.uk), which also featured regular blogs.

Another of the ways the trek was more than just a walk was a commitment to share some insights into the whole process of preparing, writing and publishing a book. I wanted to lift the lid on the dark arts involved in getting your words into print, by giving a frank and honest account of my experience. I hoped this would be interesting and helpful to others.

The whole enterprise wasn't entirely selfless. The trek was going to take place during my sixtieth year on this planet, and I wanted to mark that in some way. Whilst some might see this milestone as an opportunity to consolidate, I saw it as an opportunity for fresh challenges, to learn new skills and stretch myself. How would I cope with the walk, both physically and mentally? Was it even possible to follow a fairly random line just by using public footpaths and rights of way, especially when I'd set a self-imposed corridor of two to three miles on either side of that line?

To summarise: *Diagonal Walking* was always intended to be multi-faceted. It didn't have one purpose, it had many: tangible and intangible, practical and psychological. Perhaps the biggest challenge of all, though, was to try to gain some insight into the 'state of the nation' as it got to grips with what it had done by voting to leave the European Union two years previously. That decision was still red-raw when I set out, and it remained a running sore throughout.

It was a sore reluctant to heal through the slightly surreal summer of 2018, one marked by extremes both of weather and politics unseen for at least forty years. For all of my adult lifetime in other words. When it came to the political situation, there were times during that summer when matters looked like they might be coming to a head, only for that sense to evaporate instantly, like water dropped onto hot concrete.

All matters Brexit-related remained up in the air throughout my time on the road. At no point did I feel a sense of closure, of shaking hands and agreeing to disagree. Rather, there was continued confusion, frustration, sometimes even anger. By and large, however, these simmered below the surface, reserved for the big stage, while ordinary people got on with the business of living their lives. When it came to the practicalities of implementing the referendum decision the gap preventing closure appeared, if anything, to widen, as if we were all watching a cliff-hanger TV thriller with an unknown number of episodes. The forces driving the decision itself, though, remained much the same – hard to put a finger on, but definitely out there somewhere. The thoughts I'm about to share therefore, should be read in the context of that summer, of 'just before' what happened next, knowledge of which, dear reader, you have the privilege of knowing and I can only speculate on.

Before sharing my conclusions, there's one more thing to clear up. Minutes after finishing the walk, Annette interviewed me for a podcast. As we sat on the sea wall overlooking the English Channel staring towards a distant and perhaps suitably hidden France, one of the questions she asked me was whether there might be a *Diagonal Walking II*. Whilst acknowledging the possibility (the north-east to south-west route is kind of asking to be done), I reflected that in many ways *Diagonal Walking* was itself a follow-up to *Walking on Water*. Written on the eve of the Millennium, that book had shared the grand aim of trying to understand what made England tick. The final angle therefore, was to identify how England had changed in the first two decades of the twenty-first century.

Add all those together and you have quite an ambitious list, one probably best tackled in the same order I've set it out, so I'll start with an assessment of the success of the 'Walk With Me' idea.

My response here is a bit like the one given by the Chinese Premier Zhou Enlai (not, as is often thought, Mao Zedong) when asked if it was possible to judge the impact of the French Revolution, namely that it's too early to tell. The multiple platforms I created to communicate *Diagonal Walking* remain very much live. The completion of the walk itself was just the end of a phase of 'the project'. This book represents the next phase, and promoting it the one after that, all of which will involve further use of those channels. Early followers (and you may have been one of them) were simply founding members of the club, the early investors if you like.

I do, however, have some initial observations on my engagement in the world of social media. By far and away my most engaging account during the walk was Instagram, where I was able to gain more than 1,000 followers over the summer. Twitter was reasonably successful, whilst Facebook gained followers later on in the party, just as the slower music came on. Numbers are only one measure though, and one of the unexpected bonuses of using social media turned out to be virtual interaction whilst out on the walk, such as asking followers questions or setting occasional quizzes. There was also the occasional unsolicited praise, comment on a photo or note of encouragement, all of them gratefully received as temporary relief from the loneliness of the long-distance walker.

The podcasts and videos were fairly consistent throughout, attracting a small but dedicated band of followers, whilst the blogs and other traffic through the website underwent a steady but upward curve. It's possible that the balance of power among these different media will change as the project goes into its subsequent phases – hence the 'too early to tell' comment.

Another component of 'Walk With Me' was inviting others to accompany me in person. Around a dozen people did so, many of them friends and family, although not exclusively so. People's willingness, even eagerness, to get involved, was a genuine surprise and unexpected bonus. Countless others, previously strangers, also shared in the pleasures of a chat, the physical process of a shared walk loosening both tongues and social inhibitions, even if for only a few hundred yards or a couple of minutes, resulting in literally hundreds of 'encounters' along the way. I also managed to generate some press coverage of the walk, both in traditional print media and digitally, including online articles and even an interview on an internet radio station.

A final aim of 'Walk With Me' was to engage with third parties capable of acting as a portal to audiences who might be interested in what I was doing. Early on, I took the decision not to get sponsorship or commercial tie-ins as I wanted to keep the experience 'pure'. Whilst this did limit my scope for third-party engagement, I was able to forge informal alliances with other walking groups and media, as well as a link with a national initiative to get more people to stay in pubs (www.stayinapub.co.uk). The latter included the running of an online competition to win a copy of *Walking on Water*, and provided a welcome early bump to my Twitter following.

All things told, with hindsight I believe this level of engagement was reasonable, a seven out of ten, falling just shy of the possibly unrealistic expectations held at the outset. There are reasons for this. Foremost of these was the sheer time I found it took to engage people on social media. As the walk progressed, I was often reminded of the comment from the boxer I met early on in Hale, who said that he and his pugilist friends spent as much time developing their brand on social media as they did training. Even at that early stage, I could empathise, as I found myself spending an hour or two every evening after a long day's walking, fiddling with my iPad trying to stir the social media nest into action.

As time went on I found myself questioning whether this was something I was willing to do. I enjoyed certain aspects of the different channels, such as the videos, podcasts and sharing photos on Instagram, and I also enjoyed writing the occasional frank blog. But it all took time – time I was struggling to find. I was on my own with this; it was my project; there was no back office doing the planning, booking and updating; it was all me. And, of course, I was also the one doing the actual walking, note-taking and writing. The process became all-encompassing. I had to prioritise.

On top of this, there were two other external constraints beyond my control. The first was the weather. When I started planning the project we were still in the grip of one of the worst winters for years. What I couldn't have known was that we were about to have one of the hottest, some claim *the* hottest, summer on record. This meant tempering my walking to the conditions, planning shorter days, longer rest breaks and more days out, all of which had an impact on the time available for other things. Yes, you can sit and tweet at the same time, but when your body is screaming out for a break, sometimes you just want to rest your brain as well as your legs.

The second constraint was making sure I was in a position to release this book into the world whilst it was still relevant. Given the 'eve of Brexit' angle, I did not want to produce a book that was out of date the moment it arrived. I consoled myself with the fact that the planned Brexit Day of 29 March was mostly symbolic, with a transition period to follow. Then talk of a 'No Deal', crashing out of the Union, escalated during my walk, spooking me a little. Whatever happened, I was convinced I needed a book in my hand by early summer 2019.

A trade-off was required, between taking longer over the walk and slowly building more followers, something that was probably possible, but would be fairly laborious; or focussing on getting the walk finished (in the sunshine!) and the book written, ideally by late autumn 2018. I chose the latter. This decision was aided by the growing impression as the walk progressed that a lot of my potential audience weren't necessarily big social media users anyway. Many of the people I met during my 'encounters' were clearly interested in what I was doing, and were probably also book readers; but when offered a card detailing my website and social media addresses they looked at me as if I'd just handed them something laced with Novichok. To them, the World Wide Web was strictly for Amazon and email; Facebook, YouTube and, heaven forfend, Twitter, were for younger folk.

Then there was the issue of actually getting the book published. My initial instinct was to self-publish the book on the basis that this would give me more control, and allow me to manage its timing. As time went on, I wondered whether there might be potential to go through a publisher after all. The burden of being responsible for every aspect of the project had become a heavy one, and the prospect of offloading the actual publishing to the experts became an increasingly enticing one. Unfortunately, the traditional publishing world moves with the speed of a knackered sloth. A manuscript couldn't be considered until it was finished, and then they wanted months to consider it. As time went on, it became clear that the traditional publishing route just wasn't going to work. That my initial instinct had been right. Time spent finding this out wasn't wasted, but it was time that could have been spent on other things.

All of which brings me on to comfort zones, and whether the project allowed me to stretch mine. If conclusions around the success of 'Walk With Me' are fuzzy, those around this aspect of the project are clearer. *Diagonal Walking* allowed me to learn new skills, particularly digital ones, and gave me a deeper insight into how social media work. Take podcasts as an example. I'd initially seen these as a series of recordings of my thoughts and updates on the walk, a sort of audio-blog. It took my son Ed to point out that podcasts really needed at least two voices, to give the listener a sense that they are eavesdropping on a conversation, not a monologue. This was valuable advice, and resulted in me recording discussions (with the participants' permission) on the road, podcasts I labelled 'Diagonal Walkers'. These remain available on iTunes and offer an extra dimension to the words in this book.[20]

Given these observations on social media, was learning more about how it works a good thing? I believe it was. Interaction across the internet, in whatever form it takes, or will take in the future, is here to stay. Having an appreciation of how to participate in that conversation is one way to avoid isolating yourself from how opinions and attitudes are formed. If you don't know what (and how) others are thinking, and choose not to become involved in helping to form it, then the over-riding temptation is to fall back into established positions, which then become entrenched.

---

20 Search 'Diagonal Walking' on iTunes or download direct from www.podomatic.com.

Care is, of course, required. Over-reliance on social media can encourage polarisation, a world where only the loudest or most extreme are heard. Equally, the difference between 'the buzz', or zeitgeist, and simple 'noise' is a fine one. There is a growing body of evidence that social media can also entrench views. People with certain views follow people with the same views, which then become self-reinforcing – the 'echo chamber' theory. But isn't this what newspapers did when they were the main vehicle for transmitting news (and to a lesser extent, still do)? Ignoring social media in the twenty-first century is akin to refusing to learn how to read in the twentieth century. It's important to know how to engage. Handle with care, but don't ignore altogether.

Being an active participant in debate has never been easier – if you know how. My experience of becoming involved with social media has led me to the belief that these skills will only become more important as the limitations of the way we still conduct democracy become more apparent. Forget the twentieth or twenty-first century, our political system seems stuck in the nineteenth century. It is inevitable, in my view, that wider, digitally based, mechanisms will be used to help arrive at a sense of the collective will in the future. Not the only mechanism, but part of the mix. We are already seeing signs of this, albeit on a facile level, with a US President who interacts mainly through Twitter, where once his predecessors may have used TV broadcasts or radio fireside chats. If you are unhappy with the consequences of the policy and decisions that result, and choose to distance yourself from these new media, perhaps you are abdicating one of your responsibilities as a citizen? Social media are a work in progress. Soon, we'll probably regard Twitter and their like as quaint, but make no mistake, they'll be replaced by something else.

We are living in a transitional time when it comes to digital dialogue, but those who opted out of its early days will find it harder to join in later, when it's more developed. Opting out also leaves the field open to others, possibly with agendas we disagree with. Social media lends itself to rapid view-shaping, a gift to populists. We all need to be vigilant, and we all need to participate.

Widening the lens out from social media, impressions gained during my walk helped crystallise a view that the coming generation is much more used to ('comfortable with' might be pushing it) living in a complex multi-dimensional, and, critically, value-driven world. This is a world of 'liking' and 'sharing' rather than polarised, binary, distinctions. Even something as basic as gender, where for most of humankind the orthodoxy has been binary, they see as fluid. Their world is not one of left/right, black/white, Leave/Remain. To them, this is an antiquated way of looking at things. When they watch the generations above them operating like this they do so with growing distain or frustration. This cannot be a healthy thing.

Enough on social media. It's fair to say that the planning and execution of the walk itself, and the writing of this book, although challenging, used skills I already had. This is not to boast, simply a reflection of my life experiences so far. The greater challenge for me was more personal than practical. A natural introvert, with some learned extrovert skills (in other words, I am reasonably good at presenting a more sociable side of myself to the world), engaging with others and actively listening to what they have to say, involves an effort for me.

As such, the need to interact with others on the *Diagonal Walking* trail, to throw myself into crowded situations, and especially the need to proactively initiate contact so I could gain an appreciation of others' thoughts, was, at times, tough. The book starts with a missed opportunity to initiate such an exchange, and it wasn't an isolated incident. Many times, I'd walk away from a potential encounter annoyed with myself for letting the opportunity slip. I got better at it, and in that sense it got easier, but it was never easy.

Using Airbnbs helped. They proved an excellent way to meet and chat with people in their own homes, where they were going to feel most comfortable, and I used them whenever practicable. Incidentally, this new accommodation option is an excellent example of something that new technology and different values have made possible. This Baby Boomer was astounded by the levels of trust Airbnb owners vested in their clients: the leaving of keys under a mat and, in one instance, a single woman leaving her whole house to a stranger for the weekend.

A consideration of my various hosts gives a good indication of the cross-section of the sorts of people I was able to interact with in this way. They included people who were self-employed, working in the public services, working for corporations or retired. One was a working-from-home bookkeeper, another an HR manager for a large retailer. One ran a cattery, whilst another had just gone self-employed as an art procurer (it's complicated). I also stayed with a retired teacher and an actress, and a man living on his own who was a Housing Support Worker for people with learning disabilities. Taken together, these provided a useful contribution to the cross-section of the population I wanted to engage with. On top of these, there were traditional B&B hosts and their helpers, as well as hotel receptionists, all of whom were happy to engage with the mad man with a large blue rucksack and a few pints of sweat ingrained into his T-shirt.

This leads me on to another reflection: how happy people were generally to talk, share their thoughts and have a conversation, although with the caveat that I usually needed to make the first move. Whether this is a particularly English thing, or just part of the human condition, I can't say. As the walk went on, I appreciated these discussions more and more, and having them was a highlight of the whole experience. Furthermore, the people I met were almost universally polite, open and friendly.

Challenge can be positive, or it can be the opposite. On a handful of occasions during the walk the voice in my head started shouting: 'You're in trouble here, matey-boy.' These were the occasions when the adrenaline kicked in. One of these involved angry cows, another when I became irreparably lost. One took place on the wide-open Wanstead Flats in East London when I thought I was about to be attacked, and yet another when a probably irrational, but nevertheless very real, fear took hold of me down a quiet tree-lined track in Kent. But these only constituted a handful of occasions, which wasn't bad going for a walk of thirty-nine days.

The physical challenge posed by the walk came as a surprise. I was expecting it to be greater. I do not regard myself as particularly fit, but prior to the walk I went to the gym and asked the track-suited custodian to prepare a programme for me to set me up for the walk. I admit here that I largely ignored it, opting instead to build up muscle in my legs via the treadmill (where I was also able to watch daytime TV with a clear conscience).

The walk was tiring, of course it was, and the opportunity to flop on the bed for a couple of hours to write up notes and fiddle with social media was always welcome at the end of a day. But … the physical challenge was within my comfort zone. There were occasions when I would think to myself, 'Why are you doing this?', but there was only one answer to this question: 'Because you asked to, you idiot.' Thankfully, there were no sprained ankles or broken bones. The 'In Case Of Emergency' contact card in my wallet was never needed. I did have a bit of a blister problem early on, but I solved this with some double layer socks I bought in Liverpool, something I can heartily recommend, by the way. Blisters became only an occasional irritant afterwards.

On the subject of running sores, it's finally time to move onto the loftier ideal of the project: the attempt to gain a deeper understanding of what makes England tick, and to see if it was possible to gain a deeper understanding of the forces behind the Brexit vote in 2016. All through the summer of 2018, the news media was preoccupied with the negotiations, providing moments ranging from high political drama to the definitive Whitehall farce along the way. However, while the news media may have been preoccupied with these details, it was my experience that the general public were not. Not once during my walk, did I have a detailed, informed, debate with anyone about the pros and cons of the decision – despite making it clear I was open to one.

To this extent, my views were not challenged from outside; I had to challenge them from within. I make no apologies for stating my position as someone who believes that our future should be as part of the European Union. I understand why it might be disliked and used as a scapegoat for wider concerns, and I equally understand that it is far from perfect – but what, or who, is? At the same time, a decision had been made and I wanted to understand what had been behind it. I wanted to engage with the mood of the country, rather than become enraged by it.

At the same time, as I've already mentioned, *Diagonal Walking* was a sort of follow-up to my first book, and I wanted to get an appreciation of how the country had changed over the past nearly twenty years. It seemed to me that these two things might be connected.

First, though, some riders. This was my walk and my experience, seen through my eyes and the prisms of my upbringing, biases and prejudices. There's an infinite variety of possible permutations of this walk. Anyone doing it, at any time, in any weather conditions, would experience a different version of it. My conclusions therefore are mine and mine alone, shared here for interest. I am just an ordinary white, middle-class, fairly privileged bloke; not a professional journalist or social commentator. I started out as confused as everyone else. This element of my journey was an attempt to rationalise that confusion. There was plenty of opportunity to do this – to think, as I walked along, largely alone, through this wonderful country of ours. I found it helpful, allowing my thoughts to brew and ferment a bit, as you'll find out shortly. Maybe good old-fashioned thinking, and finding time for it, is something we could all do with more of.

Equally, my methodology was far from scientific. Although notionally based on the concept of a 'diagonal slice', a term even market researchers used only for a short while, this was only ever a pretext for the walk. In other words, and this should really go without saying but I'll say it anyway, mine was not a representative cross-section of the population, and the evidence I collected was entirely qualitative.

Let's start at the highest level. As well as open and honest people, I saw a country with some glorious countryside sandwiched between two contrasting, magnificent coasts. I saw random acts of kindness and people besotted by their dogs. I also saw a country that wanted to pull together, as it did for a few brief weeks during the Football World Cup, a sense magnified by the countrywide heatwave which meant we were all wallowing or suffering equally. I saw people who apologised when they bumped into you, even if it wasn't their fault (especially if it wasn't their fault), and I saw a wide variety of cities, towns, villages and hamlets, each existing as their own unique communities. I saw millions of individual planets all caught in their own orbits, lives spinning round on trajectories that would continue come what may, possibly altered, but still orbiting. From this perspective, it was easy to see why so many people saw Brexit in the abstract, as something that wouldn't affect them directly, so could we all just stop going on about it and just get on with it?

All along my walk there was a slight frisson whenever the subject of Brexit came up. It was somehow impolite, almost awkward, to talk about and share thoughts on the subject, and there are few things the English hate more than being impolite, although they do awkward rather well. Not once did I see any graffiti about Brexit. Nor did I see evidence of any popular movement for or against it (with the exception towards the end of the summer when a well-financed group started a campaign for a 'People's Vote'). No public meetings, no demonstrations. Brexit was the topic that barely dared speak its name.

On more than one occasion, when I asked permission to record someone for a podcast, they agreed, so long as I didn't raise Brexit. When I agreed but enquired off-mike about their reluctance, the response was typically that they didn't feel able to be articulate on the subject. At best, those who declared themselves as Leavers would express sentiments such as 'I just don't like the idea of being told what we can do in our own country' or 'I don't think it will be as bad as people make out'. When I was able to press for more, I was also struck by the level of passion, almost visceral at times, with which these views were held. Sovereignty was seen as absolute as basic human rights.

Those in the Remain camp spoke less from the heart and more from the head, of customs unions and single markets, despite the fact that probably less than five per cent of the population know the difference between the two. Less passionate, but equally committed; driven more by a sense of justice and logic, the Remain side of the argument remained convinced that facts would win the day. Few seemed to realise the debate wasn't about theory and numbers, in fact the more they were used, the more they lost their resonance.

We were all confused, and didn't know why. What was going on? There didn't seem to be a single reason, so maybe it was a combination of reasons.

Yes, there was probably a section of the population that disliked the EU and all its devilry. One of my Airbnb hosts declared herself to be a libertarian, in favour of stripping out layers of government wherever possible. Others linked the EU directly to the demise of particular industries. Still others professed a dislike of having their lives governed from afar, a sentiment often combined with a contempt for 'faceless bureaucrats'. These were often ideological objections, not always rooted in facts (the total number of civil servants working for the whole of the EU is a tenth of that for the UK government alone[21]), but that wasn't the point. These were perceptions, and ones with roots as stubborn as an old tree. There had to be more to it than that.

---

21   Source: BBC. See: https://www.bbc.co.uk/news/uk-politics-eu-referendum-36325311

Then there was the elephant in the room. The element everyone knows was part of the mix, but was the ugly secret rarely acknowledged in public. I'm talking about good old-fashioned xenophobia and, at the outer extreme, outright racism; often dressed up as patriotism. Let me state categorically that I'm not saying all Leavers are racists, but equally I don't doubt that a proportion exist on the racist scale – they usually give themselves away once they become comfortable in your presence. It would be doing the debate a disservice not to acknowledge that a section of the voting population exists which simply doesn't like foreigners, however these are defined.

It was my impression, gathered during the walk, that this, at best discomfort with, at worst antagonism towards foreigners, has become subtler than what might be termed more traditional racism. I saw very little evidence of hatred towards people of colour on my travels. What I did see, or more accurately, hear, however, were accents from Eastern Europe wherever I went. They could be heard on the streets, in shops and hotels and amongst Deliveroo guys. They could be seen in the proliferation of 'International' shops. In many people's minds they were over-busy, over-visible, over-audible – and over here!

These outward signs of immigration are significant. Research[22] has shown that people across the world tend to overestimate the degree of immigration into their country.

---

22 Source: Quoted in 'The Perils of Perception' by Bobby Duffy (Atlantic Books, 2018) using data compiled by Ipsos. See www. perils.ipsos.com for more.

For example when asked what proportion of the UK population they think are immigrants, the average guess is 25 per cent: roughly double the true figure. Furthermore, the average guess at the proportion of immigrants who are refugees or asylum seekers is about a third, when the true figure is actually a tenth.

This links back to the heart vs. head debate alluded to already, and to an established theory, charmingly called the 'backfire effect', which suggest that when people hold a view particularly strongly, facts contrary to that view can serve to entrench those views. People find alternative rationales for the supposed facts, doubting their veracity (for example 'immigrant figures don't count those entering illegally') or saying the figures don't match their experience. This is why high levels of visibility are so significant. Anyway, all news is fake, right?

Figures from the Office of National Statistics[23] show that there are around 1.4 million residents of the UK originally from Eastern Europe. The largest proportion (two thirds) come from Poland and the next largest group from Lithuania, with Bulgarians and Romanians and others also in the mix. This influx, combined with the speed it happened, seems to have generated a fear of losing control, a form of xenophobia, of distrust, not really racism (because, well, they're white aren't they?), which it has been hard for people to process, feeding the sense that 'proper' English people were losing control over their own country.

---

23 Source: Office for National Statistics, covered in *The Guardian* here: https://www.theguardian.com/world/2017/jul/10/majority-of-britain-eastern-european-residents-are-in-work

This fear has been rationalised into a legitimate and reasonable grievance that these immigrants are coming over to this country to claim 'our' benefits, a pool of money that should be the exclusive reserve of 'proper' English people whose taxes have created it. This phenomenon is sometimes labelled 'Nativism'. The fact that 'they' are actually in this country to work hard (80 per cent of these newcomers to our country are in employment[24]), and to do the jobs most 'proper' English people would rather not do, is inconvenient to this thesis and therefore conveniently brushed aside. It also assumes a 'zero sum game' theory of employment, that there is a fixed pool of jobs, a phenomenon that could be labelled 'Trumpism', as it pretty much sums up his view of the world.

Furthermore, research from the government's own expert panel,[25] the Migration Advisory Committee, has highlighted that migrants pay more in taxes than they receive in public services (i.e. not just benefits), £2,300 more a year than the average citizen, in fact. That's a statistic that doesn't get aired enough. This same committee has concluded that migration has little overall effect on levels of unemployment (their efforts create as many jobs as they 'take' from nationals), and very little impact upon wage levels. Additional evidence that this group is the new target of this new form of xenophobia, is the polling data[26] that shows that people from ethnic

---

24 See Note 20.

25 Source: Migration Advisory Committee. See: https://assets. publishing.service.gov.uk/government/uploads/system/uploads/ attachment_data/file/741926/Final_EEA_report.PDF

26 Source: The UK in a Changing Europe. See: http://ukandeu.ac.uk/ minority-ethnic-attitudes-and-the-2016-eu-referendum/

minorities often voted in favour of Brexit in order to keep these new interlopers threatening their traditional territory (running shops, operating taxis, opening restaurants) out of the country!

It is surely no coincidence that the Brexit referendum came at the very moment that annual net migration into the UK peaked, at 300,000.[27] Since the referendum, the total number of workers from the eight eastern European countries that joined the EU in 2004 has fallen by 154,000.[28] It may come as a surprise to many, but in modern times Britain has historically been a net exporter of people. It became a net importer during the 1990s, driven in part by overseas students (as I saw at Keele, these were now a strong feature of most universities, whereas they were a rarity in my day) as well as a strong economy. The wave of immigrants from the east of Europe began after those countries joined the EU. The strange thing here is that the UK, at the time, took an extremely liberal and welcoming attitude towards these new workers, in fact, much more liberal than many of our EU partners.

Equally strangely, the UK chose not to implement[29] all sorts of restrictions on migrants from fellow member states. For example, we extended a similarly open door to people from Croatia after it became a member in 2013, despite

---

27 Source: Migration Advisory Commission
28 Source: The Office for National Statistics, covered on Sky News here: https://news.sky.com/story/unemployment-climbs-while-wage-growth-improves-11553077
29 Source: Harvey Redgrave of The Tony Blair Foundation, quoted in *The Economist* 22 Sept 2018.

provisions which allowed the imposition of limits. Belgium, for example, still operating within EU laws, throws out migrants who don't get a job within six months. Equally, most other members limit access to those precious benefits until they have built up some years'-worth of contributions. In other words, if people coming into the UK from other EU states was such a problem, it could be addressed without leaving the EU.

This suggests a couple of things. First, a general ignorance of, or failure to engage with, how the EU works. This seems to highlight a basic problem amongst some when it comes to the EU – a rejection of all its works, whatever the actual facts, bringing to mind Groucho Marx's famous comment that he wouldn't want to belong to any club that would have him as a member. Why would the UK need the EU when its sovereign is head of the Commonwealth (and apparently will remain so after the Queen's death, as she recently made clear)? Why does the UK need the EU when, after all, dammit, it won a world war on its own (er …)? The UK has always felt like a reluctant member of the EU, like someone who agrees to come to a party but refuses to participate in any games, preferring instead to grumble about having to bring a bottle and to complain about the noise. It also adds to the suggestion that the referendum result wasn't driven by information, but by sentiment. This resistance to facts on the part of those preferring to leave the EU (fuelled by advice to ignore experts), and over-reliance by those preferring to remain on what they regard, rightly or wrongly, as incontrovertible truths, remained a feature of the whole Brexit debate throughout my summer walk.

Brexit has been called a class war that the middle class lost. There may be some truth in this, but I suggest it's a mistake to see it in purely class terms. The so-called 'elite' lost to a coalition whose bedrock was formed of the dispossessed and concerned working classes, for whom the EU acted as a convenient scapegoat for, well, just about everything. On top of them were a right-leaning upper-class elite safe in the knowledge that their wealth would insulate them from the economic damage of Brexit. Indeed, many of this latter group may well profit from the deregulation and general free-for-all that will follow from the jettisoning of all that dull, but often boringly necessary, stuff emanating from Brussels. Add to them, those harbouring ideological objections to EU (such as my libertarian Airbnb host, or those who fear a European superstate), and throw in the many who had equally strong psychological objections to foreigners telling us what we could and couldn't do, and you just about scraped a majority. Furthermore, you have a complex coalition, hard to pin down and categorise.

When I wrote *Walking on Water*, I saw a country at the beginning of a technological revolution. Nearly two decades later, I saw plenty of evidence of a country trying to cope with the consequences of that revolution, now in full swing and probably still with some way to go. This was exciting, but also troubling. Jobs had been lost, old industries had disappeared, high streets had been decimated. The landscape had become dotted with faceless metal boxes operating as distribution centres, offering a fraction of the jobs the old factories used to provide.

Industrial change has always been with us. I passed through many a town which defined itself in pre-industrial times through a single product: shoes, flat caps, brewing, vellum, straw hats ... but no longer. This process continued into more modern times, with other towns, Stoke with its potteries, Dagenham and Luton with its cars, suffering similar fates. With the loss of these industries went a loss of identity, of purpose, replaced by people employed in a diversity of ways, not all of them obvious, visible or tangible, and certainly not in a way that brought them together in a common cause. The sense of disconnect brought about by these changes is not a revelation, but it would be foolish not to recognise it as a reality.

The demise of the high street is a particularly visible sign of change, and one that adds further to the loss of community. This is directly attributable to technological change in the form of internet shopping, and represents a distinctive and fundamental change from the England I travelled through in 1999. If high streets offer a place for communities to gather, then we're in trouble, because they're struggling big time. Restaurants have been replaced by fast food joints, as people either can't afford to eat out, or prefer to retreat to their castle to do so, at the same time missing out on the communal benefits of preparing and sharing a meal together. Delivery services like Deliveroo, which already employs 15,000 riders, are also becoming more popular, as I saw on my walk. During 2017, the home-delivery market rose by 11 per cent[30] at a time when mid-range restaurant chains were suffering. Ironmongers, bakers and dry-cleaning outlets have been replaced by nail bars, tattoo parlours and tanning salons – the useful, in other words, by the vain and mindless.

A number of previous staples of the high street went to the wall or suffered near-death experiences during my walk, including national chains serving both the top end of the market such as House of Fraser; the very bottom, such as Poundland; and the middle, such as Toys R Us. What might be labelled experience shopping has migrated into regional centres, Liverpool for example, Lakeside, Bluewater or Maidstone, condemning the smaller centres to a slow death by a thousand store closures.

Luton and Northampton were both extreme examples of this, although the latter also offered some hope. Warned beforehand that it was, I think the phrase used was 'a shithole', I had a fun day there, largely because an attempt had been made to revitalise the town centre through a music festival. The idea of offering a platform for a community to come together and interact as a community, to show some civic pride, was a positive one. One that other towns suffering from the decline of retail, and communities gradually losing their sense of identity, might want to emulate. Northampton was doing something, even though its council was bankrupt. This suggested to me that civic pride has to come from the bottom up, not led by local authorities or driven by a website like Luton's LoveLuton.org.uk.

---

30   Source: The NPD Group, quoted in *The Economist* 17 March 2018.

Imagine what might be possible if there was more local autonomy. My experience in Higham Park suggested that once mechanisms could be found, local people did want to engage at a more micro-level. I found similar initiatives in Churchover outside Rugby with its village hall pub, and in Egerton with its attempt to create a community shop. It's at the local level where the bread and butter issues, the things that affect people every day and make a difference now, are found. Maybe it was time to reconsider the relentless centralisation of power? Not so much I want my country back, as I want my county/city/town/locale back.

Another issue it became impossible to ignore during my walk, and a clear change over the past twenty years, was the problem of homelessness. I came across regular evidence of the high levels of people living on the streets. Of sleeping bags and tents colonising shop doorways almost immediately after shopkeepers closed their doors. An article[31] I read during the walk suggested that in 2018 there were 8,000 rough sleepers on any given night; that's up from 1,800 in 2010.

Again, I'm not offering any particular insight here, the problem is well documented, but what I saw shocked me, and I felt powerless to do anything about it. There were examples of kindly souls trying to help those whose lives had reached this point (step forward Liverpool), but these were

31   No End In Sight: *The Economist* 18 August 2018.

the exception rather than the rule. How a country with the sixth biggest economy in the world (for now) can allow this to happen is damning. At the same time, there's a certain irony that at a time when people seem unduly concerned about migrant refugees across the English Channel, they appear largely indifferent to tents on their own streets.

As it happened, there was a big government policy announcement[32] during my walk with a strategy supposedly designed to eradicate the problem. The issue with this was that by the next day the announcement had become fish and chip paper. There was a sense that the government wasn't being sincere, that it was just paying lip service to the problem. More considered analysis later backed this up. Of the headline £100m in the plan, half was money already allocated to the problem and the rest was money 're-prioritised' from other programmes. Within hours, the headlines were all about Brexit again, and it struck me that the two things weren't unconnected.

Homelessness acts as a very visible reminder of how fragile the modern economy is for many people. Pay growth over the past decade has been at its lowest since Napoleonic times, and is lower than it was a decade ago. People may be in jobs (the country's unemployment rate is impressively low by European standards), but they are low-paying, stagnant jobs, offering little hope of advancement or an increase in pay. For too many, the only way to get more money is to work more hours, but even that route offers only a marginal

---

32   Source: https://www.gov.uk/government/news/new-government-initiative-to-reduce-rough-sleeping

improvement in living standards, with any extra money easily gobbled up by an unexpected bill. For these people, the system isn't working; capitalism is letting them down.

Too many people have lost hope in a brighter future. Having walked through them, it comes as little surprise to me that Stoke, Northampton and Luton voted so decisively for Brexit. They all came across to me as places tottering on the edge of viability, both financially but also, and perhaps more importantly, as entities. The referendum was a perfect chance to deliver a kick in the pants to the politicians who were supposed to be looking out for their interests.

Those same politicians were now preoccupied with a single issue, one which the country had vented its wrath on, but was now largely indifferent about. It was a strange state of affairs. There had been a narrow vote in favour of perhaps the biggest constitutional change to the country for decades, and yet no one really understood it, or was even that exercised over it. But, rather than focus their attention on the underlying reasons behind the vote, to dig deeper to understand and address its roots, the government was completely preoccupied on the symptom, rather than the cause, of the country's unease.

To make matters worse, as the so-called negotiations went on during the summer of 2018, the more it became clear that things weren't as straightforward as they'd been portrayed during the inadequate run-up to the referendum. As a consequence, not only was the government focussing on the wrong thing, it was focussing on something that they must have known it was impossible to deliver in a way that would satisfy even a significant minority of the country.

Instead of showing leadership, which involves standing above the fray, seeing the bigger picture and setting out a case for something, the government came across as obsessed with managing a problem that was unmanageable, and doing even that badly.

By the end of the summer the government was so fixated on delivering Brexit it had ruled out a new Queen's Speech, effectively abdicating from its responsibility to address other national priorities. At a time when the country is facing perhaps its greatest challenge since the end of the last war, it also has its weakest politicians, on all sides, in living memory. The irony here was that that same government was being led by a Prime Minister who had begun her term of office by setting out her stall as the champion of the JAMs – those who were 'just about managing' – when she and her colleagues were showing themselves incapable of managing themselves!

This isn't a party political point, more a comment on a whole political class. The Government was getting away with it because we had an Opposition that was either invertebrate or invisible, shying away from the real issues, often pursuing their own internecine agendas, probably in the knowledge that they couldn't do any better anyway. One argument being posited by politicians was that failure to deliver Brexit would undermine trust in politicians and the political system. This was particularly ironic given the damage they'd inflicted on their own profession over the years, not least through the expenses scandal, and a view they were perpetuating through their collective mishandling of Brexit. This wasn't just undermining the system, it was laying dynamite and pressing the plunger.

Brexit aside for one moment, this lack of leadership was doubly important because the country was facing a series of problems that were fundamental, even existential if failure to address them led to a break-up of the Union – not the European Union, but that between England and the other parts of the UK, notably Scotland and especially Northern Ireland. Politics aside, these problems also presented basic issues of morality, of respect, of fairness, all of which were themselves fuelling dissatisfaction and nurturing the sense of puzzlement I sensed all around me.

Technological change isn't the only challenge we face. Many others have been well documented elsewhere and include demographic shifts, how we organise and pay for health and social care, providing affordable housing, making our education system fit for the twenty-first century and, as I've already hinted, democracy itself. By the latter I mean, how we harness the changing ways people communicate, interact and debate: to create a proper *Demos*, in the Ancient Greek sense of a common political entity, a way for ordinary people to engage with the political process.

It feels like we're living in a country only capable of coming up with analogue responses in a digital, multi-dimensional and increasingly fluid world. Our systems are transactional rather than inspirational. On the one hand we have middle-grade managers rather than leaders, whilst in the real world we have digital masters of the universe laughing into their lattes while they develop incredible influence over our lives. So far, they have exercised this power relatively benignly, but it would be a massive assumption to think that's always going to be the case. At a time when artificial intelligence threatens yet another fresh wave of economic change, we have MPs who have to be told how WhatsApp works.

Amidst all this, it is little wonder if people regard the current democratic process as increasingly irrelevant to them, as politicians jettison their principles in favour of their careers, openly lie in their promises, actually break the law and pretend that policy papers that hold bad news don't exist (until, it turns out, they do). Instead, they 'keep calm and carry on', increasingly indifferent to the fact that their political leaders are flailing around like flags in a storm.

I don't know the answer, but think it's a question worth asking – how do we 'do' democracy in a digital and increasingly diverse age? At a time when nothing is simple (in particular Brexit, as the summer of 2018 demonstrated in spades), a simple majority no longer constitutes a mandate. Delegating decision-making for five years to MPs might have worked when you felt there was some trust or integrity in the system, but these have evaporated like early summer dew.

Our current means of exercising democracy are two-dimensional in a three-dimensional world. People, especially the younger generations, identify in all sorts of different ways, not only by nationhood, but also by sexuality, religion, region, music, ethnicity and so on. Life is complicated, and the way we conduct our *Demos* needs to reflect that. There need to be mechanisms for discussions, rather than shouting matches. Disagreement needs to be respected not vilified. Healthy debate should be something to celebrate, not regarded as a zero-sum game. As I discovered during my walk, perhaps some fresh thinking is required on how our education system encourages critical thinking, rather than a focus on knowledge? Without a different approach, the direction of travel is towards a simplistic, dogmatic form of politics, where a so-called Leader of the Free World regards it as acceptable to communicate using the vocabulary of a primary school child.

Further evidence of the inadequacy of the binary or transactional approach to politics also emerged during the walk in the increased use of ugly language to describe those who held opposing views. This was true both of politicians (Ian Duncan Smith, hang your head in shame) and newspapers. Rather than tolerance, we heard of 'traitors' or of people being told to 'like it or lump it' if they didn't favour Brexit, or even to emigrate! This isn't leadership, it's demagoguery, and use of this language poisons the democratic well, aggregating into nastiness and even violence. These examples need to be called out.

I've already highlighted the much-mooted generational gap, and an increasing awareness of this grew on me during my walk. It's difficult to point at particular evidence for this, other than the tone of the conversations and encounters I had along the way. Some, especially with older people, those whose careers were near an end or had already ended, would speak almost conspiratorially about how things were better in the old days. At a time when the future is a little bit scary, the past can offer a comforting refuge. Maybe it's always been the case that the old feel protective towards the past, which they see as their legacy, but to my subjective ears, it seems to have intensified since I last took the temperature of the nation.

One stark example of the generation gap that frequently came up during my walk was how difficult it was for the young to buy property. This was a concern raised more by their parents than the young themselves, who presumably saw becoming a homeowner as so far out of their expectations it wasn't even worth considering. Houses now cost seven times annual income, compared with three times a generation ago. This represents a significant challenge, one more that has got buried under the Brexit mountain.

To return to our propensity to take comfort in the past, this may, in part, be another response to the pace of technological change and the frightening (to some) prospects it offers, it's impossible to know for sure. England has always revelled in its heritage, and that's not necessarily a bad thing, but harking back to some golden past can be taken to an extreme.

The nearest rival to the summer of 2018 in terms of weather during my lifetime was 1976. During that summer, people stood at standpipes to get water. Forty plus years on, after privatised water companies had provided the investment in infrastructure the government was unable to find, there was only the slightest hint of restrictions. Despite this, the official Opposition's policy was to renationalise the water companies, along with other once-public services. If a return to British Rail is being taken seriously as a viable response to problems with the rail network – a service which has grown exponentially since my last trip through England – then we are definitely in trouble!

The English (at a push, the British) seem to persist in a belief that they have the best of everything in the world. This belief persists whatever evidence is put forward to challenge it. For some, this has produced what psychologists call 'cognitive dissonance': when people feel discomfort when their beliefs and values are challenged and, instead of bending with the evidence, dig their heels in deeper, seeking fresh evidence to shore up their beliefs.

The narrative persists that we have the best health system, the best education system, the best army, the best TV, the most innovative and creative people, the best comedians, the best political system (the 'Mother of all Parliaments'), the best judicial system, wigs and all, and so on. This constant reiteration must surely have helped contribute to the sense that we are capable of standing alone – despite all the evidence showing the world has become an increasingly interconnected and global place.

A refrain heard during my walk was 'we got through the war, we can get through this', suggesting Brexit could be made to work, it might just take a bit of time. Certainly, no one could accuse the Brexit cheerleader Jacob Rees-Mogg of lacking vision when he claimed during the summer that the benefits of Brexit may take fifty years to come through. Not bad when most of his colleagues were struggling to know what would be going on the following Tuesday teatime. Perhaps it's worth remembering his other moniker, that as the Hon Member for the Eighteenth Century. Maybe this was his plan all along. Maybe in his eyes the European

Union was merely a historical aberration concocted after the war, and that the future lay with a return to nation states. Because that had worked out really well, hadn't it?

During my walk, the NHS was celebrating its seventieth anniversary, so let's use our health system to test this hypothesis. Whilst not decrying the efforts of the individuals involved in delivering the service, let's stand above it and look at it as a system, and a tax-funded system at that. Shortly after completing the third leg of my walk, the Prime Minister announced a financial sticking plaster to apply to the existential problems facing the NHS. This figure was actually less than the average increase in funding historically, and still below what had been suggested as necessary just to keep it on track. Not so much a birthday present as an IOU.

This wasted opportunity for a fundamental rethink on how we fund and operate a fit-for-purpose health service was a classic 'old school' response to an ongoing problem. It supposed the only problem facing the NHS is funding, when there are clearly much deeper issues than that. The Prime Minister wasn't the only guilty party here, of course. The Leave campaign's now notorious claim that leaving the EU would free up £350m a week for the NHS was another version of the same problem. Both were examples of binary thinking: Problem? Money!

Those with a more nuanced understanding of our health system might say, 'We have an opportunity to do something really exciting here, to harness technology and gene therapy, to individualise care, to rethink how and where we deliver care and to co-ordinate health and social care.' The NHS, the world's biggest user of fax machines, is in a desperate race to become fit for the times.

What response do they get from politicians? 'Sch, sch, go away, I have more important issues on my mind right now. Can't you see I'm busy? Here's a fiver. Go to the pictures or something.'

Yes, the NHS may need more money, but there's little point in using it to paper over cracks, when what's really needed is investment. Papering over the cracks might be okay if the wall behind was otherwise solid. But, as an independent report for the BBC[33] produced to coincide with the seventieth anniversary concluded, the NHS is a 'below-average performer' compared to other countries' systems when it comes to treating fundamental conditions such as preventing deaths from heart attacks, strokes and cancer. This same report described the NHS as 'a perfectly ordinary service' produced for a 'middling level of cost'. Critically, and this is the point, it suggested that the poor performance was only partially attributable to funding.

So, two lessons. First, the NHS is not the best health system in the world, and to keep pretending it is avoids having a more fundamental discussion; and second, just throwing more money at it isn't necessarily the answer.

Another irony of the Prime Minister's focus on the 'Just About Managing', was that practically all our public services as a whole themselves fall into that category. Northamptonshire on my walk was struggling to pay for the most basic of services. It wasn't alone. Just like the NHS,

---

33   Source: BBC. See: https://www.bbc.co.uk/news/health-44567824

local authorities across the country were struggling. A welfare state designed in the twentieth century was no longer fit for purpose in a deindustrialised, digitised, dispossessed world. As I'd seen on my walk, local government, like the NHS and too many other manifestations of what the state exists to provide (prisons, schools, libraries, even footpaths), was broken.

Two contradictory dialogues seemed to be going on. One set of voices was saying our institutions and public services were the best in the world, whilst another was saying they were third world. To make things worse, these two dialogues often took place in peoples' brains at the same time. No wonder they were confused. Whilst it might be comforting to square this circle by suggesting there was nothing wrong with the institutions, they just needed to be properly funded, deeper analysis suggested this was too simplistic. More sophisticated thinking was required. However, largely because of Brexit, no one had the headspace to engage with the problem, even if we had a system of political discourse capable of doing so.

During the first twenty years of the new millennium, the economy has undergone a fundamental shift, and this became apparent to me during my walk. Wealth creation is concentrated in the hands of a relative few, while those without skills, or whose skills are no longer in demand, have found their incomes stagnate. The economy has been subject to centrifugal forces. The high streets have become magnets for consumption for its own sake (how else to explain the explosion of tattoo parlours?), rather than adding value.

People are being replaced by robots, not just in factories, but in offices and soon even in operating theatres (get used to it). In return, people are being kept busy, often, but not always, just off the breadline. Or they are being given some kind of limited self-worth or status through what a recent book by David Graeber, an anthropologist, succinctly calls 'Bullshit Jobs'.[34] These are jobs that are so pointless that even the employee cannot justify their existence. Many of these are what used to be called 'white collar jobs', and most of them are probably doomed.

This shift can work for us, or against us. Left unattended to, it has the potential to split the nation. In many senses this is already happening. Whilst absolutely not saying everyone who voted for Brexit was stupid, let's take educational attainment as a proxy, not least because these days gaining a degree involves a significant financial investment – a massive barrier if you come from a family relying on food banks (and if you come from one of those families, is it any wonder that you also struggle at school?). The numbers[35] show that 75 per cent of those with no educational qualifications voted for Brexit, whilst a similar proportion of those with university degrees voted to remain.

---

34 David Graeber: Bullshit Jobs. See review in *The Guardian* here: https://www.theguardian.com/books/2018/may/25/bullshit-jobs-a-theory-by-david-graeber-review

35 Source: The BBC. See: https://www.bbc.co.uk/news/uk-politics-38762034

This is a volatile time. The Brexit referendum couldn't have come at a worst moment: an older generation venerating the past, the JAMs looking for a way to vent their frustrations, the elites sensing an opportunity to feather their nest even deeper. Add to the mix the ugly use of posters of Syrian refugees to exploit a wider uneasiness about too many foreigners, and the dark clouds began to gather.

But there was more. A festering sense of resentment against continuing austerity. All too visible evidence to suggest that the line between failing to just about manage and being thrown onto the streets might be a thin one. Public services in ruins. A belief that the young were being left behind. A growing sense of 'us and them' – as befits the times, not just a binary 'rich and poor', but also 'young and old' and not so much 'north and south' but 'London and the rest'. Combine these together and those dark clouds became a perfect storm.

This storm operated in a climate defined by black-and-white thinking, one clouded by powerful slogans that summed up how people felt, but didn't really say anything meaningful. The Remain campaign had no powerful response to either 'I want my country back' or 'Project Fear', the irony of the latter slogan being it was those on the Leave side who were more motivated by fear – fear of what their lives had become or might become, or of outsiders coming in and undermining their already precarious living standards.

Before leaving this subject, a brief word about nationalism. The summer of 2018 was an interesting one on this front. At the beginning of the summer, the English football team jetted off to Russia with barely a fanfare, our low expectations of their chances tucked in the inside pockets of their new M&S suits. By the end of the summer, as they approached the closing stages of the tournament, the St George's flags were out in force: in flower pots, covering up windows, on umbrellas (needed as protection from the sun rather than rain), and even occasionally flying from flagpoles.

Once again, research[36] suggests a generational divide on this issue, with the young less likely to feel pride in being English than the old. That same research highlighted that qualities of humour, tradition and good manners are the characteristics most associated with being English. How terribly reassuring. We are an odd lot at times. If our pride in being English is fickle, it's probably fair to say our pride in being European is almost non-existent. In my conclusion to *Walking on Water* I made the point that you could go to almost any small town in Europe and you'd see the European flag fluttering over public buildings. This wasn't the case in England twenty years ago, and little appeared to have changed in the interim. If anything, it had gone backwards.

By the end of my walk, while I sensed people were more confused than ever about Brexit, it was possible to discern three broad camps. The first of these didn't know what was the right thing to do but just wanted to rip the plaster off.

36   Source: BBC. See: https://www.bbc.co.uk/news/uk-england-44142843

They didn't really understand it, but felt we should just get on with it. Their view seemed to be that we'd survived other crises and we'd survive this one. The second group was comprised of Remainers who felt the battle hadn't been lost yet. They believed the referendum was the result of an unscrupulous and illegal campaign and, driven by a burning sense of natural injustice and logic, felt there should be a second referendum, cunningly disguised as a People's Vote rather than a referendum, to counter those who said we'd had the referendum. Then there was the third group. They believed that a decision had been made, and that it was the right decision. That we should cut our losses and go, deal or no deal, and genuinely felt that the country would be better off on its own, even if it might take a few years for this hypothesis to be proven.

The call for a People's Vote was an interesting one, challenging to those in the Leave camp, as it made their claim to be protecting democracy a fragile one by denying the same thing. That democracy was a one-time thing. Whilst it offered a way of stopping Brexit for those who wanted it stopped, it carried its own issues. To work, the call for it needed to be overwhelming, and any subsequent vote would need to be equally conclusive. A narrow win would not hack it. It looked like a huge gamble, especially when any evidence of a marked shift in views was missing.

Where, after walking amongst the people of England, did I stand on this? I started this walk as an angry Remainer. Not, I stress, a 'remoaner' (another brilliant example of the Leave campaign's facility for pithy slogans; somehow 'Exit from Brexit' isn't in the same league). After all, I had embarked on a 400-plus-mile hike to engage. I was, however, frustrated, not just with the result, but with the process, how it had been handled and the paucity of real debate.

By the end of the walk I had become more reconciled: still in favour of remaining in the EU, more accepting that leaving was probably what was going to happen, but perhaps hoping still for some last-minute Damascene conversion to common sense. Throughout my walk, I came across an England that was resourceful, friendly, diverse, tolerant, resilient. This has given me reassurance that we will muddle through, like we always have done in the past when confronted with crises, whether self-inflicted (as I believe Brexit is) or inflicted upon us. We have always been a stoic lot, but this is going to test us to the max.

History abounds with examples of decisions, economic, political, or driven by global affairs, that many saw as fundamental disasters at the time but eventually became just that, history. The Repeal of the Corn Laws, coming off the Gold Standard, Suez – Brexit is but the latest in a long conveyor belt, only with the added complication of being economic, foreign affairs and political rolled into one. The trajectory of history isn't measured, its messy, as any student of the subject will attest.

Maybe it will all work out for the best? Maybe our countryside will flourish freed from the demands of the Common Agricultural Policy. Maybe our businesses will have to find ways of improving productivity once deprived of cheap foreign labour. Maybe the rest of the world will flock to us to secure trade deals. Maybe I should just learn to 'believe in Britain' (whatever that means). That's a lot of 'maybes'.

Whatever happens, though, there will be a cost, and that cost will come as a shock to those who least expected it. For some it will be tangible: the loss of a job, rising prices, a downturn in the housing market. But at least as significant will be the intangible losses, and these will be harder to identify and quantify. Our standing in the world for one (and yes, isn't that an irony?), lost or never made friendships, the opportunities to understand others, to get the viewpoints of others, to enrich the gene pool of decision-making. To work collaboratively and cooperatively, to give and take. To admit you don't have a monopoly on wisdom. These were driven home to me during my discussion with the Irish businesswoman Siobhán in the car park of our hotel in Toddington. All of these will be impossible to replace, and as a result, we will be the worse off for it. Respect for others will be less strong. Outward foci will be lost. We will stagnate, whilst others integrate. We will lose relevance.

Yes, we will regain an outward sense of national identity, or at least those who wanted it will. Sovereignty, whatever that is worth in an inter-connected world, will be regained. We will 'get our country back'. However, whether the gaining of a blue passport and a (largely illusory) level of control over our borders, and the ability in theory (if less so in practice) to strike trade deals with others to whom we are largely irrelevant and who need our goods less than we need theirs, will be worth it, only history will be able to judge. I think I can make a stab at a verdict, though. Maybe Brexit is something I'm destined never to understand – like tattoos, it is the triumph of the superficial rather than the considered (sorry to go on about tattoos, but seriously?)

If you've got this far in this section, it will come as no surprise to learn that in my opinion the greatest tragedy is that this is happening at a time of unprecedented opportunity. Although it may surprise some readers, when I think back to the question posed on the wall of Liverpool University: 'ARE YOU OPTIMISTIC ABOUT THE FUTURE?', my answer is a resounding 'Yes!'

However, I believe we are better placed to face the challenges of artificial intelligence, social change, an aging population, advances in healthcare, the reordering of society, affordable housing, more productive relationships with the wider world, climate change, international terrorism, migration from Africa, managing the immigration we will continue to need to rebalance our workforce, responding to wider humanitarian crises – as part of a collaborative bloc, however imperfect, rather than as a single country. It is that inestimable opportunity cost I shall grieve over.

By the time you read this, it's possible that the fog will have cleared a little. But it's equally possible that it will have set in for the duration. 'Fog in the Channel – Continent Cut Off'.[37] Maybe it just suddenly lifted, dispersed by an outbreak of common sense. Well, I did say I was an optimist. Maybe the long hot summer of 2018 was the eye of the

---

37 Although often quoted, and sometimes attributed to *The Times*, this well-known headline is almost certainly apocryphal, but it's still fun to use.

storm? Maybe it was the calm before it. Or maybe it turned out talk of a storm was over-exaggerated – those damned weather forecasters again.

Writing at the conclusion of that summer, we seem to be walking a washing line. Not a tightrope, as at least that has some tension, but a wobbly, unstable washing line. Maybe there will have been a second referendum, or People's Vote. It's possible, if still an outside bet at the time of writing. Whatever happens, hard or soft Brexit, no-deal Brexit, Blind Brexit, Botched Brexit, Barking Brexit,[38] second vote, as I type these words it appears that the best we can aspire to is the least-worst outcome. Whatever happens, there will be ill-feeling, broken trust and almost certainly anger. Attention will again divert away from 'what we can do' towards 'what ifs' and 'if onlys'.

There is a theory that sometimes you need a shock, or a series of shocks, to shake you out of a rut, and I believe we are in a rut. The danger of this theory is that no one can predict what form the reaction to that shock might be: it might bring us to our senses, but it might make us lose them, too, and result in us doing something stupid. There is precedent here after all. We have already seen the ugly side of populism, not just in the UK, but in the US, South America, Turkey and elsewhere in Europe. Revolution isn't really very English. On the other hand, it isn't unprecedented.

---

38 Given the tendency towards alliteration when describing leaving the EU, it probably shouldn't have come as a surprise that stickers proclaiming 'Bollox to Brexit' began to appear in public places towards the end of the summer.

To move away from Brexit and conclude with a broader observation, I would say that England is a country that needs to re-contract with itself. To agree both what it wants to be in the wider world, how it wants to organise itself internally as a state, and how it wants to organise and pay for things the individual can't do on their own. Assuming that the way we did things in the past was great – 'if it ain't broke don't fix it' – just doesn't cut it any more. If the Brexit vote told us anything, it told us that our society and many of our institutions are pretty creaky, if not actually damaged beyond repair, and we need to engage in some fundamental thinking. Where's the vision, the sort of thinking that gave us new towns (let's be honest, Ebbsfleet Garden City is hardly Milton Keynes when it comes to innovation)? Where's the belief that the future can, and will, be better?

England also needs to re-contract with its history. The past was not always a better place, and is unlikely to provide a great template for the future. We need to make sure it doesn't become our anchor against the prevailing tide. There also needs to be a process of recontracting between the young and the old. During my walk the suggestion was made that pensioners should be taxed more so that every twenty-five-year-old could be given a lump sum £10,000 on reaching that milestone birthday. It was an idea, even if it was one that assumed all problems could be solved with money, what I dub 'the NHS Panacea', but at least it was a suggestion. There also needs to be a discussion about how the wealth the nation creates (assuming we continue creating wealth) is captured and distributed, rewarding those who make it appropriately, but recognising that there are wider social obligations too.

The problem is, this will require mechanisms which allow us to have proper grown-up discussions, ones which recognise that there are multiple sides to an argument, and that compromises require give and take on both sides; in other words to move away from the two-dimensional, the binary, to the reality of our three-dimensional world. Are we capable of this?

As I've already suggested numerous times, an overwhelming conclusion from my walk is that I believe our current politicians (and political system) are simply not up to the job. To paraphrase Oscar Wilde's description of foxhunting, with the Brexit negotiations they have shown themselves as 'the incompetent in pursuit of the impossible'. Equally, the conduct of the referendum itself hardly offers grounds for confidence. But there are signs of hope.

The debate and subsequent referendum north of the border on Scottish independence in 2014 appeared, to this outsider at least, to have been a much more mature process. It involved passion it's true, but also reasoned discussion – at least until the establishment became worried and intervened, bullying their way to getting the result they wanted. It even had the foresight to include sixteen-year olds in the franchise, seeing as they were the ones most likely to be affected. I wonder what the outcome might have been if that had happened in the Brexit vote. We can't assume all sixteen- and seventeen-year olds would have voted for Remain (I met three along the way who, when asked, said they'd have voted the other way), but the evidence[39] suggests that most would have.

---

39   Source: BBC. See: https://www.bbc.co.uk/bbcthree/article/ b8d097b0-3ad4-4dd9-aa25-af6374292de0

Towards the end of my walk the leader of the Liberal Democrats put forward the proposal that future leaders of his party need not necessarily be Members of Parliament. The idea of tapping talent, almost on a contracted-in basis; that people other than experts, careerists or self-regarding elites, might be able to offer missing skills and insights, appears on the surface at least to be one worth exploring. Others[40] have put forward suggestions such as national 'deliberation days', inviting citizens to become involved in public community discussions, ideally just before an election.

Some glimmers perhaps?

I have no qualms in stating my own pride in England. Walking diagonally through the country has reaffirmed my affection for what it has to offer, while at the same time opening my eyes to the challenges it faces. We have much that is worth hanging on to, but we need to be realistic and open to change, rather than frightened of it, or hiding away from it in some largely mythical past.

It's going to be an interesting few years.

Maybe I will have to walk the other diagonal in twenty years' time to see how we all got on.

---

40 Source: Deliberation Day by Bruce Akerman and James Fishkin (Yale University Press). This is an American book. In the UK we are of course still 'subjects', not 'citizens'.

Finally ...

A big thank you to all those who participated, both knowingly and unknowingly in *Diagonal Walking*. This includes my diagonal walkers, Airbnb and traditional B&B hosts and those who helped in the early planning stages, before a step had been taken. Equally, those who helped knock the words into shape at the end, such as Andrew Kerr-Jarrett and Dan Coxon, thank you again. Thanks too to all the hundreds of decent people, too numerous to list, who made the walk such fun and were probably unaware they were contributing to anything in particular. Special thanks are due to Tim and Sue Graham and Simon and Judy Corble for all the Nature Table advice. The biggest thanks, however, are due to Annette for her tolerance and driving around, as well as for my absences, both physical and when I disappeared into my head. Thanks, you wonderful woman.

As I've already stated, this book is a record of my journey, furnished with details I picked up along the way. No doubt there are mistakes, and ownership of these lies with me also. If you spot any, or think you know something I didn't, please don't shoot me down in flames or give the book a one-star review. Be better than that, just let me know at nick@diagonalwalking.co.uk and share your knowledge. I might even acknowledge it in another edition. After all, sharing is part of what *Diagonal Walking* is all about.

Finally, a recommendation. If there's something you've always wanted to do, find the energy and time to do it. It won't happen unless you do.